PHP Oracle Web Development

Data Processing, Security, Caching, XML, Web Services, and AJAX

A practical guide to combining the power, performance, scalability, and reliability of Oracle Database with the ease of use, short development time, and high performance of PHP

Yuli Vasiliev

PUBLISHING

BIRMINGHAM - MUMBAI

PHP Oracle Web Development

Data Processing, Security, Caching, XML, Web Services, and AJAX

First published: August 2007

Production Reference: 1240707

Published by Packt Publishing Ltd.
32 Lincoln Road
Olton
Birmingham, B27 6PA, UK.

ISBN 978-1-847193-63-6

www.packtpub.com

Cover Image by Vinayak Chittar (vinayak.chittar@gmail.com)

Credits

Author

Yuli Vasiliev

Reviewer

Anup Nanda

Acquisition Editor

Priyanka Baruah

Technical Editor

Akshara Aware

Code Testing

Bansari Barot

Editorial Manager

Dipali Chittar

Project Manager

Patricia Weir

Indexer

Bhushan Pangaonkar

Proofreader

Chris Smith

Production Coordinator

Shantanu Zagade

Cover Designer

Shantanu Zagade

About the Author

Yuli Vasiliev is a software developer, freelance author, and a consultant currently specializing in open-source development, Oracle technologies, and service-oriented architecture (SOA). He has over 10 years of software development experience as well as several years of technical writing experience. He has written a series of technical articles for Oracle Technology Network (OTN) and *Oracle Magazine*.

About the Reviewer

Arup Nanda (arup@proligence.com) has been an Oracle DBA since 1993, when the world was slowly turning its attention to a big force to reckon with—Oracle7. But he was not so lucky; he was entrusted with a production Oracle database running Oracle 6. Since then, he has never been out of the Oracle DBA career path—weaving several interesting situations from modeling to performance tuning to backup/recovery and beyond, with lots of gray hairs to document each ORA-600. He has written several articles for publications such as *Oracle Magazine* and for *Oracle Tech Net*, he has presented at conferences such as Oracle World and IOUG Live, and he has coauthored four books. In 2003, Oracle chose him as the DBA of the Year. He lives in Danbury, Connecticut, with his wife, Anu, and their son, Anish.

Table of Contents

Preface

Oracle Database is the premier commercial database available today, providing support for a wide range of features for professional developers. It's incomparable in terms of performance, reliability, and scalability. With the advent of Oracle Database XE, a lightweight edition of Oracle Database, you now have the option to use an Oracle database for free even in a final product.

PHP is the most popular tool when it comes to building dynamic web applications. Unlike Oracle Database, PHP is an open-source product. The key reasons behind PHP's popularity are its ease of use, short development time, and high performance. Even if you are new to PHP, getting started is pretty simple. When used in a complementary way, though, PHP and Oracle allow you to build high-performance, scalable, and reliable data-driven web applications with minimum effort.

PHP Oracle Web Development: Data processing, Security, Caching, XML, Web Services, and AJAX is a 100% practical book crammed full of easy-to-follow examples. The book provides all the tools a PHP/Oracle developer needs to take advantage of the winning combination. It addresses the needs of a wide spectrum of PHP/Oracle developers, placing the emphasis on the most up-to-date topics, such as new PHP and Oracle Database features, stored procedure programming, handling transactions, security, caching, web services, and AJAX.

What This Book Covers

Chapter 1 gives an overview of the PHP and Oracle technologies, explaining why you might want to use PHP in conjunction with Oracle.

Chapter 2 covers the basics of using the PHP OCI8 extension to interact with an Oracle database from PHP. It also briefly discusses some popular alternatives to the OCI8 extension to connect to Oracle from within PHP.

Chapter 3 discusses how you can move data processing performed by your PHP/Oracle application into the database by using sophisticated SQL queries, stored PL/SQL subprograms, and database triggers.

Chapter 4 discusses the various mechanisms that can be used to perform transactions with PHP and Oracle.

Chapter 5 examines the object-oriented approach to developing PHP/Oracle applications, as an efficient means to reduce the development time and complexity, and increase the maintainability and flexibility of your applications.

Chapter 6 looks at how to effectively use the security features of both PHP and Oracle together, examining the fundamental aspects of building a secure PHP/Oracle application.

Chapter 7 discusses how to effectively use caching mechanisms available in PHP and Oracle and provides several examples of caching in action.

Chapter 8 explains how to effectively use XML techniques and technologies available in PHP and Oracle when building XML-enabled PHP/Oracle applications.

Chapter 9 shows how to build a SOAP web service exposing the functionality of a PHP/Oracle application, using the PHP SOAP extension and Oracle XML technologies.

Chapter 10 explains how AJAX and some other client-side (browser-side) JavaScript technologies can be used along with the Oracle Database technologies as well as PHP features to improve the responsiveness of PHP/Oracle applications.

Appendix A discusses how to install and configure the PHP and Oracle software components required to follow the book's examples.

Who is This Book For?

Although the book covers only the most popular and up-to-date topic areas on the use of PHP in conjunction with Oracle, the author does not make any assumption about the skill level of the reader. Packed with information in an easy-to-read format, the book is ideal for any PHP developer who deals with Oracle.

Conventions

In this book, you will find a number of styles of text that distinguish between different kinds of information. Here are some examples of these styles, and an explanation of their meaning.

There are three styles for code. Code words in text are shown as follows: "We can include other contexts through the use of the `include` directive."

A block of code will be set as follows:

```php
<?php
  //File: dbtime.php
    $dbHost = "localhost";
    $dbHostPort="1521";
    $dbServiceName = "orcl";
```

When we wish to draw your attention to a particular part of a code block, the relevant lines or items will be made bold:

```
$stmt = oci_parse($conn, $query);
 $deptno = '60';
 oci_bind_by_name($stmt, ':deptid', $deptno);
 oci_define_by_name($stmt, "EMPLOYEE_ID", $empno);
```

Any command-line input and output is written as follows:

```
# cp /usr/src/asterisk-addons/configs/cdr_mysql.conf.sample
    /etc/asterisk/cdr_mysql.conf
```

New terms and **important words** are introduced in a bold-type font. Words that you see on the screen, in menus or dialog boxes for example, appear in our text like this: "clicking the **Next** button moves you to the next screen".

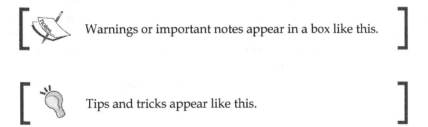

Warnings or important notes appear in a box like this.

Tips and tricks appear like this.

Reader Feedback

Feedback from our readers is always welcome. Let us know what you think about this book, what you liked or may have disliked. Reader feedback is important for us to develop titles that you really get the most out of.

To send us general feedback, simply drop an email to `feedback@packtpub.com`, making sure to mention the book title in the subject of your message.

If there is a book that you need and would like to see us publish, please send us a note in the **SUGGEST A TITLE** form on www.packtpub.com or email suggest@packtpub.com.

If there is a topic that you have expertise in and you are interested in either writing or contributing to a book, see our author guide on www.packtpub.com/authors.

Customer Support

Now that you are the proud owner of a Packt book, we have a number of things to help you to get the most from your purchase.

Downloading the Example Code for the Book

Visit http://www.packtpub.com/support, and select this book from the list of titles to download any example code or extra resources for this book. The files available for download will then be displayed.

The downloadable files contain instructions on how to use them.

Errata

Although we have taken every care to ensure the accuracy of our contents, mistakes do happen. If you find a mistake in one of our books—maybe a mistake in text or code—we would be grateful if you would report this to us. By doing this you can save other readers from frustration, and help to improve subsequent versions of this book. If you find any errata, report them by visiting http://www.packtpub.com/support, selecting your book, clicking on the **Submit Errata** link, and entering the details of your errata. Once your errata are verified, your submission will be accepted and the errata added to the list of existing errata. The existing errata can be viewed by selecting your title from http://www.packtpub.com/support.

Questions

You can contact us at questions@packtpub.com if you are having a problem with some aspect of the book, and we will do our best to address it.

1
Getting Started with PHP and Oracle

There are two kinds of database-driven applications. Ones that use databases just to store data, performing all the operations on it on the client side; and the others that use databases not only to store data, but also to process it, thus moving data processing to the data. While building the key business logic of a database-driven application inside the database is always a good idea, you should bear in mind that not all the databases available today allow you to put this into practice. However, the Oracle database offers record-breaking performance, scalability, and reliability. The partnership formed by Oracle and PHP, an open-source scripting language, is an excellent solution for building high-performance, scalable, and reliable data-driven web applications.

This chapter contains technical information that will help you to quickly start developing PHP applications on top of Oracle. It begins with a concise discussion of why you might want to use PHP in conjunction with Oracle, followed by the PHP and Oracle alternatives. Having learned what advantages the PHP/Oracle combination has over its competitors, you might want to see its strengths in action. If you don't have PHP and Oracle database software installed, you can read the *What You Need to Start* section in this chapter. This section discusses the pieces of software required to run the examples provided in this book. You could also read Appendix A *Installing PHP and Oracle Software*, which provides a quick-and-dirty guide to installing and configuring these software components to work together in your system.

Once you have all the required pieces of software installed, configured, and working properly, you are ready to build your first PHP/Oracle application. For the sake of simplicity, the sample application provided in this chapter simply obtains the current time from the database and then displays it to the user. In spite of its simplicity, the example demonstrates how to perform two basic things that every PHP/Oracle application must take care of. Specifically, it demonstrates how a PHP application can connect to an Oracle database and then interact with it.

If you have already got your feet wet with PHP/Oracle development, you probably will not be interested in reading this quick-start chapter. If so, you can move to Chapter 2, which discusses how to use PHP's OCI8 extension, providing a common way to interact with Oracle database from PHP.

Why PHP and Oracle?

With Oracle as the back-end database, you can develop and deploy data-driven PHP applications with a powerful, proven, and industry-leading infrastructure, while still taking advantage of PHP's ease of use, short development time, and high performance.

Simplicity and Flexibility

One of the key reasons behind PHP's popularity is its simplicity. So, you don't have to be a PHP guru to start building PHP applications on Oracle. All you need to learn are a few APIs, which allow you to interact with the database and handle the received data. The example discussed later in this chapter will show you how to build a simple PHP/Oracle application by using a few OCI8 functions.

PHP's Object-Oriented features, available since PHP 3 and significantly improved in PHP 5, help you create complex applications easily and quickly. Once a class has been written and debugged, you can reuse it in a number of ways. This allows you to reuse well-designed pieces of object-oriented code over and over, reducing or eliminating redundant code in your applications. For a detailed discussion of how to combine the power of object-oriented PHP and Oracle, refer to Chapter 5 *Object-Oriented Approach*.

From a PHP developer's perspective, developing PHP/Oracle applications is much easier than developing, PHP/MySQL applications. This is because, in the case of Oracle database, you may implement key business logic of the application on the database side. This not only reduces the amount of PHP code, but also improves the performance and scalability of the entire application.

If you are a PHP developer who tends to think that Oracle database represents a complicated, hard-to-drive mechanism, you should realize that—no matter how complex the Oracle insides may be—what really matters is that Oracle offers a lot of comprehensive tools intended to help you manage database objects and access data stored in the database with minimum effort. Although coverage of all the tools is beyond the scope of this book, the examples provided throughout the book will help you to obtain a good understanding of how Oracle SQL and PL/SQL—two of the most popular Oracle tools—are used to access and manipulate data, metadata, and other database resources.

Performance

Although you can process your application data on the client side in the case of Oracle database, there are many advantages of processing data inside the database. From a performance standpoint, moving processing to the data allows you to:

- Reduce the communication overhead between the web server and the database
- Conserve the web server resources
- Take advantage of optimizations and indexing techniques provided by the Oracle database

By using triggers and stored procedures, you can develop an application whose business logic resides entirely inside the database. Moving data processing to the database tier is particularly useful if your application is database intensive. This is because your application doesn't need to transfer a large amount of data between tiers while processing data inside the database; instead, it sends only the final product across the wire.

Robustness

Oracle gets high marks when it comes to performance, reliability, and scalability. Building and deploying your PHP applications on Oracle database enables you to combine the power and robustness of Oracle and the ease of use, short development time, and high performance of PHP. By using both of these technologies in a complementary way, you will be able to:

- Move key business logic of your application to the data
- Protect your application against data loss
- Take advantage of Oracle security technologies
- Leverage the power of object-oriented technology
- Build transactional applications
- Develop robust XML-enabled applications

All these capabilities make using PHP in conjunction with Oracle a natural choice when it comes to developing mission-critical, highly secure data-driven web applications.

Exploring PHP and Oracle Alternatives

Now that you have a rough idea of what the PHP/Oracle combination has to offer, it is worth taking a moment to familiarize yourself with some other popular combinations that can be used as alternatives to PHP and Oracle. Exploring such alternatives, including their advantages and disadvantages, can help you understand better whether PHP and Oracle best suit your needs or there is another combination that suits your needs better.

Although PHP supports all the major relational databases, including commercial ones such as IBM's DB2 and Microsoft SQL Server, MySQL, an open-source database, is still a popular choice among PHP developers. The major reason behind MySQL's popularity is that it is completely free under the GPL license.

Of those based on Oracle, JSF and Oracle is probably one of the most powerful combinations available. To make JSF/Oracle application development easier, Oracle offers ADF Faces, a fully compliant JSF component library including over 100 JSF components.

PHP and MySQL

MySQL is extremely popular among the open-source community that uses PHP. There are several reasons behind MySQL's popularity among PHP developers. The most significant ones are as follows:

- Completely free under the GPL license
- Low Total Cost of Ownership (TOC)
- PHP natively supports MySQL — no additional modules are required

All these factors make MySQL a natural choice for web hosts providing support for PHP. However, you should realize that the PHP/MySQL combination is a good solution for small data-driven web applications whereas professional-quality applications require much more.

JSF and Oracle

JavaServer Faces technology is a new server-side user interface (UI) component framework that is quickly becoming the standard web-application framework for J2EE applications. The biggest advantage of JavaServer Faces technology is that it enables web developers to apply the Model-View-Controller (MVC) principle, thus achieving a clean separation between the model and presentation layers of a web application. The entire user interaction with the application is handled by a front-end **Faces** servlet.

The only disadvantage the JSF and Oracle combination has compared to PHP and Oracle is that JavaServer Faces is a bit more difficult to learn than PHP.

What You Need to Start

Before you can proceed to PHP/Oracle development, you need to have PHP and Oracle database installed and working properly in your system. Moreover, to work with examples provided in this book, you will need an SQL command-line tool, such as SQL*Plus, allowing you to enter and execute SQL statements and PL/SQL code to manipulate database data, manage database objects, and perform database administration tasks.

This section briefly discusses all these pieces of software individually as well as how they fit into the big picture. For a discussion of how to install all the above software pieces and make them work together, see Appendix A *Installing PHP and Oracle Software*.

Pieces of Software Required

On jumping into a discussion of the software required for PHP/Oracle development, the first question you might ask is: "Which software components do I need to install in my system to be able to start developing PHP/Oracle applications?" Well, the list of required software components includes the following items:

- Oracle Database Server software
- An Oracle database
- Oracle Client libraries
- A web server with activated support for PHP
- An SQL command-line tool to interact with the database (or a GUI tool)

While the above list just tells you what software components you need to install, the following list outlines general steps to take to install them in your system:

- Install Oracle Database Server software. Make sure to create a database during installation.
- Install a web server. Note that, in most production environments, the web server and Oracle database server reside on different machines located within the same network. But for simplicity, you might have both the web server and Oracle database server installed on the same machine.
- Install PHP and configure the web server to use it.

- Install Oracle Client libraries. Note that you don't need to do it if the web server and Oracle database server reside on the same machine.

- Configure the PHP installation to work with Oracle.

 The above three steps are unnecessary when employing Zend Core for Oracle—a tool that allows you to install, deploy, and configure PHP to work with Oracle as quickly as possible. For a detailed discussion of Zend Core for Oracle, see the *Installing Zend Core for Oracle* section in Appendix A.

- Install an SQL command-line tool to perform database administration tasks and manipulate database objects. Note that you don't need to worry about this if you are going to connect to the database from the same machine on which the Oracle database server has been installed. In this case, Oracle SQL*Plus—standard Oracle SQL command-line tool—is installed by default.

 As a graphical alternative to Oracle SQL*Plus, you might use Oracle SQL Developer, a new, free GUI tool that can be used not only to perform database administration tasks and manipulate database objects, but also to edit and debug PL/SQL code. You can download Oracle SQL Developer from Oracle Technology Network (OTN) at: `http://www.oracle.com/technology/software/products/sql`. For more information, see the Oracle SQL Developer home page on OTN at: `http://www.oracle.com/technology/products/database/sql_developer/index.html`.

Before proceeding to the installation of the above products, it is recommended that you read through the rest of this section to get an overview of the software components mentioned above. Then, you can proceed to Appendix A *Installing PHP and Oracle Software*, which provides a quick-and-dirty guide for each step presented in the above list.

Oracle Database Considerations

This section provides a brief overview of some of the issues related to the Oracle Database, which you need to be familiar with before installing Oracle Database software in your system.

Understanding the Oracle Database

Looking through the list of the software components that need to be installed in your system, you might notice that it distinguishes between Oracle Database Server software and an Oracle database. If you are new to Oracle, this may sound confusing to you. This needs a little explanation.

According to the Oracle terminology, an Oracle database is simply a collection of user and control data stored on a disk and is treated as a unit. It is obvious that a database itself is useless — you need software to operate it.

 An Oracle database server consists of an Oracle database and an Oracle instance. While an Oracle database represents a collection of files that hold the database data and metadata, an Oracle instance represents the combination of the background processes operating on a database and shared memory used by those processes.

During the installation of the Oracle Database software, you have the option of creating a database or installing the software. It means that you can either install the Oracle software components designed to operate on a database and create a database itself or install only the Oracle software components. You might want to choose the later if, for example, you already have a database created and you want to use it with the newly installed software.

Choosing Between Oracle Database Editions

At the time of writing this book, the latest production release of Oracle's database was Oracle Database 10g Release 2, which is available in several editions outlined below:

- Oracle Database 10g Express Edition — a starter database for DBAs and developers. Being completely free of charge, this no-frills edition of Oracle Database supports up to 4 GB of user data and executes on one processor only. Built on the same core code as Oracle Database 10g Release 2, Express Edition provides the same set of integrated programming interfaces available in the other editions of Oracle Database 10g and can be easily upgraded to Standard or Enterprise Edition.

- Oracle Database 10g Standard Edition One — a full-featured Oracle database that is ideal for small- to-medium-sized business environments. Standard Edition One provides the proven performance, ease of use, reliability and security of Oracle Database at a low cost. It can only be licensed on servers supporting up to two CPUs.

- Oracle Database 10g Standard Edition — an ideal choice for medium-sized business environments. Unlike Standard Edition One, Standard Edition supports Real Application Clusters, an Oracle technology that enables the clustering of the Oracle Database, comprising several Oracle instances running on multiple clustered computers so that they operate as a single system. Standard Edition can be licensed on single or clustered servers with up to four processors.

- Oracle Database 10g Enterprise Edition—ideal for enterprises that have to operate on large amounts of information. Enterprise Edition contains all of the components of the Oracle Database, offering enterprise-class performance as well as reliable and secure data management for mission-critical applications.

 For more information on the Oracle Database product family, see Oracle white papers and Oracle documentation available on the OTN web site at: `http://www.oracle.com/technology`.

You can choose the edition of Oracle Database that best suits your needs and budget. As for the examples provided in this book, they should work with any of the above editions, including Oracle Database Express Edition. Unless otherwise noted, all examples provided in this book will work with Oracle Database 10g Release 2, or higher, irrespective of its edition.

Obtaining Oracle Database Software

Since most of the Oracle products are available on a commercial basis, you may be asking yourself: "Is there any way to try Oracle software for free in order to determine if it suits my needs or not?" The Oracle Software Downloads page on the Oracle website gives us the following information: **All software downloads are free, and each comes with a development license that allows you to use full versions of the products only while developing and prototyping your applications. You can buy Oracle products with full-use licenses at any time from the online Oracle Store or from your Oracle sales representative**.

What this means in practice is that you can download for free any piece of Oracle software today, for example, Oracle Database Enterprise Edition, play with it while developing and prototyping your applications, and then pay for that piece of software only if you decide to use it in your final product. If you are not still satisfied with it and would like to keep using an Oracle database for free even in a final product, consider Oracle Database Express Edition—a lightweight Oracle database that is free to develop, deploy, and distribute.

All Oracle Database 10g software is available for download from Oracle Technology Network (OTN). For Oracle Database 10g Enterprise/Standard Editions, you start by visiting the following OTN page:

```
http://www.oracle.com/technology/software/products/database/
oracle10g/index.html
```

For Oracle Database 10g Express Edition Editions, visit the following OTN page:

```
http://www.oracle.com/technology/software/products/database/xe/index.html
```

Oracle Database software is easy to install regardless of which edition of the database you choose. The *Installing Oracle Database Software* section in Appendix A provides the basic steps to install Oracle Database 10g on both Windows and UNIX systems. For detailed information on how to install Oracle Database software, see Oracle documentation: the Oracle Database Installation Guide for your operating system platform. Oracle documentation is available from the documentation section of the OTN website at:

```
http://www.oracle.com/technology/documentation/index.html
```

Besides the detailed installation steps specific to your operating system, the Oracle Database Installation Guide provides information on the issues to consider before installing the software and discusses platform-specific post-installation tasks that must be performed before you start using the database. It is highly recommended that you familiarize yourself with this information before installing Oracle Database software.

PHP Considerations

If you have already got your feet wet with PHP, you probably know that PHP is a server-side scripting language, which means that PHP code is executed on a web server. Therefore, before you install PHP, you must have a web server installed and working in your system.

Apache HTTP Server

Although PHP has support for most of the web servers worth mentioning, including Microsoft Internet Information Server, Personal Web Server, Netscape, and iPlanet servers, and many others, Apache/PHP remains the most popular combination among developers. Oracle itself incorporates open-source Apache technology in some of its products. For example, Oracle HTTP Server 10g, the web server component of Oracle database, is based on the proven technology of both Apache 1.3 and Apache 2.0.

The Apache HTTP server is distributed under the Apache License, a free software/ open-source license authored by The Apache Software Foundation (ASF). The current version of the Apache License can be found on the licenses page of the Apache website at:

```
http://www.apache.org/licenses/
```

You can download the Apache HTTP server from the download page of the Apache website at:

```
http://httpd.apache.org/download.cgi
```

This page also contains a link to the Apache HTTP Server Documentation index, which in turn contains a link to the *Compiling and Installing* document.

 Oracle recommends that you install a web server on another machine but on the same network as the database server. However, for simplicity, you can install both an Oracle database server and a web server, which will communicate with that database server, on the same machine.

For instructions on how to install Apache in your system, see the *Installing Apache HTTP Server* section in Appendix A.

Why PHP 5

Although PHP 4 is still very popular, the examples provided throughout this book assume that you will use PHP 5. We decided on PHP 5 because it offers a lot of new features and improvements that are not available in its predecessors.

One of the significant improvements in PHP 5 is the new object model, which allows you to leverage the power and flexibility of object-oriented programming in a number of useful ways. In particular, you can take advantage of interfaces, abstract classes, private/public/protected access modifiers, static members and methods, exception handling, and other features that are usually found in other object-oriented languages, such as Java, but were not available in prior releases of PHP.

 Chapter 5 *Object-Oriented Approach* explains in detail how all these new object features of PHP 5 can be used in PHP/Oracle development.

Another significant improvement in PHP 5 is its renewed XML support; SAX, DOM, and XSLT extensions are now based on the single library, namely libxml2, thus allowing for better interoperability between the XML extensions.

 Chapter 8 *XML-enabled Applications* discusses how to build and deploy robust XML-enabled PHP applications on Oracle Database.

While PHP 4 lacked native SOAP support, PHP 5 introduces the SOAP extension. Written in C, this built-in extension can serve as a good alternative to the PEAR::SOAP package.

 Chapter 9 *Web services* discusses how to create a SOAP web service using PHP 5's SOAP extension, on top of the Oracle database.

Obtaining PHP

PHP is licensed under the PHP License, a BSD-style license. For more information, visit the License Information page of the php.net website at:

```
http://www.php.net/license/
```

The current recommended releases of PHP are available for download from the downloads page of the php.net site at:

```
http://www.php.net/downloads.php
```

From this page, download the latest stable release of PHP 5 and then follow the installation steps—provided in the *Installing PHP* section in Appendix A. For further assistance along the way, you may consult the Installation and Configuration manual available on the php.net website at:

```
http://www.php.net/manual/install.php
```

Alternatively, you can read the install.txt file that is shipped with PHP.

Making PHP and Oracle Work Together

As you will learn in Chapter 2 *PHP and Oracle Connection*, there are several ways in which PHP can interact with Oracle. However, it is important to realize that most of these ways are based on using APIs provided by the PHP OCI8 extension, which is not enabled by default. To enable it in your existing PHP installation, you have to perform the following general steps:

- Install the Oracle client libraries needed by the PHP OCI8 extension.
- On UNIX-like systems, recompile PHP to support the OCI8 extension. On Windows, uncomment the OCI8 extension line in php.ini.
- Restart the web server.

As you can see from the above, you have to install the Oracle client libraries before you can enable the OCI8 extension in your existing PHP installation.

Oracle Instant Client

Consider Oracle Instant Client, a package containing the Oracle client libraries required to run OCI, OCCI, and JDBC-OCI applications. Note that Oracle Instant Client comes with a free license for both development and production environments.

If you have both the database and web server installed on the same computer then you already have all the required Oracle components—no Instant Client is required. However, in this case you still have to explicitly enable the OCI8 extension in your PHP installation.

You can download a copy of Oracle Instant Client specific to your platform from the Instant Client web page on OTN at:

```
http://www.oracle.com/technology/tech/oci/instantclient/
instantclient.html
```

Looking through this page, you may notice that there are in fact several Instant Client Packages available for download. You should choose the Basic Instant Client Package. It includes all the files required to run OCI, OCCI, and JDBC-OCI applications.

For a detailed instruction on how to install Oracle Instant Client and then enable the OCI8 extension, see the *Enabling the OCI8 Extension in an Existing PHP Installation* section in Appendix A.

Zend Core for Oracle

As you learned in the previous sections, making PHP and Oracle software work together is a process involving many tedious tasks. You have to find, download, install, deploy, and configure a number of software pieces to get the job done.

You might significantly speed up and simplify the whole process by taking advantage of Zend Core for Oracle, a pre-built stack that delivers a rapid development and deployment foundation for Oracle-driven PHP applications. In particular, Zend Core for Oracle saves you the trouble of performing the following steps:

- Installing PHP and configuring the web server to use it
- Installing Oracle Client libraries
- Configuring the PHP installation to work with Oracle

Moreover, Zend Core for Oracle provides the following features:

- Updated OCI8 driver re-factored for reliability and performance
- GUI-based tool that makes it easier to change the PHP configuration
- Easy access to PHP, PEAR and Zend Core for Oracle documentation

The installation steps in the *Installing Zend Core for Oracle* section in Appendix A will help you install this tool in your system.

Using Oracle SQL*Plus

After an Oracle Database server and a web server with activated support for PHP, which has the OCI8 extension enabled, are installed and working correctly, you can proceed to developing PHP/Oracle applications. However, before moving on, you might want to install another piece of software in your system in order to make your development work easier.

Why Use SQL*Plus in PHP/Oracle Development?

While using the PHP OCI8 extension you can execute any valid SQL statement or PL/SQL block against an Oracle database from your PHP script, it is generally not a good idea to do so when you need to perform a database administration task or create a database object.

 The fact is that these kinds of tasks are usually performed with the help of batch scripts executed against the database. However, executing batch scripts from PHP is a tricky task and so you might want to use a more appropriate tool for this purpose.

The simplest way to perform the above tasks is to use an SQL command-line tool that will allow you to execute SQL statements and PL/SQL blocks in a batch or individually, and display the results of each statement once it has been executed.

Consider Oracle SQL*Plus—an interactive and batch query command-line tool that is installed by default with every Oracle Database installation. Most of the examples in this book assume that you will use SQL*Plus when it comes to performing database administration or creating database objects. Since SQL*Plus is installed by default when installing the Oracle Database software, you don't need to install it again if you are going to use a local database. Otherwise, you might take advantage of SQL*Plus Instant Client—a stand-alone SQL*Plus command-line tool that allows you to communicate with a remote database.

This section discusses how to use SQL*Plus to interact with an Oracle database. The *Installing SQL*Plus Instant Client* section in Appendix A describes the installation steps to install SQL*Plus Instant Client in your system, assuming you will work with a remote database. For detailed information on how to use Oracle SQL*Plus, see Oracle documentation: *SQL*Plus User's Guide and Reference*.

> From now on, we won't distinguish between SQL*Plus and SQL*Plus Instant Client—references will be made to SQL*Plus.

Connecting to a Database with SQL*Plus

To connect to a database with SQL*Plus, you specify the database using an Oracle Net connection identifier. For example, you might use the following Easy Connect syntax to connect as hr/hr to the orcl database running on yourmachine:1521 within yourdomain:

```
sqlplus hr/hr@//yourmachine.yourdomain:1521/orcl
```

However, if you are connecting to a local database you might use a simpler syntax:

```
sqlplus hr/hr
```

> HR/HR is a demonstration database schema that is installed by default when you choose the **Basic Installation** and **Create Starter Database** options during Oracle Database installation. Some examples in this book use the default tables from this database schema.

If your HR/HR database schema is locked, you will see the following error message:

```
ERROR:
ORA-28000: the account is locked
```

To unlock the HR database account, first connect as SYSTEM database user:

```
sqlplus system/system_pswd@//yourmachine.yourdomain:1521/orcl
```

And then enter the following SQL statement at the SQL> prompt:

```
ALTER USER HR IDENTIFIED BY hr ACCOUNT UNLOCK;
```

Now, to connect as hr/hr, you don't have to open another SQL*Plus session. From an existing SQL*Plus session, enter a CONNECT command as follows:

```
CONNECT hr/hr@//yourmachine.yourdomain:1521/orcl;
```

To connect to the database, all the above examples employ the Easy Connect Naming feature that first appeared in Oracle Database 10g Release 1. You may find this method very convenient because it enables you to connect to a database server without first configuring net service names.

Warning: the Easy Connect Naming feature can be used only in a TCP/IP environment.

Alternatively, you might use the Local Naming method to connect to a database. The local naming method uses a localized configuration `tnsnames.ora` file to store net service names and their connect descriptors. So, you first create a connect descriptor in the `tnsnames.ora` file and then you can refer to that descriptor by name.

Normally, the `tnsnames.ora` file can be found in the `[ORACLE_HOME]\network\admin` directory on the client machine. However, if you are connecting to a remote database by means of SQL*Plus Instant Client, you should take into account that neither SQL*Plus Instant Client nor Basic Instant Client comes with a `tnsnames.ora` file and so you will have to create it yourself. For example, if you have installed the Instant Client to the `c:\instantclient_10_2` directory, create the `c:\instantclient_10_2\network\admin\` directory and then create a plain-text `tnsnames.ora` file in that directory.

Next, set the `ORACLE_HOME` environment variable to `c:\instantclient_10_2\`. Finally, create a connect descriptor in the `tnsnames.ora` file. For example, you might create the following connect descriptor for the `orcl` database running on `yourmachine:1521` within `yourdomain`:

```
ORCL10g =
  (DESCRIPTION =
    (ADDRESS = (PROTOCOL = TCP)(HOST = yourmachine.yourdomain)
                                            (PORT = 1521))
    (CONNECT_DATA =
      (SERVICE_NAME = orcl)
    )
  )
```

Once you have saved this entry in the `tnsnames.ora` file, you can then connect to the specified database with SQL*Plus as follows:

```
sqlplus hr/hr@orcl10g
```

For further discussion of how to use the Easy Connect Naming and Local Naming method, see the *Connecting to a Database* section, which discusses these Oracle Net Services features from a PHP developer standpoint.

Running Scripts in SQL*Plus

As you saw in the previous subsection, executing an SQL statement in SQL*Plus is very simple. To do this, you simply enter the SQL statement at the SQL> prompt. For example, you might enter the following statement at the SQL> prompt to obtain the current date from the database:

```
SELECT SYSDATE FROM DUAL;
```

Once you press the *Enter* key, the above should produce a result that might look like the following:

```
SYSDATE
---------
20-MAR-06
```

However, note that entering statements at the SQL> prompt manually may be an acceptable solution when dealing with a single statement that you are not going to use frequently in the future. Otherwise, you might want to save the statement or statements in a script and then run this script when necessary.

To create a script in SQL*Plus, you can use your operating system's default text editor. To do this, you simply enter the EDIT command followed by the name of the script file you want to create or edit. For example, if you want to create a dbdate.sql script, you have to enter the following command at the SQL> prompt:

```
EDIT dbdate
```

As a result, the dbdate.sql file is opened in the editor so that you can insert the desired statement or statements into the script. For simplicity, you might insert into the dbdate.sql script the same SQL statement as in the above example:

```
SELECT SYSDATE FROM DUAL;
```

Once you have saved the dbdate.sql script with the editor, you can then run it by entering the START command followed by the name of the script as follows:

```
START dbdate
```

This should produce the same output as in the previous example.

Now, if you want to edit the dbdate.sql script without leaving SQL*Plus, you can do it with the help of the EDIT command, as shown below:

```
EDIT dbdate
```

This should open the dbdate.sql file with the editor for editing. You can edit the script as needed and then save the changes and quit the editor. For example, you might replace the existing SQL statement in the dbdate.sql script with the following:

```
SELECT TO_CHAR(SYSDATE, 'MM-DD-YYYY HH:MI:SS') FROM DUAL;
```

So, the next time you run the dbdate.sql script with the START command, it will produce output that looks like:

```
TO_CHAR(SYSDATE,'MM
-------------------
03-20-2006 04:50:07
```

Here, the script outputs the current date and time.

No doubt you have realized, the dbdate.sql script is a toy example. In a real-world situation, you might need to create a script containing more than one statement. As noted previously, using batch scripts can be very handy when you need to perform database administration tasks or create database objects.

Putting It All Together

Now that you have a rough idea of what each piece of software required for PHP/Oracle development is used for, let's look at how all these components interact with each other to get the job done. Let's summarize what each piece does individually to better understand its role in the entire architecture.

The following table gives a summary description for each piece of software you need to have installed to get started.

Software component	Functional description
Oracle Database Server software	Provides concurrent access to the database data while still delivering high performance. Also prevents unauthorized access to the data and provides efficient mechanism for backup and recovery.
Oracle Database	Provides physical and logical structures in which user and control data is stored. A database is mounted and opened by an instance (may be more than one instance in the case of using Real Application Clusters).
Apache HTTP Server	Provides secure, efficient, and feature-rich web server services. Provides the ability to incorporate new functionality in the form of third-party modules.
PHP	Provides a way to add dynamic content into HTML. Supports a wide range of relational databases.

Software component	Functional description
Oracle Instant Client	Provides the Oracle client libraries that allow client software to interact with an Oracle Database server.
Zend Core for Oracle	Contains all the client-side components required for PHP/Oracle development. Specifically, it contains an Apache HTTP server, PHP, and Oracle client libraries. All the components are configured so that you can quickly start developing PHP/Oracle applications.

While the above table gives a short functional description of each software component needed to start developing PHP/Oracle applications, the following figure illustrates how all these components fit together, giving you a high-level view of PHP/Oracle interactions.

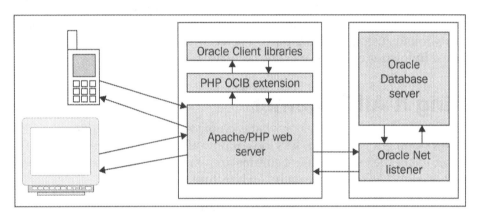

As you can see in the above figure, the web server sends connection requests to the Oracle Net listener, a process that listens for client connection requests, rather than to the Oracle database server directly. The listener in turn forwards those requests to the database server. But what is not shown in the figure is that the web server and Oracle database server start communicating directly with one another once a connection is established.

Creating Your First PHP/Oracle Application

Using the information provided in the *What You Need to Start* section earlier in this chapter, as well as the information provided in Appendix A *Installing PHP and Oracle Software,* you can easily install all the required pieces of software in your system. Once you are done with it, you are ready to create your first PHP/Oracle applications. The example provided in this section consists of one PHP script: dbtime.php. All this simple script does is display the current time obtained from the database. The result is a single string that should look like this:

```
The current time is 07:30:20
```

The following figure shows what this looks like in a web browser:

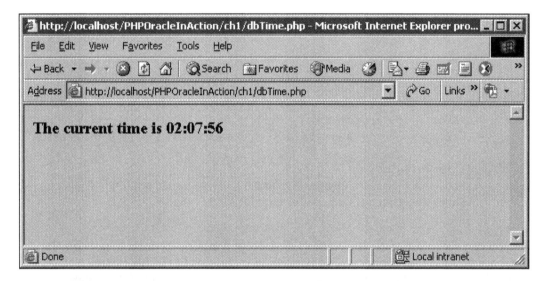

Despite the simplicity of the results produced, this PHP script is a good example of how a PHP application can interact with Oracle by means of PHP's OCI8 functions. To display a simple string representing the current time, dbtime.php performs the following sequence of steps:

- Connects to the Oracle database
- Executes a SELECT query against the database
- Fetches the received result and then displays it to the user

Now that you know what the script does behind the scene in order to display a simple string representing the current time, you might want to look at the code. The dbtime.php script code is shown below:

```php
<?php
 //File: dbtime.php
   $dbHost = "localhost";
   $dbHostPort="1521";
   $dbServiceName = "orcl";
   $usr = "hr";
   $pswd = "hr";
   $dbConnStr = "(DESCRIPTION=(ADDRESS=(PROTOCOL=TCP)
            (HOST=".$dbHost.")(PORT=".$dbHostPort."))
              (CONNECT_DATA=(SERVICE_NAME=".$dbServiceName.")))";
   if(!$dbConn = oci_connect($usr,$pswd,$dbConnStr)) {
      $err = oci_error();
      trigger_error('Could not establish a connection: '
                              . $err['message'], E_USER_ERROR);
   };
   $strSQL = "SELECT TO_CHAR(SYSDATE, 'HH:MI:SS') ctime FROM DUAL";
   $stmt = oci_parse($dbConn,$strSQL);
   if (!oci_execute($stmt)) {
      $err = oci_error($stmt);
      trigger_error('Query failed: ' . $err['message'], E_USER_ERROR);
   };
   oci_fetch($stmt);
   $rslt = oci_result($stmt, 'CTIME');
   print "<h3>The current time is ".$rslt."</h3>";
 ?>
```

As you can see in the code, the connect descriptor contains location details for the database you want to connect to. In particular, it consists of the host name, the port on which the Oracle Net listener process is running, and the SID of the database. For further discussion, see the *Connecting to a Database* subsection later in this section.

This example assumes that you have HR/HR demonstration schema installed in your database. For the sake of this example, though, you could use any other database schema. For this, you simply set the $usr and $pswd variables to appropriate values.

To establish a connection to the Oracle Database server, you use the oci_connect function. This function returns a connection identifier that is then used in the other OCI8 calls in this script.

Besides `oci_connect`, there are two other OCI8 functions that you can use to establish a connection to the database: `oci_new_connect` and `oci_pconnect`. For detailed discussion of the OCI8 connection functions see Chapter 4 *Transactions*.

Another important thing to note in the script is the use of the `oci_error` function. When used to obtain a connection error, the `oci_error` function is invoked without a parameter. Otherwise, you pass an appropriate connection identifier returned by the `oci_connect` function.

In this example, the `trigger_error` function triggers an error and then stops execution because you pass predefined constant `E_USER_ERROR` as the third parameter.

 The `trigger_error` function is covered in more detail in Chapter 2, section *Using the trigger_error Function*.

The query discussed in this example contains two standard Oracle SQL functions: `SYSDATE`, used here to obtain the current time from the operating system on which the database resides, and `TO_CHAR`, used here to convert a `DATE` value returned by `SYSDATE` to a string of characters.

Another thing to note here is the use of the column alias in the query. This will allow you to refer to the query result by its alias, in this example: `ctime`, later in the `oci_result` function. Otherwise, you would have to deal with a column name, which in this case is `TO_CHAR(SYSDATE, 'HH:MI:SS')`.

After the query string is defined, you use the `oci_parse` function that prepares the SQL statement for execution.

 `oci_parse` doesn't look for errors in the SQL query. You have to execute the query to check if it is valid.

`oci_execute` returns a Boolean value: true on success and false on failure. Using the `IF-THEN` statement allows you to take appropriate steps in case of a failure. In this example, if `oci_execute` returns false, the script generates the error and stops execution.

Normally you use the `oci_fetch` function in a loop to fetch the next row into the result buffer. In this example, however, the result consists of one row only.

After the current row has been fetched by `oci_fetch`, you use `oci_result` to obtain the field's value from that row. As mentioned, in this particular case the query result consists of one row that contains one field.

 Regardless of the way in which you specified a column name or a column alias name in the query, Oracle returns all field names in uppercase. So, you must specify all field names in uppercase when calling the `oci_return` function. Specifically, in this example you must use CTIME instead of `ctime`.

Connecting to a Database

No doubt you have realized that before your application can make use of the database data, it must first connect to the database. While the PHP OCI8 extension provides the `oci_connect` function for just this purpose, Oracle in fact allows you to configure connectivity information in several ways. This section discusses how to use the Local Naming and Easy Connect Naming Oracle methods when connecting to an Oracle database from PHP.

Using the Local Naming Method

By specifying `localhost` as the host name in the connect descriptor in the above example, you tell `oci_connect` that the database you are connecting to is local. In a real-world situation, however, you might need to establish a connection to a remote database. To do this, you can use either the IP address or network name of the host machine on which the Oracle Net listener is running. For example, if your Oracle database server resides on the computer whose network name is `MyServer` and IP address is `192.168.100.1`, you might use either `HOST = MyServer` or `HOST = 192.168.100.1` in the connect descriptor.

 Using a connect descriptor is a common way of providing information required for establishing a connection to a remote database.

To make using connect descriptors easier, you might define them in the `tnsnames.ora` file, which is normally located in the `ORACLE_HOME/network/admin` directory on the client machine. Once you have a connect descriptor defined in the `tnsnames.ora` file, you can then refer to that descriptor by name. Doing so saves you the trouble of defining descriptor connections in your application code. For example, you might define the following connect descriptor in `tnsnames.ora`:

```
ORCL10gR2 =
  (DESCRIPTION =
```

```
    (ADDRESS = (PROTOCOL = TCP)(HOST = localhost)(PORT = 1521))
    (CONNECT_DATA =
      (SERVER = DEDICATED)
      (SERVICE_NAME = orcl)
    )
  )
```

Once you have the above entry saved in the `tnsnames.ora` file, you can then pass the name that maps to the connect descriptor, namely, `ORCL10gR2`, as the third parameter to `oci_connect`, rather than passing the string representing the connect descriptor itself:

```
$dbDescName = "ORCLR10gR2";
$dbConn = oci_connect($usr,$pswd,$dbDescName);
```

It is important to note that you may not pass the third parameter to `oci_connect` at all if the database you are connecting to is local.

Using the Easy Connect Method

For TCP/IP environments, you might make use of Oracle Database 10g's Easy Connect Naming Method feature, which can eliminate the need for service name lookup in the `tnsnames.ora` file. We touched on this feature in the *Using Oracle SQL*Plus* section earlier in this chapter, when discussing some of the ways you can connect to a remote database with SQL*Plus. If you recall, the Easy Connect Naming method enables you to connect to an Oracle database server by simply providing the database user/password combination and the server computer's host name along with two optional parameters, namely, the service name of the database and the port on which the listener will accept connections. Note, however, that you cannot omit the service name when it comes to defining the third parameter of `oci_connect`:

```
$dbEasyConn = "//MyDbServer/orcl";
$dbConn = oci_connect($usr,$pswd,$dbEasyConn);
```

To specify an optional port, you use the following syntax:

```
$dbEasyConn = "//MyDbServer:1521/orcl";
```

It is important to realize that `orcl` in the above examples is not the name of a connect descriptor defined in the `tnsnames.ora` file, but the service name of the database.

 The service name defaults to the global database name—a name consisting of the database name and domain name, which are specified during the installation or database creation.

As you can see, the Easy Connect Naming method provides an easy-to-use syntax enabling you to connect to a database server without any configuration.

Issuing an SQL Statement Against the Database

In the example discussed earlier in this chapter, you used the oci_execute function to execute a SELECT statement against the database. It is important to note that oci_execute's use is not limited to QUERY operations—you can use this OCI8 function to execute any SQL or PL/SQL statements performing QUERY, DML, and DDL operations.

As mentioned, oci_execute returns a Boolean value: true on success and false on failure. In the case of a failure, you likely will want your script to perform certain actions in response. For example, you might use the trigger_error PHP function to either generate an error and stop execution or generate a warning and continue execution. Whether error_trigger stops script execution or not depends on what predefined error level constant you are passing to this function as the second parameter. For example, if you want the script to generate a warning message and continue execution, you must use the E_USER_WARNING predefined constant:

```
$err = oci_error();
trigger_error('Query failed: ' . $err['message'], E_USER_WARNING);
```

To terminate execution, you use the E_USER_ERROR constant.

Fetching and Displaying Results

If the oci_execute call returns true, you can then move on to fetching the results. Of course, this makes sense only when you are dealing with a QUERY operation—that is, you are issuing a SELECT statement.

There are several ways to fetch the result data using the PHP OCI8 extension. The example discussed earlier in this chapter demonstrates the use of oci_fetch in conjunction with oci_result:

```
oci_fetch($stmt);
$rslt = oci_result($stmt, 'CTIME');
print "<h3>The current time is ".$rslt."</h3>";
```

You use oci_fetch to fetch the next row from the result data into the internal result buffer. Then, you use oci_result to retrieve the CTIME field's value from the fetched row.

It is important to note that with `oci_fetch` and `oci_result` you are not limited to using associative indices—you can use numeric indices as well. So, you might rewrite the above code as follows:

```
oci_fetch($stmt);
$rslt = oci_result($stmt, 1);
print "<h3>The current time is ".$rslt."</h3>";
```

While using `oci_fetch` assumes that you will then use `oci_result` to retrieve the fetched data from the internal result buffer, there are OCI8 fetch functions that fetch the next row from the result data directly into a PHP array, thus eliminating the need to use `oci_result`. One of these functions is `oci_fetch_array`. With this function, you can reduce the above three lines of code to the following two:

```
$rslt = oci_fetch_array($stmt, OCI_ASSOC);
print "<h3>The current time is ".$rslt['CTIME']."</h3>";
```

Or by using numeric indices:

```
$rslt = oci_fetch_array($stmt, OCI_NUM);
print "<h3>The current time is ".$rslt[0]."</h3>";
```

For further discussion on OCI8 fetch functions, see Chapter 2 *PHP and Oracle Connection.*

Summary

If you have made up your mind to take advantage of the capabilities that the PHP/Oracle combination provides, the first obvious step is to make sure that you have PHP and Oracle database software installed and working properly. This chapter in conjunction with Appendix A *Installing PHP and Oracle Software* takes you through the basics of getting your PHP/Oracle development environment installed and configured. You learned that making PHP work with Oracle database is in fact a piece of cake, especially if you employ Zend Core for Oracle—a package that includes all the client libraries needed to work with Oracle from a PHP environment.

Every PHP/Oracle application does at least two things: connecting to the database and executing an SQL statement or statements against it. For example, imagine an application that collects user input and then executes an SQL pass-through query to send the data to the database. In practice, however, you normally need to create an application that takes care of two more things: fetching the retrieved data from the database and displaying it to the user. The example discussed in this chapter contains each of the steps mentioned above. Specifically, it shows you how to: connect to the database, issue a query against it, and then fetch and display the results to the user.

This is a common set of operations, which almost every lightweight PHP front-end application has to deal with.

Now that you've got a basic understanding of how a PHP/Oracle application works, it's time to move on to more advanced uses. The next chapter deals with some of the most interesting aspects of PHP/Oracle application development and deployment.

2
PHP and Oracle Connection

The sample in Chapter 1 represents a simple example of how the OCI8 functions can be used to interact with Oracle. However, besides OCI8, there are some other ways for Oracle and PHP to interact with each other. For example, you may choose from a number of open-source libraries such as PEAR DB and ADOdb, which provide a level of data abstraction. You might also create a set of your own PHP functions on top of the OCI8 extension to encapsulate its low-level functionality.

However, it is important to realize that using another level of data abstraction can simplify the development process, but using direct database calls made through the OCI8 functions allows you to take full advantage of the Oracle database features and build faster and more reliable applications. That is why, in the examples throughout this book, the OCI8 extension is used as the primary way to communicate with an Oracle database.

This chapter covers the basics of using the PHP OCI8 extension to interact with an Oracle database from PHP. Covering them at this stage will ensure that you can go further and understand specific topics discussed in the subsequent chapters. It also briefly discusses some popular alternatives to the OCI8 extension available today.

Introducing the PHP OCI8 Extension

As a matter of fact, when it comes to working with Oracle, many PHP developers prefer the PHP OCI8 extension to any other tool enabling PHP and Oracle to interact with each other because OCI8 offers a lot of capabilities that the other tools lack.

 One word of warning: Although the PHP OCI8 extension provides a common way to communicate with Oracle database from PHP, it is not enabled by default. Refer to the *Making PHP and Oracle Work Together* section in Chapter 1 for information on how to enable PHP OCI8 extension in your PHP installation.

This section briefly discusses why you might want to use the OCI8 extension and then explains how SQL statements are processed with OCI8.

Why Use OCI8 Extension

One of the key differences between the OCI8 extension and the other popular tools such as PEAR DB, ADOdb, and PDO, which can also be used to access Oracle database from PHP, is that OCI8 was developed exclusively for interacting with Oracle database and hence provides a lot of options for PHP/Oracle developers. With the OCI8 extension, you can employ a connection cache when connecting to the database, bind PHP variables to Oracle placeholders, access and manipulate Oracle collections, handle transactions, and deal with LOBs, to name only a few possibilities.

However, the key advantage of using the OCI8 extension is that it allows you to control all phases of SQL statement execution, thus allowing a very fine-grained control over script execution itself. The next subsection briefly outlines each step in processing an SQL statement by means of OCI8.

Processing SQL Statements with OCI8

From the example discussed in Chapter 1, you learned which steps are required when it comes to executing an SQL statement by means of the OCI8 extension. Nevertheless, there may be some circumstances that require some additional steps. This subsection outlines the general steps to be taken while processing an SQL statement with the help of OCI8 functions. However, functions can vary depending on the situation. The OCI8 extension offers many more functions for processing SQL statements than the ones mentioned in the following steps.

Another thing to note is that some steps involved in processing an SQL statement are not common to all types of SQL statements. For example, fetching the retrieved results makes sense only when dealing with a query (SELECT) statement, while taking care to explicitly commit or roll back the transaction makes sense only when performing a DML (INSERT, UPDATE, or DELETE) operation. However, it is important to note that there are also steps common to all SQL statements, regardless of the type of statement. For example, you must always perform the parsing and executing operations, whether you are dealing with a query or DML operation. Here are the general steps involved in processing a SELECT statement:

- Step 1 (required): Prepare the SQL statement for execution by using the oci_parse function.

- Step 2 (optional): If the statement contains placeholders for values that will be supplied by the application at run time, you use the `oci_bind_by_name` function that allows you to create an association between a PHP script variable and an Oracle placeholder.

> Although Step 2 is optional, Oracle recommends using bind variables wherever they make sense. Doing so can significantly improve the performance of your application. For further discussion, see the *Using Bind Variables* section later in this chapter.

- Step 3 (optional): You can define PHP variables to fetch SQL columns presented in the SELECT list. To do this, you use the `oci_define_by_name` function.

- Step 4 (optional): You can use the `oci_set_prefetch` function to set the number of records to be prefetched after a successful call to `oci_execute`. By default, this number is set to 1. By setting it to a larger number, you can reduce the overhead associated with moving the data over the network, at the cost of increased memory usage.

- Step 5 (required): Execute the parsed statement by using the `oci_execute` function.

- Step 6 (optional): Make sure to check what the `oci_execute` function returns. If `oci_execute` returns false, this indicates that the query failed. In this case, you can take an appropriate action and make use of the `oci_error` function that allows you to retrieve the error description and the Oracle error code.

- Step 7 (required): Fetch the results of the query. To do this, you can use one of the fetch functions available in OCI8. For example, you might use the `oci_fetch_all` function to fetch all rows from the retrieved result set into a user-defined array. You might also fetch the retrieved data into the internal result buffer by using the `oci_fetch` function and then employ the `oci_result` function to read the fetched results. If you defined variables to fetch SQL columns, you can use these variables to access the retrieved results.

> For details on the fetch functions available in OCI8, see the *Fetching Results* section later in this chapter.

Here are the general steps involved in processing a DML statement:

- Step 1 (required): Prepare the SQL statement for execution by using the `oci_parse` function.

- Step 2 (optional): If the statement contains placeholders, use the `oci_bind_by_name` function.

- Step 3 (required): Execute the parsed statement by using the `oci_execute` function. By default, an executed statement is committed automatically. However, setting the mode parameter to `OCI_DEFAULT` allows you to create a transaction that can be committed later by explicitly calling `oci_commit` or rolled back by `oci_rollback`.

- Step 4 (optional): Make sure to check what the `oci_execute` function returns.

- Step 5 (optional): If you are interested in knowing the number of rows affected during statement execution, you can use the `oci_num_rows` function.

- Step 6 (optional): If you have set the mode parameter of `oci_execute` to `OCI_DEFAULT`, you should take care to explicitly commit or roll back the transaction. Not doing so will result in rolling back the transaction when the script ends or you close the connection.

Now that you are familiar with the basics of processing SQL statements with OCI8, it is time to move on and build an application that will demonstrate how an SQL statement can be processed using OCI8 APIs in practice. The `sqlproc.php` script shown in the following listing demonstrates how to process a `SELECT` statement, using all the steps outlined earlier involved in processing a `SELECT` statement. In particular, `sqlproc.php` accesses the `employees` table from the default `HR/HR` demonstration schema and displays some important fields of the records representing employees who work in the Department whose `department_id` is `60`. The output of this script is shown in the following figure:

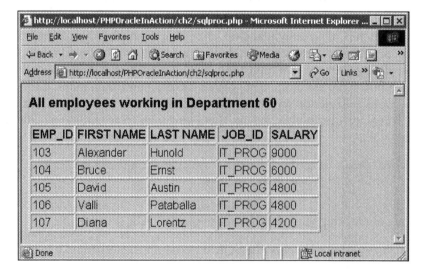

Here is the code for the `sqlproc.php` script:

```php
<?php
//File: sqlproc.php
if (!$conn = oci_connect('hr', 'hr', '//localhost/orcl')) {
    $err = oci_error();
    trigger_error('Could not establish a connection: ' .
                              $err['message'], E_USER_ERROR);
}
$query = 'SELECT EMPLOYEE_ID, FIRST_NAME, LAST_NAME, JOB_ID,
            SALARY FROM EMPLOYEES WHERE department_id = :deptid';
$stmt = oci_parse($conn, $query);
$deptno = '60';
oci_bind_by_name($stmt, ':deptid', $deptno);
oci_define_by_name($stmt, "EMPLOYEE_ID", $empno);
oci_define_by_name($stmt, "FIRST_NAME", $firstname);
oci_define_by_name($stmt, "LAST_NAME", $lastname);
oci_define_by_name($stmt, "JOB_ID", $jobid);
oci_define_by_name($stmt, "SALARY", $salary);
if (!oci_set_prefetch($stmt, 5)) {
    trigger_error('Failed to set the number of rows to be
                              prefetched', E_USER_WARNING);
}
if (!oci_execute($stmt, OCI_DEFAULT)) {
    $err = oci_error($stmt);
    trigger_error('Query failed: ' . $err['message'], E_USER_ERROR);
}
print '<h3>'.'All employees working in Department '.$deptno.'</h3>';
print '<table border="1">';
print '<th>EMP_ID</th>
        <th>FIRST NAME</th>
        <th>LAST NAME</th>
        <th>JOB_ID</th>
        <th>SALARY</th>';
while (oci_fetch($stmt)) {
    print '<tr>';
    print '<td>'.$empno.'</td>';
    print '<td>'.$firstname.'</td>';
    print '<td>'.$lastname.'</td>';
    print '<td>'.$jobid.'</td>';
    print '<td>'.$salary.'</td>';
    print '</tr>';
}
print '</table>';
?>
```

As you can see, the select list of the query used in this example contains only those columns of the `employees` table that you will use later in the script.

From a performance standpoint, it is always a good idea to specify only those columns in the query select list that you really need, instead of specifying *, which means that all columns will be returned.

The oci_bind_by_name function is used here to associate the $deptno PHP script variable with the deptid: Oracle placeholder. Using placeholders makes your program more flexible, allowing you to operate with SQL statements and PL/SQL blocks that contain input data to be supplied at run time. For further information, see the *Using Bind Variables* section later in this chapter.

Then, you define PHP variables to fetch SQL columns using the oci_define_by_name function. Doing so will allow you to access the fetched data through the corresponding PHP variables once you have fetched the next row of the retrieved data. This approach makes it easier to produce more readable code.

In this example, if the oci_set_prefetch function returns false, the script triggers a warning by calling the trigger_error function with E_USER_WARNING as the second parameter so that execution continues. When your application runs into a problem that is beyond its limits, it is always a good idea to trigger a warning rather than a fatal error. For more information on handling errors, see the *Handling Errors* section later in this chapter.

Normally, the oci_fetch function fetches the next row from the result data into the internal result buffer only. Then, you use the oci_result function to retrieve the value of the desired field in the fetched row. However, in this example you need not employ the oci_return function since you can access the fetched data through the PHP variables defined for fetches before executing the query.

While the example presented in the above listing demonstrates some important steps involved in processing an SQL statement with OCI8, you'll see more examples and descriptions of the use of OCI8 APIs in the subsequent sections of this chapter.

Connecting to Oracle with OCI8

Before diving into the details of processing SQL statements, it is worthwhile to take a moment to look at another important step, which must be taken before the application can start processing an SQL statement. As you have no doubt guessed, this step involves getting a connection to the database.

As you saw in the *Connecting to a Database* section of Chapter 1, Oracle offers several methods for configuring connectivity information for client connections to an Oracle database server. In particular, you learned how to use the local naming and easy connect naming Oracle methods when connecting to Oracle from PHP.

After a brief discussion of how to compose a connection string that can be used to connect to Oracle, this section discusses the OCI8 functions that are used to establish a connection itself.

Defining a Connection String

If your web/PHP server and Oracle database server is connected using TCP/IP, the simplest method for configuring information required to connect to Oracle from PHP is to use the easy connect naming method discussed in the *Connecting to a Database* section in the previous chapter. The biggest advantage of this method is that it allows the client application to connect to an Oracle database server without configuring net service names, thus eliminating the need to create a `tnsnames.ora` configuration file on the client side.

The easy connect naming method is a new Oracle Database 10g feature. So, if you are used to dealing with connect descriptors defined in the `tnsnames.ora` file but want to switch to the easy connect naming method, you might want to see an example demonstrating how this new method can be used instead of the customary way of configuring connectivity information.

Suppose you have the following connect descriptor in the local `tnsnames.ora` file:

```
(DESCRIPTION=
 (ADDRESS=(PROTOCOL=TCP)(HOST=dbserverhost)(PORT=1521))
 (CONNECT_DATA=
  (SERVICE_NAME=orcl)))
```

Using the easy connect naming syntax, you could convert the above descriptor into the following TCP/IP connect string:

```
//dbserverhost:1521/orcl
```

However, in practice you might use a shorter syntax form:

```
//dbserverhost/orcl
```

When using the easy connect naming method, the `port` parameter in a connect descriptor can be omitted if your database server listening port number is 1521.

To seee an example of the easy connect naming syntax when connecting to the database with the help of the `oci_connect` function, you can turn back to the `sqlproc.php` script discussed earlier in this chapter.

OCI8 Functions for Connecting to Oracle

So far, you have seen a few examples of using the `oci_connect` function to connect to an Oracle database server from PHP. However, note, that the OCI8 extension offers three different functions for this purpose — namely `oci_connect`, `oci_pconnect`, and `oci_new_connect`. These functions are summarized in the following table:

OCI8 function for connecting	Description
`oci_connect`	Returns a database connection handle that is then used by some other OCI8 APIs. `oci_connect` uses a database connection cache so that each subsequent call to this function with the same parameters during script execution will return the same connection handle as the first call.
`oci_pconnect`	Returns a handle that refers to a persistent connection established to an Oracle database server. `oci_pconnect` uses a connection cache to reuse connections between requests, thus reducing overhead on each subsequent page load.
`oci_new_connect`	Returns a handle that refers to a new connection established to an Oracle database server. `oci_new_connect` doesn't use a connetion cache and establishes a distinctly new connection each time you call it.

Now that you know which OCI8 functions can be used to establish a connection to an Oracle database server, let's discuss when one might be more appropriate than the others.

In most cases, you will be happy using `oci_connect` when it comes to obtaining a connection to an Oracle database server. You are not supposed to use `oci_connect` in the following cases:

- When you need to maintain transactional isolation when dealing with more than one transaction, opened concurrently in your script.

- When you need to establish a persistent database connection, which can be reused between requests.

The `oci_new_connect` function establishes a distinctly new connection to a database server each time you call it and thereby can be used in situations where you need to separate transactions. Using `oci_new_connect`, you can apply commits and rollbacks to the specified connection only. By contrast, using `oci_connect` assumes that commits and rollbacks are applied to all open transactions in the page. This is because `oci_connect` doesn't establish a new connection if you have already established a connection with the same parameters. Instead, it will return the identifier of the already opened connection.

The `oci_pconnect` function establishes a persistent connection to an Oracle database server. A persistent connection is not closed when the script execution ends. So, the application may have a single persistent connection open against the Oracle database server, thus eliminating the overhead of opening and terminating connections when starting another instance of the application.

Parsing and Executing SQL Statements with OCI8

Whether you are dealing with a query operation, selecting data from a database, or performing a DML operation, modifying database data, both parsing (preparing for execution) and executing are required when it comes to processing an SQL statement with OCI8. Besides these required steps, there may be a few optional steps, such as binding PHP variables to Oracle placeholders that you can perform after you have parsed the statement, but have not yet executed it.

Preparing SQL Statements for Execution

Once a connection to the database is established and the query string is defined, you can go ahead and prepare the statement for execution using the `oci_parse` function, passing to this function the database connection and the SQL statement string as the arguments.

As you saw in the `sqlproc.php` script discussed earlier in this chapter, `oci_parse` returns the statement identifier that can be then passed to `oci_bind_by_name`, `oci_define_by_name`, `oci_set_prefetch`, and `oci_execute` as the first argument.

One word of warning: it is important to realize that oci_parse doesn't validate the SQL statement you pass to it. You have to execute the statement, using oci_execute, to check to see if it is valid.

Using Bind Variables

Besides the fact that using bind variables allow you to build more flexible applications, because it makes it possible for the user to supply input data at run time, it may also significantly improve performance of your application. The fact is that using bind variables, you can parse an SQL statement once and then execute it many times.

From an Oracle database server perspective, once a statement is parsed, it is shared within the shared pool so that the parse tree and execution plan for the statement can be reused by multiple applications. When bind variables are used in a statement, regardless of the fact that their actual values may change from execution to execution, Oracle reuses the metadata for the statement, which is stored in the shared pool, thus avoiding repeated parses.

Finally, using bind variables allows you to avoid concatenating SQL statements, thus preventing SQL injection attacks.

From the sqlproc.php script discussed earlier, you learned how bind variables can be used when dealing with a SELECT statement. The bindvars.php script shown below demonstrates how you can use bind variables when inserting new rows in the departments database table from the HR/HR demonstration schema:

```php
<?php
//File: bindvars.php
  if(!$dbConn = oci_connect('hr', 'hr', '//localhost/orcl')) {
      $err = oci_error();
      trigger_error('Could not establish a connection: ' .
                          $err['message'], E_USER_ERROR);
  };
$depts = array(array("deptno" => 330, "deptname" => 'Research'),
          array("deptno" => 340, "deptname" => 'DB Development'));
$query = 'INSERT INTO departments (department_id, department_name)
                      VALUES(:dept_id, :dept_name)';
$stmt = oci_parse($dbConn, $query);
foreach ($depts as $dept) {
  oci_bind_by_name($stmt, ':dept_id', $dept['deptno'], 4);
```

```
    oci_bind_by_name($stmt, ':dept_name', $dept['deptname'], 30);
    if (!oci_execute($stmt)){
        $err = oci_error($stmt);
        trigger_error('Insertion failed: ' .
                        $err['message'], E_USER_WARNING);
      } else {
        print 'Row inserted! <br />';
      }
    }
  ?>
```

Using bind variables in this example allows you to parse the statement only once and then execute it in a loop several times, each time rebinding the same variables but with different values.

In this example, you explicitly specify the maximum length for the bind variable value when calling the oci_bind_by_name function. In particular, you set the maximum length for the $dept['deptno'] array field variable to 4, and for $dept['deptname'] to 30, thus limiting the maximum length for the values of these bind variables to 4 and 30 characters respectively. To understand where these numbers come from, you should examine the departments table structure. For that, you might connect to the database as HR/HR from SQL*Plus and issue the following query:

```
DESCRIBE departments
```

The result should look like the following figure:

```
SQL> DESCRIBE departments
 Name                                      Null?    Type
 ---------------------------------------- -------- ----------------------------
 DEPARTMENT_ID                             NOT NULL NUMBER(4)
 DEPARTMENT_NAME                           NOT NULL VARCHAR2(30)
 MANAGER_ID                                         NUMBER(6)
 LOCATION_ID                                        NUMBER(4)

SQL> |
```

As you can see in the figure, the department_id column is of type NUMBER and limited to a length of 4 digits. The department_name column is of type VARCHAR2 up to 30 characters in length.

Another thing to notice here is the execution mode used for oci_execute. Since you didn't specify the execution mode for the oci_execute functions explicitly, it is performed in the default OCI_COMMIT_ON_SUCCESS mode, which means that the statement is committed automatically. If insertion fails, the script triggers a warning and execution continues. In a real-world situation, however, you might want to explicitly create a transaction and then commit it only if all the rows have been inserted successfully. Transactions are discussed in detail in Chapter 4 *Transactions*.

Executing SQL Statements

As you saw in the previous examples, you use the oci_execute function to execute a previously parsed statement. This function takes the statement identifier returned by oci_parse as the first parameter, and can take the execution mode as the optional second parameter. The default execution mode is OCI_COMMIT_ON_SUCCESS. In this mode, the executed statement is committed automatically. If you want to create a transaction, you must specify OCI_DEFAULT as the execution mode.

> For discussion on how to handle transactions by means of OCI8, refer to Chapter 4 *Transactions*.

When performing a SELECT statement with the oci_execute function, the query results are held in memory and not available to you immediately. To make use of this data, you must fetch it using one of the OCI8 functions discussed in the *OCI8 Functions for Fetching* section later in this chapter.

Whether you perform a query or a DML operation, oci_execute returns a true on success or false on failure. So, it is always a good idea to make sure that the execution has been completed successfully, triggering an error or warning in case of a failure. Handling errors is discussed in the next section.

Handling Errors

Even though your code doesn't contain programming errors, such as syntax/parse or include/require errors, you may still bump into a run-time error during execution of the script. For example, oci_connect may fail because the database server is temporarily unavailable, and oci_execute may fail simply due to the fact that the table specified in the statement doesn't exist any longer. It is obvious that in most cases such problems are beyond your immediate control. And since there is no guaranteed way of preventing the above problems from occurring, it is always a good idea to employ a mechanism allowing you to handle run-time errors correctly.

Using the oci_error Function

A typical OCI8 function returns a status code indicating the success of the operation. If it returns false, your script can call the oci_error function to obtain information about the error that occurred. Normally, you pass the appropriate resource handle as the parameter to the oci_error function. For connection errors, you call oci_error with no parameter. In both cases, oci_error returns an associative array containing information relating to the error. A common example of oci_error in action involves using this function in conjunction with trigger_error, as shown below:

```
$err = oci_error($stmt);
trigger_error($err['message']);
```

You saw a similar error handling block of code in each example discussed previously in this book.

Using the trigger_error Function

The most popular approach to handling run-time errors in PHP involves using the trigger_error function. When something goes wrong, you make a call to this function, specifying the message describing the error. Optionally, you can pass a predefined constant representing the type of error to trigger as the second parameter. The following table lists the predefined constants representing the types of errors used with trigger_error function:

Predefined constant	Description
E_USER_ERROR	Instructs trigger_error to trigger a fatal error. Terminates the execution of the rest of the script. This level of error is usually specified when it doesn't make much sense to let the script continue to execute.
E_USER_WARNING	Instructs trigger_error to trigger a warning (non-fatal error). This level of error allows your code to continue execution. A warning is usually issued when a non-critical error occurs.
E_USER_NOTICE	Instructs trigger_error to trigger a notice. This will allow the script to continue execution. A notice is normally issued in response to an event that is not necessarily an error, but could happen in the normal course of running a script.

In the following code fragment, you pass E_USER_ERROR as the second parameter to the trigger_error function, which means that the execution of the rest of your script will stop when a connection error occurs.

```
if(!$dbConn = oci_connect('hr', 'hr'))
{
$err = oci_error();
trigger_error('Failed to obtain a connection: '
          .$err['message'], E_USER_ERROR);
}
```

It is important to realize that `trigger_error` doesn't necessarily have to be used for triggering errors. Generally, you can use `trigger_error` as a notification mechanism for all unexpected events occurring during execution of the script.

Using Exceptions

For handling errors, PHP 5 offers a new build-in mechanism based on the use of exceptions. You create and throw an instance of the built-in `Exception` class in response to an error that occurs in your object code. The following code fragment shows exceptions in action:

```
...
try {
  if(!$dbConn = oci_connect('hr', 'hr')) {
    $err = oci_error();
    throw new Exception('Failed to obtain a connection:
                                  '.$err['message']);
  }
...// If an exception is thrown this code is not executed.
} catch (Exception $e) {
  print $e->getMessage()."\n";
}
...// Continue execution
?>
```

The above code looks nice and simple. However, before you decide whether you want to use exceptions in your applications, you should consider the following issue. Using exceptions comes at a cost, which is the performance. That's why, in most cases, it is not a good idea to employ exceptions just as a notification mechanism for unexpected events. Where exceptions fit nicely is the object-oriented world. So they are discussed in greater detail in Chapter 5 *Object-Oriented Approach* later in this book.

Fetching Results with OCI8

If the `oci_execute` call returns `true`, you can then move on to fetching the results. Of course, this makes sense only if you are dealing with a query operation. This section provides a practical description of the fetch functions available in OCI8 as well as code samples showing a few different ways to fetch the retrieved data.

OCI8 Functions for Fetching

The PHP OCI8 extension offers several functions that can be used to fetch the result data. These functions are listed in the following table:

OCI8 fetching function	Description
oci_fetch_assoc	Returns the next row from the result data as an associative array, thus allowing for the fields to be referenced by name. If there are no more rows to be fetched, it returns false.
oci_fetch_row	Returns the next row from the result data as a numeric array. If there are no more rows to be fetched, it returns false.
oci_fetch_array	Returns the next row from the result data as an array. An optional second parameter allows you to specify the kind of array you want to get (associative, numeric, or both). If there are no more rows to be fetched, it returns false.
oci_fetch	Retrieves the next row from the result data and sends it to the internal result buffer. Then, oci_result is used to retrieve the data from the buffer.
oci_fetch_all	Fetches all the retrieved rows at once and sends them into a user-defined array. Returns the number of fetched rows or false in the event of an error.
oci_fetch_object	Returns the next row from the result data as an object whose attributes correspond to the columns specified in the select list of the statement. If there are no more rows to be fetched, it returns false.

As you can see from the table, OCI8 offers three different functions to fetch the next row from the result data into a user-defined array, namely oci_fetch_assoc, oci_fetch_row, and oci_fetch_array. While oci_fetch_assoc and oci_fetch_row can be used to retrieve the next row as an associative or numeric array respectively, oci_fetch_array allows you to either have one or both the arrays. You also have oci_fetch to fetch the next row from the result data. However, it differs from the above functions in that it fetches the next row into the internal result buffer and not into a user-defined array. You then use the oci_result function to access the data stored in that buffer.

While each of the above functions fetches the next row in one way or another, in some situations, you might want to fetch all the retrieved rows into a two-dimensional array at once. This is where oci_fetch_all comes in very handy.

Fetching the Next Row

Although `oci_fetch_array` can be insignificantly slower than the other OCI8 functions in fetching the next row into a user-defined array, you may find it more useful in many ways. Here is an example of using the `oci_fetch_array` function to fetch the data retrieved from the database.

```
...
$query = 'SELECT employee_id, first_name, last_name FROM employees';
...
print '<table border="1">';
 while ($emp = oci_fetch_array($stmt, OCI_ASSOC))
 {
   print '<tr>';
   print '<td>'.$emp['EMPLOYEE_ID'].'</td>';
   print '<td>'.$emp['FIRST_NAME'].' '.$emp['LAST_NAME'].'</td>';
   print '</tr>';
 }
 print '</table>';
```

In the above example, you make a call to the `oci_fetch_array` function specifying `OCI_ASSOC` as the second optional parameter. This tells `oci_fetch_array` to return the next row from the result data as an associative array.

> By default, `oci_fetch_array` returns an array with both associative and numeric indices. Although you may be satisfied with this default behavior, it is a good practice to explicitly specify the type of array you want to get.

Here is how you could use a combination of constants when specifying the second parameter of `oci_fetch_array`:

```
...
$query = 'SELECT * FROM employees';
...
print '<table border="1">';
 while ($emp = oci_fetch_array($stmt, OCI_RETURN_NULLS+OCI_NUM)) {
   print '<tr>';
     foreach ($emp as $item) {
       print '<td>'.($item?htmlentities($item):' ').'</td>';
     }
     print '</tr>';
 }
 print '</table>';
...
```

In the above example, you specify OCI_RETURN_NULLS+OCI_NUM as the second parameter of oci_fetch_array. This combination tells the function to return the next row as a numeric array, creating empty elements for the NULL fields.

Fetching All the Rows

Sometimes you might want to fetch all the retrieved rows into a user-defined array at once. For example, this approach may be handy when you implement a function that encapsulates SELECT statement processing, including fetching the retrieved data, and then returns all the fetched records as an array to the calling code. In this case, fetching the rows one at a time would definitely be an unnecessary step. An example of such function is shown below:

```php
<?php
//File: getEmployees.php
function getEmployees($deptno) {
  if(!$rsConnection = oci_connect('hr', 'hr', '//localhost/orcl')) {
      $err = oci_error();
      trigger_error('Could not establish a connection: ' .
                    $err['message'], E_USER_ERROR);
   };
  $strSQL = "SELECT * FROM employees WHERE department_id =:deptid";
  $rsStatement = oci_parse($rsConnection,$strSQL);
  oci_bind_by_name($rsStatement, ":deptid", $deptno, 4);
  if (!oci_execute($rsStatement)) {
   $err = oci_error($stmt);
   trigger_error('Query failed: ' .
                    $err['message'], E_USER_WARNING);
   return false;
  }
  $nrows = oci_fetch_all($rsStatement, $employees);
  return array ($nrows, $ employees);
 }
?>
```

In the above script, oci_fetch_all fetches all the retrieved rows into the employees two-dimensional array. This example demonstrates how you can employ a list to return multiple values from a function. The function discussed here returns the number of retrieved rows and the array containing these rows as a single array.

To test the `getEmployees` function from this script, you need to create a script that will call this function, passing the ID of a department as the parameter. Such a script is shown below:

```php
<?php
  //File: deptEmployees.php
require_once 'getEmployees.php';
$deptno = 60;
if(list($nrows, $employess) = getEmployees($deptno)){
 print '<h3>'.'All employees working in Department '.$deptno.'</h3>';
 if ($nrows > 0) {
  print "<table border=1>";
  print "<tr>\n";
  while (list($key, $value) = each($employees)) {
   print "<th>$key</th>\n";
  }
  print "</tr>\n";
  print "</tr>\n";
  for ($i = 0; $i < $nrows; $i++) {
     print "<tr>\n";
     foreach ($employees as $emp) {
        print "<td>$emp[$i]</td>\n";
     }
     print "</tr>\n";
  }
  print "</table>\n";
 } else {
  echo "No employees found<br />\n";
 }
}
?>
```

Using custom functions to encapsulate SQL statement processing can be useful especially when you need to cache results retrieved from the database. In order to achieve this, you could cache function calls using the PEAR::Cache_Lite package.

 Using the PEAR::Cache_Lite package is discussed in extensive detail in Chapter 7 *Caching*.

Alternatives to PHP OCI8 Extension

Now that you are familiar with how to use OCI8 APIs to access Oracle database from PHP, it is worthwhile to take a moment to briefly touch on the other tools that can be used as alternatives to the OCI8 extension. This will not only give you an overview of some popular tools other than the OCI8 extension that can be used to build PHP/Oracle applications, but it can also help you understand whether OCI8 is the best choice for a particular application or there is another tool that fits your needs better.

As mentioned previously, there are several open-source libraries that can be used to communicate with Oracle from PHP. This section briefly touches upon the most popular two, namely PEAR DB and ADOdb, as well as the PHP Data Objects (PDO) extension that provides a lightweight interface for accessing databases in PHP. Finally, it discusses how you might benefit from creating your own library on top of the OCI8 extension.

Using PEAR DB

PEAR DB is a database abstraction layer providing a single API for interacting with most of the databases supported by PHP. You install the PEAR DB package using the PEAR Installer, as shown below:

```
$ pear install DB
```

For more information on how to install PEAR and its packages, see PEAR documentation available on the PEAR Documentation page of the PEAR website at:

http://pear.php.net/manual/

Once you have installed the PEAR DB package, you might want to see it in action. Turning back to the example discussed in Chapter 1, you might rewrite it with PEAR DB as shown in the following example:

```php
<?php
//File: dbtime_pear.php
require_once 'DB.php';
$dbh = DB::connect("oci8://hr:hr@localhost:1521/orcl");
if(DB::isError($dbh)) {
  die($dbh->getMessage());
}
$dbh->setFetchMode(DB_FETCHMODE_ASSOC);
$rslt = $dbh->query("SELECT TO_CHAR(SYSDATE, 'HH:MI:SS')
              ctime FROM DUAL");
if (PEAR::isError($rslt)) {
```

```
              die($res->getMessage());
    }
    $rslt->fetchInto($row);
    print "<h3>The current time is ".$row['CTIME']."</h3>";
?>
```

As you can see in the above script, the `connect` method of a DB object is used to connect to a database. It requires a valid Data Source Name (DSN) as the first parameter, which can be either a string or an array. In this example, the DSN is a string consisting of the database driver name as used in PHP, database user name and password, host name where the database resides, port on which the database server listens for connection requests, and the service name of the database.

Note that the `connect` method is a universal DB connection method that is used to connect to all databases supported by PEAR DB. For example, when connecting to a MySQL database, the DSN passed to the `connect` method might look like the following:

```
mysql://usr:pswd@hostname/db_name
```

The `query` method performs a query passed as an argument. Note that the query method eliminates the need for a prepare method, thus simplifying coding. Alternatively, PEAR DB allows you to use the `prepare` and `execute` method combination. In the above example, you might replace the `query` function with the `prepare` and `execute` method combination as follows:

```
$sth = $dbh->prepare("SELECT TO_CHAR(SYSDATE, 'HH:MI:SS')
                                       ctime FROM DUAL");
$rslt = $dbh->execute($sth);
```

However, in this particular case, the above replacement would not make sense. The `prepare` and `execute` method combination provides more power and flexibility when it comes to performing the same query several times — each time with different arguments. The following code snippet demonstrates how you could insert several rows into a `customers` table using the DB's `prepare` and `execute` methods:

```
$custs = array(array(1, 'Maya Silver'),
               array(2, 'Tom Jamison'),
               array(3, 'Ann Nelson'));
$sth = $dbh->prepare('INSERT INTO customers VALUES(?, ?)');
foreach ($custs as $row) {
    $dbh->execute($sth, $row);
}
```

Now, if you compare the `dbtime.php` script discussed in Chapter 1 to the `dbtime_pear.php` script discussed in this section, you may note that the latter is shorter and seems to be more readable. So, you might be asking yourself: "Why not prefer PEAR DB API to using OCI8 functions?" Well, the main advantage of PEAR DB is that it provides a way to rapidly develop portable and reusable database solutions—you use a single API for all databases supported.

On the other hand, it is important to remember that DB is written in PHP, which in practice means that it is slower than using built-in PHP functions directly. Moreover, providing one common API for accessing different databases, PEAR DB in fact lacks some Oracle-specific functionality, such as support for LOBs and REF cursors (this is true for PEAR DB 1.6 at least).

So, the use of PEAR DB makes sense in the following situations:

- When you need to quickly build an application where high performance is not required.
- When you need to build a portable application that can be easily migrated from one database to another.
- When you use other PEAR packages.

As for the last situation mentioned in the above list, it is important to note that although choosing PEAR DB seems to be a reasonable way to go when you are planning to use other PEAR packages, you actually don't have to follow this rule. In many situations, using the OCI8 APIs in conjunction with some PEAR libraries still results in better performance than using PEAR DB APIs with PEAR libraries.

Using ADOdb

ADOdb is another popular database abstraction layer designed to simplify coding database-driven PHP applications. Like PEAR DB, ADOdb supports a wide range of SQL databases, providing a unified API for accessing all databases. For detailed information about how to install and then use ADOdb, visit the following web page:

```
http://phplens.com/lens/adodb/docs-adodb.htm
```

While the above web page includes a lot of detailed examples on how to interact with databases using ADOdb library, the following example shows a simple ADOdb/Oracle application obtaining the current time from the database:

```php
<?php
//File:dbtimeADOdb.php
require_once "adodb\adodb.inc.php";
if (!$db = NewADOConnection("oci8://hr:hr@localhost:1521/orcl")){
```

```
      die("Connection failed");}
  $db->SetFetchMode(ADODB_FETCH_ASSOC);
  if (!$rs = $db->Execute("SELECT TO_CHAR(SYSDATE, 'HH:MI:SS')
                    ctime FROM DUAL")){
    die("Query failed: ".$db->ErrorMsg());}
  $row = $rs->FetchRow();
  print "<h3>The current time is ".$row['CTIME']."</h3>";
  ?>
```

As you can see, the NewADOConnection method is used to create a Connection object through which you can then access the database. Like PEAR DB's connect method, NewADOConnection takes a Data Source Name (DSN) as a parameter. Note that in this example the DSN passed to the NewADOConnection function is the same as the one used with the PEAR DB's connect method in the previous example.

The Execute function performs the query and returns a recordset object whose FetchRow method then is used to fetch the retrieved rows. In this example, only one row is retrieved and so there is no need to call FetchRow in a loop. If you are using the same query several times during script execution, it makes sense to take advantage of the Prepare function.

Generally, ADOdb provides more sophisticated functionality compared to PEAR DB, when it comes to building applications interacting with Oracle. For example, unlike PEAR DB, ADOdb supports LOBs and REF cursors. However, ADOdb is similar to PEAR DB in that it is a high-level database abstraction layer designed to hide the differences between the different database APIs. Practically, this means that you can build an application quickly using OCI8 functions directly in your code, rather than using ADOdb APIs.

Using PDO

PDO (PHP Data Objects) is a new PHP 5 extension providing a data-access abstraction layer. Like PEAR DB and ADOdb, PDO provides a programming interface for accessing different databases in PHP. However, PDO is different in that it is a built-in C extension rather than a high-level API library written in PHP itself.

 In PHP 5.0, you can install PDO as a PECL extension. Starting with PHP 5.1, PDO is included in the distribution. For detailed information on PDO, see PDO documentation at: http://www.php.net/pdo.

Here is a simple application using PDO to interact with Oracle:

```php
<?php
//File:dbtimePDO.php
try {
  $dbh = new PDO('oci:host=localhost;dbname=orcl', 'hr', 'hr');
  foreach ($dbh->query("SELECT TO_CHAR(SYSDATE, 'HH:MI:SS')
                        ctime FROM DUAL") as $row) {
    print "<h3>The current time is ".$row['CTIME']."</h3>";
  }
  $dbh = null;
} catch (PDOException $e) {
    die("Error!: " . $e->getMessage() );
}
?>
```

Creating Your Own Library on Top of OCI8

Another way to simplify coding PHP applications interacting with Oracle is to create a set of your own PHP functions built on top of the OCI8 extension. This approach allows you to encapsulate repeated code in a function so it can be reused by multiple applications. The connect.php script shown below contains the GetConnection function that simplifies the process of obtaining a database connection.

```php
<?php
  //File: connect.php
  function GetConnection(
              $usr,
              $pswd,
              $dbServiceName = "orcl",
              $dbHost = "localhost",
              $dbHostPort="1521")
  {
    $dbConnStr = "(DESCRIPTION=(ADDRESS=(PROTOCOL=TCP)
                  (HOST=".$dbHost.")(PORT=".$dbHostPort."))
                  (CONNECT_DATA=(SERVICE_NAME=".$dbServiceName.")))";
    if(!$dbConn = oci_connect($usr,$pswd,$dbConnStr)) {
       $err = oci_error();
       trigger_error('Failed to connect ' . $err['message']);
       return false;
    }
    return $dbConn;
  }
?>
```

Looking through the previous code of the GetConnection function, you may note that the function doesn't trigger a fatal error when it fails to obtain a connection. Instead, GetConnection returns false to the calling code. This allows the calling code to decide whether to stop execution or not when failing to obtain a connection.

Once you have defined the GetConnection function, you can use it in your scripts to obtain a connection to a database. The following example demonstrates how you might rewrite the dbtime.php script discussed in Chapter 1, using the above GetConnection function:

```php
<?php
//File: dbtime2.php
require_once "connect.php";
$usr = "hr";
$pswd = "hr";
if(!$dbConn = GetConnection($usr,$pswd))
{
    die('Could not establish a connection:');
};
$strSQL = "SELECT TO_CHAR(SYSDATE, 'HH:MI:SS') ctime FROM DUAL";
$stmt = oci_parse($dbConn,$strSQL);
if (!oci_execute($stmt))
{
    $err = oci_error($stmt);
    trigger_error('Failed to execute the
    query: ' . $err['message'], E_USER_ERROR);
};
oci_fetch($stmt);
$rslt = oci_result($stmt, 'CTIME');
print "<h3>The current time is ".$rslt."</h3>";
?>
```

As you can see from the listing, using custom functions can help you produce shorter and thus more readable code.

Summary

OCI8 provides the most powerful way to interact with Oracle from PHP. Developed exclusively for interacting with Oracle database, OCI8 offers more options than any high-level database abstraction layer does.

When developing a PHP/Oracle application, you normally start by creating the code responsible for obtaining a database connection. With OCI8, you can choose between three different connecting functions: `oci_connect`, `oci_pconnect`, and `oci_new_connect`. While using `oci_connect` will be appropriate for most general uses, you should use `oci_new_connect` instead when it comes to dealing with transactions. When you want to reduce overhead on each subsequent page load, you may use `oci_pconnect` to obtain a persistent connection that is not closed when the script execution ends.

Once you have obtained a connection, you can start processing the SQL statement. With OCI8, the required steps involved in SQL statement processing include parsing and executing. You perform these steps using `oci_parse` and `oci_execute` respectively. Also, there may be a few optional steps in SQL processing, where the most interesting one is binding PHP variables to Oracle placeholders. You perform it using the `oci_bind_by_name` function.

If something goes wrong when calling an OCI8 function, the information on the error can be obtained by calling the `oci_error` function, which is commonly used in conjunction with `trigger_error`.

By now, you should have a clear understanding of the steps involved in developing PHP code interacting with Oracle by means of OCI8. In the next chapter, you'll learn how to implement the business logic of your application inside the database.

3

Data Processing

Data processing is essential for any data-driven application. Whether you access database data or modify it, you perform data processing in one way or another. While in simple cases, data processing may involve a few steps, more sophisticated solutions typically perform multiple operations on the data, with branch logic based on the success or failure of any single operation involved.

For most PHP/Oracle applications, data processing takes place partly at the web/PHP server and partly at the Oracle database server. Even if you are dealing with an application that simply outputs the results of a query, you will need to perform at least two general steps: retrieve data from the database and then display the results to the user. In this case, the database server processes the query, producing the results, and the web/PHP server is responsible for formatting and displaying the query results. In more complex cases, you may have to perform some additional processing to get the job done. For example, you might need to calculate the sum of a particular column of the result set, or concatenate two columns into a single column.

The performance of a data processing operation often depends heavily on the way the operation is implemented and therefore on the place where it is performed—at the database server or web/PHP server. While some operations on the data may be performed at either the database server or web/PHP server, it is always a good idea to move data processing to the data rather than moving the data to the processing. Putting it simply, when developing a PHP/Oracle application, in most cases it is better to implement the key business logic of the application inside the database so that the data processing takes place at the database server rather than at the web/PHP server. Doing so can significantly enhance the performance and scalability of your application.

This chapter discusses the most common ways to implement the key business logic of a PHP/Oracle application inside an Oracle database. In particular, it discusses how you can move data processing to the data by using sophisticated SQL queries, stored PL/SQL subprograms, and database triggers.

Implementing the Business Logic of a PHP/Oracle Application

When developing the business logic of your PHP/Oracle application, you have a number of choices. The first choice is to implement the key business logic of the application entirely in PHP, so that the data is processed on the web/PHP server. The situations where you might want to employ this technique are outlined in the *When to Move the Data to the Processing* subsection discussed later in this section.

The second choice is to implement business logic entirely inside the database, so that the data is processed on the database server. The advantages of this technique are outlined in the *Advantages of Moving the Processing to the Data* subsection discussed later in this section.

However, in a real-world situation it is often not possible to implement the business logic of an application entirely inside a database, or entirely in PHP. So, you normally use a bit of both the above techniques. In fact, this is the most common way of implementing the business logic of a data-driven application—the data is processed partly on the web/PHP server and partly on the database server.

When to Move the Data to the Processing

Although implementing business logic inside the database is preferable for most typical PHP/Oracle applications, there are still some situations in which you might prefer to write the key business logic of your application in PHP. The situations are as follows:

- When you need to develop a portable and reusable database solution that can be used with a database other than Oracle.
- When you need to implement the business logic of your application using the tested pieces of PHP code that you already use in other applications.
- When the database server you are using is heavily loaded. So, you might be interested in offloading data processing from the database server to the web/PHP server.

If none of the situations listed above applies, it is highly recommended that you consider implementing the key business logic of your application inside the database.

Advantages of Moving the Processing to the Data

While developing a PHP application that interacts with Oracle, you should always bear in mind that a well-designed PHP/Oracle application performs the bulk of data processing on the database server rather than on the web/PHP server. Generally, implementing the key business logic of a PHP/Oracle application inside the database can help you accomplish the following goals:

- Enhance the performance
- Increase the scalability
- Improve the security

The following table summarizes concrete benefits that can be achieved when implementing the key business logic of a PHP/Oracle application inside the database:

Benefit	Description
Producing re-usable solutions	By creating a common set of stored subprograms inside the database, you can easily share business logic across applications.
Centralizing control over business logic	Implementing business logic of a PHP/Oracle application inside the database gives you centralized control over that business logic, and therefore allows you to produce a more maintainable solution.
Reducing network overhead	When performing data processing inside the database, the application doesn't need to transfer a large amount of data between tiers; instead, it sends only the final product across the wire.
Avoiding redundant coding	When implementing the business logic of a PHP/Oracle application inside the database, you normally have to work less than writing it in PHP—Oracle tools are extremely effective when it comes to implementing data processing operations.
Taking advantage of Oracle's built-in functionality	Because of the tight coupling between Oracle's built-in tools, such as Oracle SQL and PL/SQL, and database data, you may achieve a better performance using these tools when it comes to processing the data stored in the database.
Building more secure applications	By utilizing Oracle security features, you can effectively protect your application data from unauthorized access, giving trusted users easy access to that data at the same time.

As the table shows, there are several advantages of implementing the business logic of a PHP/Oracle application inside the database. Specifically, this can significantly enhance the performance, scalability, and security of your application.

Ways of Implementing Business Logic Inside the Database

Now that you know the major advantages of performing data processing inside the database, it's time to move on and discuss the ways in which this can be accomplished. The first question you might ask is "which Oracle features should I use to implement the business logic of my application inside an Oracle database?". While the answer to this question may vary depending on the situation, there are several Oracle features that are used in almost any Oracle-backed application. These features are listed in the following table:

Feature	Description
SQL statements	A SQL statement is an instruction passed to the database to perform a certain operation on information stored in the database. Specifically, it is passed to the SQL compiler, which in turn generates a procedure to perform the desired task. A SQL statement may have a very sophisticated structure, combining subqueries to different database objects and using a variety of built-in Oracle SQL functions.
Stored subprograms	A stored subprogram, procedure, or function, is a named program unit stored inside the database, used to access and manipulate database information, usually consisting of PL/SQL constructs and SQL statements. Stored subprograms can take parameters.
Database triggers	Like a stored procedure or function, a database trigger is a subprogram stored inside the database. A trigger is associated with a database table, view, or database event such as instance startup or shutdown, and is automatically invoked when a certain event occurs, for example, updating a row in the associated table.

It is important to note that each of the features outlined in the table represents a program unit running on an Oracle database server. The following figure gives a conceptual depiction of how these program units interact with each other.

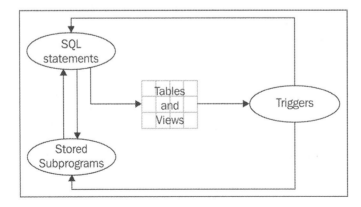

As can be seen from the previous diagram, in the long run, only SQL statements provide a way to access and modify database data and metadata. Both stored subprograms and triggers must employ SQL statements when it comes to operating on database data or metadata.

Also notice that triggers cannot be called directly from SQL statements or stored subprograms. Instead, triggers are fired implicitly whenever a triggering event, such as an insertion of a new row into a certain table, occurs. Nevertheless, you can still call the stored subprograms and issue SQL statements from triggers.

While the previous figure gives a high-level view of how program units of different types interact with each other inside the database, the rest of this chapter discusses these Oracle database features in detail, presenting several examples of using them to effectively implement the business logic of a PHP/Oracle application.

Interaction between Components Implementing Business Logic

Now that you know which program units can be used to implement the business logic of a PHP/Oracle application inside the database and have a rough idea of how they interact with each other, let's take a look at how these program units interact with the other program components implementing the business logic of a PHP/Oracle application. The following figure gives a high-level view of this interaction.

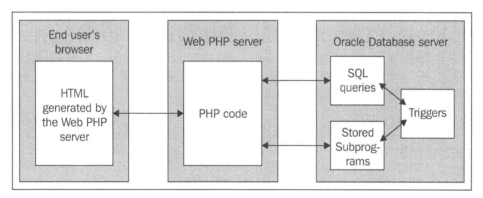

From the previous figure you can see how application processing is done. In particular, it shows that PHP code is processed on the web/PHP server, while SQL statements, stored subprograms, and database triggers are executed on the database server. You directly call SQL statements and stored subprograms from your PHP code, whereas database triggers are normally invoked in response to the events triggered by operations implemented using single SQL statements or stored subprograms.

Once all this processing is done, the web/PHP server sends the generated HTML tags to the end user's browser. In practice, this means that some business logic may also be implemented in a client-side scripting language. For example, the HTML page generated by the web/PHP server may contain JavaScript scripts that are returned as part of that HTML page and are run in the browser on an end-user machine.

Using Complex SQL Statements

While developing PHP/Oracle applications, you may find that implementing some data processing operations by means of PHP can be very difficult to accomplish, as well as inefficient in terms of performance. For example, using PHP, if you need to calculate the average value of all the values in a specific database table column with a numeric data type, first you will have to retrieve all these values from the database and then process them using custom PHP code. Obviously, this solution increases the network overhead and slows down the performance. In this case, using the AVG built-in Oracle SQL function in the query would allow you to achieve the same general result with less overhead.

From the examples given in the preceding chapters, you learned how to use SQL statements to access data stored in the database. This section discusses how you can design SQL statements to offload data processing from the web/PHP server to the database server.

Employing Oracle SQL Functions in Queries

In some situations, you don't need to write stored subprograms to move some business logic from PHP to the database. Instead, you simply design a SQL query that contains built-in Oracle SQL functions for getting the job done.

 While the examples provided in this section demonstrate using just a few of the Oracle SQL functions, Oracle actually offers a variety of built-in functions, which can be used in SQL queries. For detailed information, see Oracle documentation: *Oracle Database SQL Reference*.

Oracle SQL Functions versus PHP Data Processing

Consider the following example. Suppose you need to concatenate two columns in the result set into a single column. Say, you want the first and last names of employees to appear in a single table column when displaying in the browser, as shown in the following figure:

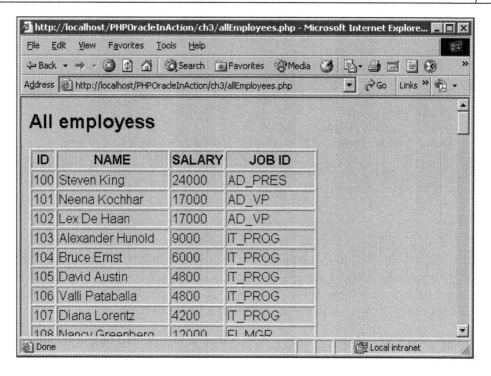

To accomplish this, you can either issue a query against the employees table, so that it returns the first_name and last_name columns and then concatenate these columns into a single column in PHP, or issue a query that will return the already concatenated names, using Oracle built-in SQL function CONCAT in the select list of the query. In the former case, to achieve the results shown in the previous figure, you might build the following PHP script:

```php
<?php
  //File: allEmployees.php
  if(!$rsConnection = oci_connect('hr', 'hr', '//localhost/orcl')) {
      $err = oci_error();
      trigger_error('Could not establish a connection: '
                              . $err['message'], E_USER_ERROR);
  };
  $query = 'SELECT employee_id, first_name, last_name,
                              salary, job_id FROM employees';
  $stmt = oci_parse($rsConnection,$query);
  if (!oci_execute($stmt)) {
   $err = oci_error($stmt);
   trigger_error('Query failed: ' . $err['message'], E_USER_ERROR);
  }
  print '<h2>All employess</h2>';
```

```
      print '<table border="1">';
       print '<th>ID</th>';
       print '<th>NAME</th>';
       print '<th>SALARY</th>';
       print '<th>JOB ID</th>';
       while ($emp = oci_fetch_array($stmt, OCI_ASSOC)) {
        print '<tr>';
        print '<td>'.$emp['EMPLOYEE_ID'].'</td>';
        print '<td>'.$emp['FIRST_NAME'].' '.$emp[
                          'LAST_NAME'].'</td>';
        print '<td>'.$emp['SALARY'].'</td>';
        print '<td>'.$emp['JOB_ID'].'</td>';
        print '</tr>';
      }
     print '</table>';
   ?>
```

Looking through the previous script, you may notice that both the `first_name` and `last_name` columns are included in the select list of the query. This means that each of these columns will appear in the result set as a single column.

In this example, you call `oci_fetch_array` with the `OCI_ASSOC` flag to obtain the return row data as an associative array.

Then, you concatenate the first name and last name of an employee together in the way strings are normally concatenated in PHP.

The following example demonstrates how the same concatenation can be accomplished using the Oracle SQL function CONCAT in the select list of the query.

```
     $query = "SELECT employee_id, CONCAT(CONCAT(first_name,'
             '),last_name) ename, salary, job_id FROM employees";
   ...
      print '<table border="1">';
       print '<th>ID</th>';
       print '<th>NAME</th>';
       print '<th>SALARY</th>';
       print '<th>JOB ID</th>';
       while ($emp = oci_fetch_array($stmt, OCI_ASSOC)) {
        print '<tr>';
        print '<td>'.$emp['EMPLOYEE_ID'].'</td>';
        print '<td>'.$emp['ENAME'].'</td>';
        print '<td>'.$emp['SALARY'].'</td>';
        print '<td>'.$emp['JOB_ID'].'</td>';
        print '</tr>';
      }
     print '</table>';
```

Note the use of Oracle SQL's built-in CONCAT function in the query. The fact is that the CONCAT function concatenates only two strings per call. However, in this particular case, you need to concatenate three strings, namely: the first name of an employee, his or her last name, and a separating space between them. To achieve this, you call CONCAT twice.

Note that ENAME is a alias, which you used in the query for the CONCAT(CONCAT(... column. It is always a good idea to use an alias for a column that has such a long name.

Although the previous snippet is fairly simple, it does serve to illustrate the point. In particular, it shows how a data processing operation implemented in PHP can instead be implemented using a built-in Oracle function specified in the select list of a query.

Aggregate Functions

In the previous example, you saw how an Oracle SQL function can be used to operate on the values of fields in the same record, returning a single result for every row in the result set. However, in some situations, you may need to operate on groups of rows, producing a single result row for each group. This is where Oracle SQL aggregate functions come in handy. The following example shows using the MAX aggregate function to calculate the maximum value in a certain column of a database table.

Suppose you need to find the highest salary of all employees present in the employees table. Although the required processing may be implemented in PHP, using Oracle SQL built-in function MAX in the select list of the query also results in an efficient solution. The following code fragment demonstrates the MAX function in action:

```
$query = 'SELECT MAX(salary) maxsal FROM employees';
$sal = oci_fetch_array($stmt, OCI_ASSOC);
print '<h3>'.'The max salary is: '.$sal['MAXSAL'].'</h3>';
```

Now that you've seen the use of the MAX Oracle SQL function, try to figure out how much code you would have to write if you decided to implement the same functionality in PHP. Another thing to consider here is the performance. Whatever PHP code you write to determine the maximum value in a table column, you will first have to retrieve all the values presented in this column from the database, thus increasing network overhead.

The GROUP BY Clause

Often, you don't need to apply aggregate functions to all the rows in a queried table. Instead, you might want to divide the rows of a queried table into groups and then apply the aggregate functions to each group, retrieving a single result row for each group. To achieve such functionality, you might use the GROUP BY clause in the query, as discussed in the following example.

Suppose you need to determine the highest salary in each department from the employee records stored in the employees table. To achieve this, you might rewrite the above code fragment as follows:

```
$query = 'SELECT department_id, MAX(salary) maxsal
                    FROM employees GROUP BY department_id;';
while ($sal = oci_fetch_array($stmt, OCI_ASSOC)) {
 print '<h3>'.'The max salary in department
      '.$sal['DEPARTMENT_ID'].' is: '.$sal['MAXSAL'].'</h3>';
}
```

As you can see, this is still a very easy task to accomplish using the MAX function and the GROUP BY clause in the query. In contrast, a PHP-based solution would require much more coding and would be inefficient in terms of performance, due to the same reason mentioned in the preceding example.

Using Join Queries

So far, we've used SQL queries issued against a single database table. However, often, you need to retrieve information stored in more than one table. In such situations, using join queries comes in very handy.

 A join query is a query that combines information from two or more tables or views.

Without join queries, you would have to issue single queries against each table you need to retrieve information from, and then process the retrieved data as needed, using business logic implemented in PHP.

Probably the easiest way to understand join queries is to look at an example. Turning back to the allEmployees.php script's output shown in the previous figure in the *Oracle SQL Functions versus PHP Data Processing* section earlier, you may notice that the last column in the table contains the job IDs of employees instead of their real job titles. Of course, in a real-world situation, you probably will want to see the real job titles in this column, as shown in the following figure:

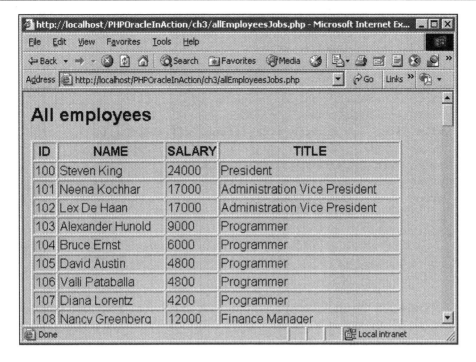

However, the fact is that the employees table queried in the allEmployees.php script contains only employees' job IDs in the job_id column, while the corresponding job titles are stored in the job_title column of another table, namely jobs, which, like the employees table, resides in the HR/HR demonstration database schema by default. One way to solve this problem is to develop a join query whose result set will include the desired columns from both the employees and jobs tables. The following script shows such a join query in action.

```php
<?php
//File: allEmployeesJobs.php
if(!$rsConnection = oci_connect('hr', 'hr', '//localhost/orcl')) {
    $err = oci_error();
    trigger_error('Could not establish a connection: '
                            . $err['message'], E_USER_ERROR);
};
$query = "SELECT employee_id, CONCAT(CONCAT(first_name,'
                    '),last_name) ename, salary, job_title FROM
                    employees e, jobs j WHERE e.job_id=j.job_id";

$stmt = oci_parse($rsConnection,$query);
if (!oci_execute($stmt)) {
 $err = oci_error($stmt);
 trigger_error('Query failed: ' . $err['message'], E_USER_ERROR);
```

```
    }
    print '<h2>All employees</h2>';
    print '<table border="1">';
     print '<th>ID</th>';
     print '<th>NAME</th>';
     print '<th>SALARY</th>';
     print '<th>TITLE</th>';
    while ($emp = oci_fetch_array($stmt, OCI_ASSOC)) {
      print '<tr>';
      print '<td>'.$emp['EMPLOYEE_ID'].'</td>';
      print '<td>'.$emp['ENAME'].'</td>';
      print '<td>'.$emp['SALARY'].'</td>';
      print '<td>'.$emp['JOB_TITLE'].'</td>';
      print '</tr>';
    }
    print '</table>';
   ?>
```

In the query used in the above script, you join the employees and jobs tables based on the join condition comparing their job_id columns. When referencing these columns, use the table aliases to avoid ambiguity.

 When designing a join query, whether you are referencing a table column in the select list or in a join condition, if the joined tables have the name of that column in common, you have to use either the table name or its alias to explicitly specify to which table the column belongs. Neglecting to do so will result in the following Oracle error:
ORA-00918: column ambiguously defined.

In the case of the fetching functions like oci_fetch_array used in this example, there is no difference whether you are executing a query against a single table or dealing with a join query. In either case, these functions will fetch the next row from the result set into an array, whether the result set contains data retrieved from one table or view or from several tables and/or views.

If you have fetched the row into an associative array, as in this example, you refer to the array fields using column names or their aliases specified in the select list of the join query.

Taking Advantage of Views

Although SQL queries are performed on the database server, it is the responsibility of a PHP developer to design the queries required to obtain the necessary information from a database. As you saw in the preceding sections, often there is a need to build complex SQL queries that use Oracle SQL functions and obtain information from more than one table. Obviously, there are very few PHP developers who have the advanced skills required to efficiently build such complex SQL queries.

One possible way to solve the above problem is to use database views.

A view is a customized representation of the data contained in one or more database tables or other views. A view can be thought of as a stored query or a virtual table. This is because a view does not actually contain data, but contains is a SELECT statement whose result set forms the virtual table. The actual tables referenced by the SELECT statement of a view are referred to as the base tables of the view.

In essence, views provide an efficient way of implementing business logic inside the database. The queries that define views are not only performed at the database server, but also stored inside the database, thus hiding data complexity from application developers.

The Key Benefits of Using Views

Now that you know what views are, let's look at how they can be useful in simplifying the development of applications. Here are the key benefits of using views when developing PHP applications on top of Oracle:

- Views can be used to hide data complexity, concealing the details related to the data processing from PHP developers developing SQL queries. Using views makes it possible for people developing PHP code for PHP/Oracle applications to take advantage of the existing queries stored inside the database, rather than designing them from scratch. Since the queries issued against a view are defined in a manner that is similar to that for a single database table, a PHP developer doesn't actually have to be an expert in SQL to obtain required database data available through the views.

- Views can be used to insulate applications from modifications in structures of base tables. If the changes applied to the base tables' structures affect columns referenced in a view, you may have to re-create the view so that those changes in turn do not require rewriting SQL queries issued against the view.

- Views can be used to provide an additional level of security. Using views, you can restrict a user to a predetermined set of rows or columns of a base table or tables. For a detailed discussion on how views can be used to protect application data stored in the database, see Chapter 6 *Security*.

Now that you have a basic grasp of when database views can be useful, it's time to look at an example of them in practice. The following subsection provides an example of when you might have to create a view to make it easier for the PHP developer to build a SQL query retrieving data stored in several database tables.

Hiding Data Complexity with Views

As you learned in the *Using Join Queries* section earlier in this chapter, join queries can be useful when you need to retrieve information stored in more than one table. In particular, you saw how to build a join query on two tables. However, in a real-world situation, you often need to develop a join between more than two tables. In such cases, you have to include several join conditions in your query. However, with more join conditions, your query increases in complexity, sometimes to the point where it is difficult to understand and manage.

Turning back to the join query used in the `allEmployeesJobs.php` script discussed in the *Using Join Queries* section earlier in this chapter, for example, you might want to add a column containing the name of the department for each employee. This information is stored in the `department_name` column of the `departments` table, which resides in the `HR/HR` demonstration database schema by default, like `employees` and `jobs` — the other two tables referenced in the query. So, to include the `department_name` column into the query's select list, you first have to add a join condition comparing the `department_id` column of `employees` to the `department_id` column of `departments`. As a result, you should have a join of three tables, namely `employees`, `jobs`, and `departments`. The code fragment below shows this join query in action.

```
$query =
    "SELECT employee_id, CONCAT(CONCAT(first_name,' '),last_name)
    ename, salary, job_title, department_name FROM employees e,
    jobs j, departments d
    WHERE e.job_id=j.job_id AND e.department_id=d.department_id";
print '<h2>All employees</h2>';
print '<table border="1">';
 print '<th>ID</th>';
 print '<th>NAME</th>';
 print '<th>SALARY</th>';
 print '<th>TITLE</th>';
 print '<th>DEPARTMENT</th>';
 while ($emp = oci_fetch_array($stmt, OCI_ASSOC)) {
```

```
    print '<tr>';
    print '<td>'.$emp['EMPLOYEE_ID'].'</td>';
    print '<td>'.$emp['ENAME'].'</td>';
    print '<td>'.$emp['SALARY'].'</td>';
    print '<td>'.$emp['JOB_TITLE'].'</td>';
    print '<td>'.$emp['DEPARTMENT_NAME'].'</td>';
    print '</tr>';
}
print '</table>';
```

The query used in the above snippet is an example of a complex query. It uses an Oracle SQL function in the select list and retrieves data from three database tables, containing two join conditions in the WHERE clause.

One approach to hide the complexity of the query, used in the above code fragment inside the database is to create a view for that query. This can be done very easily from SQL*Plus. You run SQL*Plus, connecting to the database as hr/hr, and then execute the following SQL statement:

```
CREATE OR REPLACE VIEW employees_v AS SELECT employee_id,
    CONCAT(CONCAT(first_name,' '),last_name) ename, salary,
    job_title, department_name FROM employees e, jobs j, departments d
    WHERE e.job_id=j.job_id AND e.department_id=d.department_id;
```

Once the above view has been created, you can issue queries against it. For example, you might replace the query string used in the above script with the following one:

```
$query = 'SELECT * FROM employees_v';
```

Although this new query string is much simpler than the previous one, you will obtain exactly the same result set in both cases.

Using the WHERE Clause

As you saw in the preceding example, you can issue SQL queries against a view in the same way as you issue them against a regular database table. Any column specified in the select list of the view's SELECT statement may be referenced in a query issued against that view. What this means in practice is that you have to include in the view's select lists all the base tables' columns that you may need to refer to in the queries issued against the view, regardless of whether a given column will be referenced in the SELECT or WHERE clause of a query.

Suppose you want to recreate the employees_v view discussed above so that you can restrict the queries issued against that view to return only the records representing employees working in a particular department, by specifying the condition in the WHERE clause that equates the department_id column to the given department ID.

To achieve this, you need to modify the SELECT statement of the employees_v view so that the view's select list includes the department_id column of the employees table. You can perform this from SQL*Plus. Assuming that you're connected to the database as hr/hr, issue the following SQL statement:

```
CREATE OR REPLACE VIEW employees_v AS SELECT employee_id,
    CONCAT(CONCAT(first_name,' '),last_name) ename, salary,
    job_title, department_name, e.department_id FROM employees e,
    jobs j, departments d WHERE e.job_id=j.job_id AND
    e.department_id=d.department_id;
```

The script below illustrates how you could put the above view into action:

```php
<?php
  //File: displayEmployees.php
  function displayEmployees($deptno) {
    $query = 'SELECT employee_id, ename, salary, job_title,
    department_name FROM employees_v WHERE department_id =:deptid';
...
    oci_bind_by_name($rsStatement, ":deptid", $deptno, 4);
...
    print '<h2>All employees</h2>';
    print '<table border="1">';
     print '<th>ID</th>';
     print '<th>NAME</th>';
     print '<th>SALARY</th>';
     print '<th>TITLE</th>';
     print '<th>DEPARTMENT</th>';
    while ($emp = oci_fetch_array($stmt, OCI_ASSOC)) {
     print '<tr>';
      print '<td>'.$emp['EMPLOYEE_ID'].'</td>';
      print '<td>'.$emp['ENAME'].'</td>';
      print '<td>'.$emp['SALARY'].'</td>';
      print '<td>'.$emp['JOB_TITLE'].'</td>';
      print '<td>'.$emp['DEPARTMENT_NAME'].'</td>';
     print '</tr>';
    }
    print '</table>';
  ...
}
?>
```

In the `displayEmployees.php` script shown opposite, you don't specify * in the select list of the query to avoid moving unnecessary data from the database. Instead, you specify only those columns of the `employees_v` view that contain information you need to display. So, you exclude the `department_id` column from the select list of the query because you are not going to display information stored in this column.

The only reason why you have included the `department_id` column of the `employees` table in the select list of the `employees_v`'s SELECT statement is that it allows you to refer to that column in the WHERE clause of queries issued against the `employees_v` view, restricting the results to only those rows where the `department_id` values match the condition specified.

Using Stored Subprograms

Employing a view is definitely the best way to go when you need to store a single SQL query in the database, hiding query complexity from the application developer. However, in practice you may need to implement a stored program unit that encapsulates a set of SQL statements and control-of-flow statements, such as loops and conditional statements, grouped together and processed with a single call. In such situations, Oracle recommends using stored subprograms.

What are Stored Subprograms?

Stored subprograms can be thought of as building blocks to create high-performance, maintainable, and secure database-driven applications.

 A stored subprogram is a named program unit stored inside a database, ready to be executed. It runs in the database server, can take parameters and return values, and can be called by many users.

Looking through the above definition, you may notice that it says nothing about the programming language in which a stored subprogram can be implemented. The fact is that you have several choices when it comes to implementing an Oracle Database stored subprogram. In particular, you can use PL/SQL, Java, C, or any other programming language that lets you create subprograms callable by C. However, if you want to create a stored subprogram that will run within the address space of the database server, you must use either PL/SQL or Java.

For example, you might prefer to use Java when you already have a Java application that interacts with Oracle and meets your requirements, and you want to move the application code to the database to take advantage of the computing resources of the database server, avoid network bottlenecks, and reuse the application classes in other applications.

Although Java provides full access to Oracle data, PL/SQL, because of its tight integration with the Oracle database server, is, in most cases, the natural choice when it comes to implementing stored subprograms inside an Oracle database. All the examples of stored subprograms given in this book are written in PL/SQL.

The following code is an example of a PL/SQL subprogram. The dept_func function shown here takes a department ID as the parameter and returns the corresponding department name as the result. The primary purpose of this example is to illustrate how a PL/SQL subprogram is organized. The details on how to create PL/SQL subprograms and how to call them from PHP are discussed in subsequent sections later in this chapter.

```
FUNCTION dept_func(deptno NUMBER)
RETURN VARCHAR2 AS
   dept_name VARCHAR2(30);
BEGIN
   SELECT department_name INTO dept_name FROM departments WHERE
department_id=deptno;
   RETURN dept_name;
EXCEPTION
   WHEN NO_DATA_FOUND THEN
      RETURN 'No such department';
END;
```

A PL/SQL subprogram spec begins with the keyword FUNCTION or PROCEDURE followed by the subprogram name. The optional list of parameters must appear in parentheses. The parentheses must be omitted if the subprogram takes no parameters. The spec of a function ends with the RETURN clause that specifies the datatype of the return value.

In the above example, you have the PL/SQL function dept_func that takes one parameter of type NUMBER and returns a value of type VARCHAR2.

In the optional declarative part of a PL/SQL subprogram, you define types, variables, exceptions, and other items that will be manipulated in the executable part. In this example, you declare the only variable in the declarative part, namely dept_name, which is then used to hold a department name retrieved by the SELECT statement run in the executable part.

The executable part is required. It starts with the BEGIN keyword and ends with the END or EXCEPTION keyword, depending whether the subprogram has an optional exception-handling part or not. The executable part cannot be empty—at least one statement must be included. In the case of a function, at least one RETURN statement must appear in the executable part.

The optional exception-handling part is intended to deal with exceptions raised during execution. In this particular example, you handle an exception that is raised when the SELECT statement defined in the executable part returns no row.

Advantages of Stored Subprograms

Stored procedures provide an efficient way of the implementing business logic of your PHP/Oracle application at the database server level, thus increasing application performance, scalability, and security. Specifically, by employing stored subprograms in your PHP/Oracle applications, you can achieve the following benefits:

- Performance improvements: Since subprograms are stored inside a database in a compiled form, when called, they are immediately loaded into the shared memory of a database instance and can be shared by many applications. Another thing to note here is that using stored subprograms can help you reduce network overhead. You need to make only a single call over the network to run a stored subprogram that may encapsulate a series of SQL statements to be processed on the database server.

- Reusability: Using stored subprograms can help you to achieve a consistent implementation of business logic across applications. For example, you might create a set of stored subprograms to perform the most common tasks faced by your applications.

- Maintainability: Using stored subprograms makes maintenance and enhancement easier. Although you can create a reference to a stored subprogram from PHP code as well as from within other stored subprograms, it doesn't automatically mean that you have to modify the calling code once the stored subprogram has been modified. A well-designed application assumes that changing the internals of a certain subprogram will not require modifying the code calling it.

- Security: Stored subprograms can be used as a security mechanism. For example, you can implement a stored function that will manipulate data stored in a database table. Then, you grant users privileges to execute this function, instead of granting them privileges to issue SQL statements against that table directly.

As you no doubt have realized, stored subprograms provide a powerful way of implementing the business logic of your application inside a database, enabling you to create reliable, maintainable, and reusable PHP/Oracle solutions. In general, when developing a PHP/Oracle application, you should use stored subprograms whenever possible.

An Example of When to Use a Stored Subprogram

As stated earlier, stored subprograms can be especially useful when you deal with a task that is implemented as a series of SQL statements. The following example is intended to demonstrate a situation in which you might want to create a stored subprogram to perform two SQL statements with a single call.

Suppose you need to develop a PHP/Oracle application accessing sensitive data stored in the database. In such situation, you'll no doubt want to implement a secure mechanism preventing unauthorized access to sensitive information. One common approach to this task is to make sure that users log in, and determine their rights before they can access certain information. To implement this functionality, you might perform the following steps:

1. Create a new database schema, in which you create a table, say, `accounts`, to store users' accounts, and another table, say, `logons`, to store information about users' logons.

2. Build the PHP code that will check a user/password combination against the `accounts` table and establish a new session, setting a session variable to the user name, upon successful authentication. Also, build the code that will insert a row into the `logons` table once a user is authenticated.

3. Implement a security mechanism inside the database that will allow only authenticated users to access the data.

While the most common ways to implement step 3 are discussed in Chapter 6 *Security*, this section discusses how to implement steps 1 and 2. The main focus here is on implementing step 2. In particular, you'll learn how to implement an authentication system in PHP and then how to move the authentication logic implemented in PHP to the database, accomplishing that by creating a PL/SQL stored subprogram.

Before you proceed with the procedures outlined in step 2 you need to accomplish a series of tasks outlined in step 1. Specifically, you need to create a new database schema to work with and then create the `accounts` and `logons` database tables in that schema. You can perform all these tasks from SQL*Plus by issuing the following statements:

```
CONN /AS sysdba

CREATE USER usr IDENTIFIED BY usr;

GRANT connect, resource TO usr;

CONN usr/usr

CREATE TABLE accounts (usr_id      VARCHAR2(10)   PRIMARY KEY,
                       full_name   VARCHAR2(20),
                       pswd        VARCHAR2(10)   NOT NULL
                      );

CREATE TABLE logons (usr_id    VARCHAR2(10)   REFERENCES accounts,
                     log_time  DATE
                    );

CREATE INDEX ind_usr_id ON logons(usr_id);

INSERT INTO accounts VALUES ('bob', 'Bob Robinson', 'pswd');

COMMIT;
```

By issuing the above SQL statements, you create the usr user and then grant the privileges to that user that will be required to work with the database object stored in the usr/usr schema.

Next, you create the accounts table and then define a primary key on the usr_id column of that table to guarantee that the value of the usr_id field for each row is unique within the table and is not null.

When creating the logons table, you define a foreign key on the usr_id column that references the primary key on the usr_id column of the accounts table to guarantee that each row in the logons table will be assigned to a row in the accounts table.

Then, you create an index on the usr_id foreign key column of the logons table to speed up queries issued against that table. Oracle recommends that you define indexes on the foreign keys to have faster access to data.

Next, you insert a row into the accounts table, since you need to have at least one row in the accounts table to be able to test your authentication system.

When issued, the COMMIT statement ends the current transaction, making the changes made by the data modification language (DML) operations within the transaction permanent. In this example, you issue the COMMIT statement to make the changes made by the INSERT action performed above permanent.

You don't need to issue a COMMIT statement to make the changes made by data definition language (DDL) operations like CREATE TABLE permanent. In such cases, Oracle commits changes implicitly, upon completion of a single DDL operation. For further discussion, see Chapter 4 *Transactions*.

Once you have performed the statements discussed above, you can proceed to implement an authentication system in PHP, as outlined in step 2 at the beginning of this section. For simplicity, you might build a single PHP function implementing the required functionality, as shown in the following script:

```php
<?php
//File: userLogin.php
function login($usr, $pswd) {
if(!$rsConnection = oci_connect('usr', 'usr', '//localhost/orcl')) {
    $err = oci_error();
    trigger_error('Could not establish a connection: ' .
                $err['message'], E_USER_ERROR);
};
$query = "SELECT full_name FROM accounts
                WHERE usr_id = :userid AND pswd = :passwd";
$stmt = oci_parse($rsConnection,$query);
oci_bind_by_name($stmt, ':userid', $usr);
oci_bind_by_name($stmt, ':passwd', $pswd);
if (!oci_execute($stmt)) {
 $err = oci_error($stmt);
 trigger_error('Query failed: ' . $err['message'], E_USER_ERROR);
}
if ($arr = oci_fetch_array($stmt, OCI_ASSOC)) {
  print "Hello, ".$arr['FULL_NAME'];
  session_start();
  $_SESSION['user']=$usr;
} else {
  print "Wrong user/password combination";
  return false;
}
oci_free_statement($stmt);
$query = "INSERT INTO logons VALUES (:userid, SYSDATE)";
$stmt = oci_parse($rsConnection,$query);
oci_bind_by_name($stmt, ':userid', $usr);
if (!oci_execute($stmt)) {
 $err = oci_error($stmt);
 trigger_error('Insertion failed: ' . $err['message'],
                                    E_USER_WARNING);
```

```
    }
    return true;
    }
?>
```

In the previous script, you define the query that is used to check if a given user account exists in the `accounts` table.

Once a query is parsed, you bind PHP variables to the placeholders used in that query. In this particular example, you bind the PHP variables representing the user name and password to the placeholders used in the query.

Upon successful authentication, you print a hello message including the full name of the authenticated user, and also establish a new session. In this example, you create a new session variable and set it to the ID of the authenticated user.

Then, assuming successful authentication, you insert a new row into the `logons` table.

As you can see, the `login` function shown in the script opposite takes the user name and password as parameters and validates the user against the database. Upon successful authentication, it establishes a new session and sets the session variable `user` to the name of the authenticated user, so that it can be used in the other application scripts. While Chapter 6 *Security* discusses in detail how PHP session variables can be used in conjunction with a security mechanism implemented inside the database, the `testLogin.php` script shown below simply checks whether the `login` function works as expected.

```php
<?php
  //File: testLogin.php
  require_once "userLogin.php";
  if (login('bob','pswd')) {
    if (isset($_SESSION['user'])) {
      print '<p>'.'Your account name: '.$_SESSION['user'].'</p>';
    } else {
      print '<p>'.'Session variable representing the account
                            name is not set'.'</p>';
    }
  }else {
      print '<p>'.'Authentication failed'.'</p>';
  }
?>
```

The `testLogin.php` script should produce the following output:

```
Hello, Bob Robinson
Your account name: bob
```

Now that you have an authentication system implemented in PHP, it's time to look at how you can move the authentication logic from PHP to the database, thus achieving the benefits of moving data processing inside the database, discussed in the *Advantages of Stored Subprograms* section earlier in this chapter. The following section discusses how the authentication logic implemented in the `login` function discussed here might be implemented in a PL/SQL subprogram instead.

Creating Stored Subprograms

Turning back to the `login` function discussed in the preceding section, you may notice that it issues two SQL statements against the database. The first statement is a query issued against the `accounts` table. The second is an INSERT statement issued against the `logons` table. In this situation, it would be a good idea to create a PL/SQL stored subprogram that will encapsulate both these statements, thus moving the data processing from PHP to the database.

 When implementing a stored subprogram, you have two choices—you can either create a function or procedure. Both stored procedures and stored functions are commonly referred to as stored procedures. In fact, a procedure differs from a function only in that a function always returns a single value to the caller, while a procedure does not.

The following SQL statement shows how to create a PL/SQL function that will authenticate users against the database, returning true upon successful authentication and false otherwise. You can create the PL/SQL function shown below in SQL*Plus, when connected as usr/usr:

```
CREATE OR REPLACE FUNCTION auth(user IN VARCHAR2, password IN
VARCHAR2, fullname OUT VARCHAR2, msg OUT VARCHAR2 )
RETURN NUMBER AS
BEGIN
  BEGIN
    SELECT full_name INTO fullname FROM accounts
                    WHERE usr_id=user AND pswd=password;
  EXCEPTION
    WHEN NO_DATA_FOUND THEN
      msg:='Wrong user/password combination';
      RETURN 0;
  END;
```

```
BEGIN
  INSERT INTO logons VALUES(user, SYSDATE);
  COMMIT;
EXCEPTION
  WHEN OTHERS THEN
    msg:='Failed to insert a row into the logons table';
    RETURN 1;
END;
RETURN 1;
END;
/
```

In the above code, note the use of IN and OUT parameters in the parameter list of the function specification. You pass user and password as IN parameters to the function because you don't need to change the values of these parameters in the function. In contrast, you specify fullname and msg as OUT parameters because you compute their values in the function and want to make these values available to the caller of the function.

Besides IN and OUT parameters, PL/SQL also lets you specify IN OUT parameters in the parameter list of a subprogram specification. You use IN OUT parameters when you need to pass initial values to a subprogram and then return updated values to the calling code.

In this example, the executable part of the function consists of two blocks. In the first block, you issue a query against the accounts table, looking for the row corresponding to the specified user/password combination. If the query fails to find this row, PL/SQL raises a NO_DATA_FOUND exception and transfers control to the exception-handling part of the block, in which you set the value of the msg variable to a string containing the message saying that the given user/password combination is wrong, and then you complete the execution of the function and return false to the caller.

The second block is performed only if the query in the first block has returned a row, which means that the authentication has been successful. Here, you simply create a new record in the logons table. This record contains two fields, namely user_id and log_time. The former contains the ID of the authenticated user, as specified in the accounts table. The latter contains the date and time when the authentication occurred.

Finally, note the use of the single slash (/) on the last line of the above statement. It activates the CREATE FUNCTION statement. You must use the same technique when creating a stored procedure with the CREATE PROCEDURE statement.

Calling Stored Subprograms from PHP

Now that you have the auth PL/SQL stored function created, you can call it from
PHP in much the same way you call SQL statements. The following script shows
how you can modify the login function originally used in the userLogin.php script
discussed in the *An Example of When to Use a Stored Subprogram* section earlier,
so that it calls the auth stored function, which implements the application's
authentication logic.

```php
<?php
//File: userLogin.php
function login($usr, $pswd) {
if(!$rsConnection = oci_connect('usr', 'usr', '//localhost/orcl')) {
    $err = oci_error();
    trigger_error('Could not establish a connection: ' .
                        $err['message'], E_USER_ERROR);
};
$query = "BEGIN :rslt:=auth(:usrid, :pwd, :fullname, :msg); END;";
$stmt = oci_parse($rsConnection,$query);
oci_bind_by_name($stmt, ':rslt', $func_rslt,1);
oci_bind_by_name($stmt, ':usrid', $usr, 10);
oci_bind_by_name($stmt, ':pwd', $pswd, 10);
oci_bind_by_name($stmt, ':fullname', $full_name, 20);
oci_bind_by_name($stmt, ':msg', $err_msg, 100);
if (!oci_execute($stmt)) {
 $err = oci_error($stmt);
 trigger_error('Function call failed: ' .
                        $err['message'], E_USER_ERROR);
}
if ($func_rslt) {
  print "Hello, ".$full_name;
  session_start();
  $_SESSION['user']=$usr;
} else {
  print $err_msg;
  return false;
}
if (isset($err_msg)){
 print '<p><i>'.'Warning: '.$err_msg.'</i></p>';
}
return true;
}
?>
```

In the previous script, note the use of placeholders in the PL/SQL block to be executed. Whether you are dealing with an IN, OUT, or IN OUT parameter, or the return value of a PL/SQL stored function, you must use a placeholder that will be then bound to a PHP variable, by using the oci_bind_by_name function.

It is important to realize that the oci_bind_by_name function doesn't let you specify whether the bind variable is used for input or output—this is determined at run time. That is why you bind all the PHP variables to the Oracle placeholders in the same way, regardless of whether you are dealing with an IN, OUT, or IN OUT parameter, or use a bind variable to obtain the return value of the auth function.

Then, you check whether the auth function has returned 0 or 1. The former means that the authentication failed, while the latter indicates successful authentication.

Upon successful authentication, you print a welcome message and set the user session variable to the ID of the authenticated user. If the authentication fails, you print an error message generated in the auth stored function and then stop the execution of the login PHP function, returning false to the calling code.

If you look through the code of the auth stored function shown in the preceding section, you may notice that this function still returns true upon failure to insert a new record into the logons table. However, in this case, it sets the msg output parameter to the string containing a warning message. That is why you check to see whether the err_msg variable in the logon function—which is bound to the msg output parameter of the auth stored function—is set up, regardless of whether the auth stored function returns true or false.

Using Triggers

In some situations, you may need to create a stored subprogram that will be invoked implicitly when a certain action occurs. For example, you might need to create a procedure that will be invoked whenever a certain DML operation (INSERT, UPDATE, or DELETE) is issued against a given table or view. You can also choose a combination of DML operations, each of which will fire the procedure. To handle such tasks, the Oracle database offers triggers.

 A database trigger is an event-driven stored subprogram that is invoked automatically in response to a certain event.

The following sections discuss how to create a trigger on a database table. This is the most common use of triggers. In chapter 6 *Security*, you'll see an example of a system trigger created on the LOGON event, to be fired whenever a user is connected to the database.

For more information on triggers, see Oracle documentation: chapter *Coding Triggers* in the *Oracle Database Application Developer's Guide–Fundamentals* book.

Creating Triggers

The simplest way to see how Oracle database triggers work is with the help of an example. The following example shows how you might create a BEFORE INSERT OR UPDATE trigger on the accounts table used in the preceding examples in this chapter.

```
CREATE OR REPLACE TRIGGER accounts_trigger
   BEFORE INSERT OR UPDATE OF usr_id
   ON accounts
   FOR EACH ROW
DECLARE
   not_allowed_symbol EXCEPTION;
BEGIN
   IF REGEXP_INSTR(:new.usr_id,'[[:digit:]]{1}')=1 THEN
     RAISE not_allowed_symbol;
   END IF;
 EXCEPTION
   WHEN not_allowed_symbol
   THEN
       RAISE_APPLICATION_ERROR (-20500,
         'This record cannot be inserted or updated because usr_id
begins with a digit');
   END;
   /
```

In the previous example, you created a trigger that will be invoked when any INSERT or UPDATE operation — which affects the usr_id column in the accounts table — is performed. You use the BEFORE keyword to handle the new values of the row fields before they are written to the disk. You use the FOR EACH ROW clause to be able to examine the data for each row that is affected.

In the DECLARE block of the trigger, you define a user-defined exception not_allowed_symbol.

Then, with the IF statement, you simply check if the value of the usr_id field of the affected row begins with a digit. If so, you raise a not_allowed_symbol exception and pass control to the not_allowed_symbol exception handler.

In the `not_allowed_symbol` exception handler, you call the `RAISE_APPLICATION_ERROR` function to stop the execution of the current `INSERT` or `UPDATE` statement and return the user-defined message to the caller.

Finally, you define a single slash (/) on the last line of the trigger to activate the `CREATE TRIGGER` statement.

Firing Triggers

To make sure that the `accounts_trigger` trigger discussed in the preceding section works as expected, you may connect to the database as `usr/usr` via SQL*Plus and then issue the following `INSERT` statement:

```
INSERT INTO accounts VALUES('2tom','Tom Johnson','pswd');
```

Since you are trying to insert a row whose `usr_id` field contains a value that begins with a digit, the `accounts_trigger` trigger will fire. As a result, you should see the following error message:

```
ERROR at line 1:
ORA-20500: This record cannot be inserted or updated because usr_id
begins with a digit
ORA-06512: at "USR.ACCOUNTS_TRIGGER", line 10
ORA-04088: error during execution of trigger 'USR.ACCOUNTS_TRIGGER'
```

However, you should have no problem when attempting to perform the following `INSERT` statement:

```
INSERT INTO accounts VALUES('tom','Tom Johnson','pswd');

1 row created.
```

Calling Stored Procedures from a Trigger

The best thing about triggers is that they let you call stored procedures and functions. Suppose you already have a stored procedure or procedures that implement the functionality that you need to implement in the trigger. In such cases, it is always a good idea to call an existing stored procedure or procedures from the trigger, rather than implementing the required functionality from scratch.

Going back to the `accounts_trigger` trigger discussed in the *Creating Triggers* section earlier, you might, for example, move the code that validates the ID of a user to a single PL/SQL function, thus increasing reusability and maintainability. The following example shows how you might create such a function using the `CREATE OR REPLACE FUNCTION` statement. To perform the statement shown overleaf, you must connect to the database as `usr/usr`.

```
CREATE OR REPLACE FUNCTION checkUserid(usrid IN VARCHAR2) RETURN
BOOLEAN AS
BEGIN
   IF REGEXP_INSTR(usrid,'[[:digit:]]{1}')=1 THEN
     RETURN true;
   END IF;
 RETURN false;
END;
/
```

Once you have the `checkUserid` function created, you can modify the
`accounts_trigger` trigger as follows:

```
CREATE OR REPLACE TRIGGER accounts_trigger
   BEFORE INSERT OR UPDATE OF usr_id
   ON accounts
   FOR EACH ROW
DECLARE
   not_allowed_symbol EXCEPTION;
BEGIN
   IF checkUserid(:new.usr_id) THEN
     RAISE not_allowed_symbol;
   END IF;
 EXCEPTION
   WHEN not_allowed_symbol
   THEN
      RAISE_APPLICATION_ERROR (-20500,
         'This record cannot be inserted or updated because usr_id
            begins with a digit');
END;
/
```

The most important thing to note here is that the changes made to the
`accounts_trigger` trigger did not affect its functionality — it will still be fired
when any INSERT or UPDATE operation affecting the `usr_id` column in the `accounts`
table is performed, preventing those modifications where the new value of `usr_id`
begins with a digit.

Summary

Whether you are developing a new PHP/Oracle application or redesigning an existing one, probably the first decision you have to make is where you should implement the key business logic of the application. While making this decision, you should bear in mind that implementing the key business logic of your application inside the database can significantly enhance the performance and scalability of your application.

In this chapter, you examined the most common ways to implement business logic of a PHP/Oracle application inside an Oracle database. You learned that in some cases you don't even need to write PL/SQL code to move the key business logic of your application to the database. Instead, you need to develop a sophisticated SQL query that will return the required data from the database, so that no further processing of that data is required.

Although Oracle SQL provides a powerful way to access and manipulate database data, it lacks some important features normally found in procedural programming languages. To handle tasks where you need to specify the sequence of steps to be performed, Oracle offers PL/SQL – a procedural language that lets you create procedural code encapsulating SQL statements and control-of-flow statements grouped together and processed with a single call. This chapter provided a series of examples demonstrating how to create stored subprograms, including triggers, with PL/SQL.

By this point, you should be familiar with the ways of implementing the key business logic of a PHP/Oracle application inside an Oracle database and have a good hand on them. The next chapter examines how to build transactional applications with PHP and Oracle, providing examples that illustrate how you can benefit from having the key business logic of a transactional PHP/Oracle application implemented inside the database.

4

Transactions

To guarantee that the data you are working on is always correct, you have to use transactions. In a nutshell, transactions provide a mechanism that makes it possible for you to safely modify database data, bringing the database from one consistent state to another.

A classic example of transactions in action involves banking operations such as transferring money from one bank account to another. Say you need to transfer money from a savings account to a checking account. To accomplish this operation, you have to at least perform the following two steps: decrement the savings account and increment the checking account. It is obvious that in this situation it is important to treat both the operations as a single unit of work, to maintain the balance in the accounts. So, neither of the operations can be performed separately—either both of them should be complete, or neither of them—you must ensure that either both the operations are completed successfully or both are not done. In this situation, a transaction is exactly what you need.

This chapter discusses the various mechanisms that can be used to perform transactions with PHP and Oracle. It begins with a brief overview of transactions, which is important in understanding how transactions work in general. The chapter then explains in detail how to make use of transactions in PHP/Oracle applications in a number of different ways.

Overview of Transactions

Before you can start building your own transactional PHP/Oracle applications, you have to familiarize yourself with the basics of transactions and get an idea of how they can be performed with PHP and Oracle. This section takes a brief look at transactions and covers the following:

- What transactions are and why you may want to use them
- How to perform transactions with PHP and Oracle
- How to organize a PHP/Oracle application to effectively control transactions

Since the above topics may be better understood with the help of examples, this section provides a couple of simple examples on how transactions could be used in PHP/Oracle applications.

What is a Transaction?

In general terms, a transaction is an action or series of actions that take the system from one consistent state to another. From the point of view of a developer who builds database-driven applications, a transaction can be thought of as an indivisible set of operations that brings the database from one consistent state to another.

 A transaction is a logical unit of work containing one or more SQL statements that can be either all committed or all rolled back.

This means that all the SQL statements within a transaction must complete successfully so that the entire transaction can be committed, making the changes made by all DML statements in the transaction permanent. Graphically, it might look like the following figure:

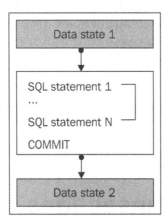

As you can see from the figure, the SQL statements composing the transaction take the data on which they operate from one consistent state to another. The transaction must be committed so that its effects can be applied to the database, thus bringing the data to the next consistent state. Otherwise, all the changes made by the SQL statements within the transaction are rolled back, thus bringing the data into the state that it was before the transaction took place.

If a severe error, such as a hardware failure, occurs during the transaction execution then the effects of the transaction are automatically rolled back. However, in some situations, you might want to manually roll back a transaction that has been successfully completed (but not yet committed), depending on a condition you specify. The following figure illustrates it graphically:

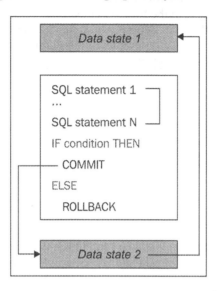

As you can see from the diagram, once all the statements composing the transaction have been successfully completed, you have the choice of either committing the transaction or rolling it back.

What are ACID Rules?

ACID is an acronym for Atomicity, Consistency, Isolation, and Durability. Any DBMS (database management system) that supports transactions must conform to the above characteristics. These are summarized in the following table:

Property	Description
Atomicity	A transaction is an atomic unit of work. This means that either all the operations within a transaction are performed or none of them are performed.
Consistency	A transaction brings the database from one consistent state to another. This means that no integrity constraints must be violated during the transaction execution. If a transaction violates any data integrity rule, then it is rolled back.

Property	Description
Isolation	Changes made by the operations within a transaction should not be visible to other simultaneous transactions until the transaction has committed.
Durability	Once the transaction is committed, all of the modifications made in the transaction become permanent and visible to other transactions. Durability guaranties that if a transaction is successfully committed it will not be undone in the case of system failure.

The Oracle database supports all of the ACID properties listed in the table. So, when developing transactional applications on top of Oracle, you don't need to design custom schemas that will guarantee the consistency and integrity of your data; instead, it is always better to use Oracle transactions, thus letting the database worry about these problems.

How Transactions Work in Oracle

This section provides a quick overview of Oracle transactions. For detailed information on how transactions work in Oracle see Oracle documentation: chapter *Transaction Management* in the *Oracle Database Concepts* manual.

In Oracle, you don't begin a transaction explicitly—it begins implicitly when you perform the first executable SQL statement. However, there are several situations that cause a transaction to end. The following table lists these situations:

Situation	Description
A COMMIT statement is issued	When issued, a COMMIT statement ends the current transaction, making the changes made by the SQL statements within this transaction permanent.
A ROLLBACK statement is issued	When issued, a ROLLBACK statement ends the current transaction, rolling back all the changes made by the SQL statements within the transaction.
A DDL statement is issued	If a DDL statement is issued, Oracle first commits the current transaction and then performs and commits the DDL statement in a new, single statement transaction.
A connection is closed	When a connection is closed, Oracle automatically commits the current transaction on that connection.
Execution of the program terminates abnormally	If execution of the program terminates abnormally, Oracle automatically rolls back the current transaction.

As you can see in the table, a transaction is always either committed or rolled back, whether or not you commit it or roll it back explicitly.

However, note that it is always a good practice to explicitly commit or roll back transactions, rather than relying on the default behavior of Oracle. The fact is that the default transactional behavior of an application may vary depending on the tool the application uses to connect to Oracle.

For example, when it comes to PHP scripts that interact with Oracle via the OCI8 extension, you cannot rely on the fact that the active transaction on a connection will be automatically committed when you close that connection. In that case, the active transaction is rolled back when you close the connection, or when the script ends.

In contrast, if you disconnect from the database in SQL*Plus using a DISCONNECT statement, or connect as another user using a CONNECT statement, or close the SQL*Plus session with the help of the EXIT SQL*Plus command, then the active transaction on the connection will be committed.

 To prevent unexpected behavior in applications, it is always a good idea to explicitly commit or roll back a transaction rather than relying on the default transactional behavior of your application.

Using Transactions in PHP/Oracle Applications

As mentioned in the preceding section, in Oracle you can explicitly either commit a transaction or roll it back, using the COMMIT or ROLLBACK statements respectively. To perform these statements from PHP code, you don't need to use the oci_parse and oci_execute functions as you do it when it comes to performing other SQL statements, such as SELECT or INSERT. Instead, you use the oci_commit and oci_rollback OCI8 functions.

The following PHP script demonstrates how to explicitly commit or rollback a transaction from PHP when dealing with DML operations. What this script does is attempt to update those records in the employees table that represent employees whose job ID is ST_MAN (Stock Manager), increasing their salaries by 10 percent. If it fails to update one or more of these rows, then the entire transaction is rolled back, setting the updated salary fields back to their original values. The following steps summarize the process:

- Step 1: Issues a query against the employees table to obtain the number of rows representing stock managers.

- Step 2: Opens a transaction and performs the UPDATE operation against the employees table, attempting to increase stock managers' salaries by 10 percent.

- Step 3: Rolls back the transaction if the number of records affected by the UPDATE operation is less than the number of all the records representing stock managers. Otherwise, it commits the transaction.

Now, let's look at the code for the script to see how the above steps can be implemented in PHP, using the OCI8 functions.

```php
<?php
//File: trans.php
if(!$dbConn = oci_connect('hr', 'hr', '//localhost/orcl')) {
    $err = oci_error();
    trigger_error('Could not establish a connection: ' .
                              $err['message'], E_USER_ERROR);
};
$query = "SELECT count(*) num_rows FROM employees
                          WHERE job_id='ST_MAN'";
$stmt = oci_parse($dbConn,$query);
if (!oci_execute($stmt)) {
  $err = oci_error($stmt);
  trigger_error('Query failed: ' . $err['message'], E_USER_ERROR);
};
oci_fetch($stmt);
$numrows = oci_result($stmt, 'NUM_ROWS');
oci_free_statement($stmt);
$query = "UPDATE employees e
SET salary = salary*1.1
WHERE e.job_id='ST_MAN' AND salary*1.1
  BETWEEN (SELECT min_salary FROM jobs j WHERE j.job_id=e.job_id)
  AND     (SELECT max_salary FROM jobs j WHERE j.job_id=e.job_id)";
$stmt = oci_parse($dbConn,$query);
if (!oci_execute($stmt, OCI_DEFAULT)) {
  $err = oci_error($stmt);
  trigger_error('Update failed: ' . $err['message'], E_USER_ERROR);
}
$updrows = oci_num_rows($stmt);
print "Tried to update ".$numrows." rows.<br />";
print "Managed to update ".$updrows." rows.<br />";
if ($updrows<$numrows) {
    if (!oci_rollback($dbConn)) {
        $err = oci_error($dbConn);
        trigger_error('Failed to rollback transaction:
                    '.$err['message'], E_USER_ERROR);
    }
    print "Transaction is rolled back";
```

```
    } else {
        if (!oci_commit($dbConn)) {
              $err = oci_error($dbConn);
              trigger_error('Failed to commit transaction:
                             '.$err['message'], E_USER_ERROR);
        }
        print "Transaction is committed";
    }
  ?>
```

In the above script, you define the query that will return the number of records representing stock managers. In the select list of the query, you use the count function to obtain the number of rows matching the criteria specified in the WHERE clause of the query. In this particular example, count(*) will return the number of records representing the employees whose job_id is ST_MAN.

In this example, you obtain the number of records representing stock managers from the result buffer, using the oci_fetch/oci_result function combination. You don't need to use a loop here because the query returns a single row containing only one field, namely num_rows.

Next, you perform the query that updates the salary column in the employees table, increasing salaries of stock managers by 10%. It updates the salary only if the value of the new salary is still between the minimum and maximum salary specified for the stock manager in the jobs table.

In this example, you execute the UPDATE statement in the OCI_DEFAULT execution mode. Doing so opens a transaction, which will allow you to explicitly commit or roll back the changes made by the UPDATE operation later in the script. It is interesting to note that the default execution mode is OCI_COMMIT_ON_SUCCESS in which the statement is committed automatically upon successful execution.

 Oracle documentation states that applications should always explicitly commit or roll back transactions before program termination. However, when using PHP OCI8 extension, you don't have to do so if you execute SQL statements in the OCI_COMMIT_ON_SUCCESS mode. In that mode, an SQL statement is committed automatically upon successful execution (just as if you explicitly committed immediately after executing the statement). If a severe error prevents the successful execution of an SQL statement, Oracle automatically rolls back all the changes made by that statement.

In the above script, you call the oci_num_rows function to get the number of rows affected by the UPDATE operation. Once you know the number of records representing stock managers and how many of them were actually updated, you can compare these numbers to find out if they are equal.

In this example, you simply roll back the transaction if the number of updated rows is less than the total number of records representing stock managers. This makes sense given that you don't want to have some stock managers' records updated and others not.

Having the changes rolled back in this situation is crucial—this makes it possible for you to make use of another script that will be able to update each stock manager record in a proper way. For example, in a real-world situation, you would probably want to set the salary of a stock manager to the maximum allowed value if a 10 percent raise exceeds that value.

If the UPDATE operation has affected all of the records representing stock managers, you commit the transaction with the help of the `oci_commit` function, making the changes made permanent.

Another thing to note here is the error handling mechanism used. If an error occurs during the execution of `oci_rollback` or `oci_commit`, you pass the connection identifier as the parameter to the `oci_error` function, which returns the error message describing the error that has occurred.

Structuring a PHP/Oracle Application to Control Transactions

If you recall from Chapter 3, it is generally a good idea to have the key business logic of a PHP/Oracle application implemented inside the database. As discussed in that chapter, in simple cases, you don't even need to write PL/SQL code to move the data processing to the data—instead, you can design a complex SQL query that, when issued, instructs the database server to perform all the necessary data processing.

Turning back to the example discussed in the preceding section, you might modify the UPDATE statement used there so that it updates the records representing stock managers only if the new salary of each and every stock manager is still between the minimum and maximum salary specified for the stock manager in the `jobs` table, thus eliminating the need to perform a separate query that returns the number of stock manager records satisfying the above condition, and, therefore, reducing the amount of code that must be written to implement the desired behavior.

In essence, this new UPDATE combines all the three steps outlined at the beginning of the preceding section within a single statement. You don't even need now to explicitly commit or roll back the UPDATE operation. Instead, you can execute that UPDATE statement in the OCI_COMMIT_ON_SUCCESS mode, which guarantees that the operation is automatically committed upon successful execution, or rolled back otherwise.

The following script shows the new UPDATE statement in action:

```php
<?php
//File: transQuery.php
if(!$dbConn = oci_connect('hr', 'hr', '//localhost/orcl')) {
    $err = oci_error();
    trigger_error('Could not establish a connection: ' .
                       $err['message'], E_USER_ERROR);
};
$jobno = 'ST_MAN';
$query = "
UPDATE (SELECT salary, job_id FROM employees WHERE
  (SELECT count(*) FROM employees WHERE job_id=:jobid AND
    salary*1.1 BETWEEN (SELECT min_salary FROM jobs WHERE
                         job_id=:jobid) AND
                    (SELECT max_salary FROM jobs WHERE
                         job_id=:jobid)) IN
  (SELECT count(*) FROM employees WHERE job_id=:jobid)
  ) emp
 SET emp.salary = salary*1.1
 WHERE emp.job_id=:jobid";
$stmt = oci_parse($dbConn,$query);
oci_bind_by_name($stmt, ':jobid', $jobno);
if (!oci_execute($stmt, OCI_COMMIT_ON_SUCCESS)) {
  $err = oci_error($stmt);
  trigger_error('Query failed: ' . $err['message'], E_USER_ERROR);
};
$updrows = oci_num_rows($stmt);
if ($updrows>0) {
   print "Transaction is committed";
} else {
   print "Transaction is rolled back";
}
?>
```

Here, you define the UPDATE statement that will update all the records representing stock managers, increasing their salaries by 10%, provided that each and every new salary doesn't exceed the maximum salary defined for the stock manager in the jobs table. If at least one new salary exceeds the maximum salary, the UPDATE statement will update no rows.

To achieve this functionality, rather than specifying the `employees` table in the `dml_table_expression_clause` of the UPDATE statement, you specify the SELECT statement that returns either all the records from the `employees` table or none of them, depending on whether or not all the records that satisfy the condition in the WHERE clause of the UPDATE statement (all records representing stock managers, in this case) can be updated so that the new salary in each of the records being updated does not exceed the maximum salary.

> This SELECT statement is referred to as an inline view. Unlike regular views discussed in the *Taking Advantage of Views* section in Chapter 3, inline views are not database schema objects but subqueries that can be referenced only within their containing statements, using aliases.

In this example, using the `emp` inline view in the UPDATE statement eliminates the need to separately perform the query that returns the number of records representing stock managers and then figure out whether that number is equal to the number of rows actually affected by the UPDATE statement. Now the script has to perform only one SQL statement to get the job done, thus reducing the script execution time significantly.

> The above is a good example of how you can benefit from moving the key business logic of a PHP/Oracle application from PHP to Oracle. In this example, rather than using two separate statements and analyzing their results in PHP, you employ only one SQL statement that makes the database server perform all the required data processing.

Also note how binding is performed in this example. You bind the `jobno` PHP variable to the `jobid` placeholder used in the UPDATE statement. It is interesting to note that the `jobid` placeholder appears in the statement more than one time.

Unlike the previous example where the UPDATE statement was executed in the `OCI_DEFAULT` mode, which explicitly opens a transaction, in this example you execute the statement in the `OCI_COMMIT_ON_SUCCESS` mode, thus committing the UPDATE operation automatically upon successful execution.

> As mentioned earlier, `OCI_COMMIT_ON_SUCCESS` is the default execution mode. This means that you do not need to explicitly specify it when calling `oci_execute`. In this example, it is specified explicitly just to emphasize the point.

In the previous example, you still use the oci_num_rows function to obtain the number of rows affected by the UPDATE statement. However, this time you don't need to compare that number with the total number of records representing stock managers, as you did it in the preceding example. All you need to find out here is whether or not the number of rows affected by the UPDATE statement is greater than 0.

If the number of updated rows is greater than 0, this automatically means that the UPDATE operation has modified all the records representing stock managers and has been successfully committed. In this case, all you need to do is output a message informing the user that the transaction is committed.

If the number of updated rows is equal to 0, this means that the UPDATE operation did not affect any rows. In this case, all you have to do is to output a message informing the user that the transaction is rolled back. However, in reality the transaction has committed but no rows were affected by the UPDATE operation.

Developing Transactional Code

So far, you have seen a few simple examples that showed the basics of how Oracle transactions work in PHP. This section takes you through more complex examples of using transactions in PHP/Oracle applications.

Controlling Transactions from PHP

As you learned from the examples discussed earlier in this chapter, the oci_execute function allows you to execute an SQL statement in one of two modes—OCI_COMMIT_ON_SUCCESS mode and OCI_DEFAULT mode.

While statements are automatically committed when run in the OCI_COMMIT_ON_SUCCESS mode, you have to explicitly call oci_commit or oci_rollback to commit or roll back the transaction respectively, when specifying the OCI_DEFAULT mode.

However, it is interesting to note that a transaction created when a statement is executed in the OCI_DEFAULT mode may still be committed without calling oci_commit. To accomplish this, all you need to do is to execute a subsequent statement in the OCI_COMMIT_ON_SUCCESS mode.

The above technique can be applied when you're grouping two or more statements into a single transaction. To guarantee that the entire transaction will be rolled back when the execution of one of the statements within the transaction fails or you get results telling you that the transaction must be undone, you may simply stop the script execution by calling, say, the trigger_error function with E_USER_ERROR as the second parameter, thus rolling back the transaction without calling oci_rollback.

You may be wondering why we need a discussion on how to implicitly end an Oracle transaction from PHP, rather than explicitly calling `oci_commit` or `oci_rollback`. After all, the latter is the recommended method for ending transactions. Well, the main purpose of this discussion is to give you a better understanding of how Oracle transactions work in PHP scripts that interact with the database via the OCI8 extension.

The example discussed in this section uses the data structures that were defined in the *An Example of When to Use a Stored Subprogram* section in Chapter 3. However, before you proceed with the example, you need to alter these data structures as shown below. You can perform the SQL statements shown in the following listing via SQL*Plus when connected as `usr/usr`.

```
ALTER TABLE accounts
     ADD (num_logons INT);
UPDATE accounts
     SET num_logons = 0;
COMMIT;
DELETE logons;
ALTER TABLE logons
     ADD CONSTRAINT log_time_day
     CHECK (RTRIM(TO_CHAR(log_time, 'Day'))
       NOT IN ('Saturday', 'Sunday'));
```

By issuing the ALTER TABLE statement in the above example, you add a `num_logons` column of `INT` to the `accounts` table. This column will accumulate the number of successful logons for each user account. For that, you will have to increase the number of logons stored in the `num_logons` field once the user is successfully authenticated.

Of course, you can still do without it, querying the `logons` table like this:

```
SELECT count(*) FROM logons WHERE usr_id='bob';
```

However, as the number of logons grows, the above would be a very expensive operation just to know how many logons a given user has performed.

Once you have added the `num_logons` column to the `accounts` table, you have to set the initial value for that column to 0. Alternatively, you might have issued the ALTER TABLE statement, using the DEFAULT clause for the `num_logons` column as follows:

```
ALTER TABLE accounts
     ADD (num_logons INT DEFAULT 0);
```

In this example, you explicitly commit the transaction to make the changes made by the UPDATE operation permanent.

In the next step you delete all the rows in the logons table. This step is required to guarantee that the check constraint, which will be defined in the next step, is not violated. In this example, you may omit this step if the logons table contains no records created on Saturday or Sunday, and so the check constraint defined in the next step will not be violated. Otherwise, when trying to perform the ALTER TABLE, you will receive the following error message:

```
ERROR at line 2:
ORA-02293: cannot validate (USR.LOG_TIME_DAY) - check constraint
violated
```

Here, you define the check constraint on the log_time column of the logons table. This constraint prevents inserting new rows into the logons table on Saturday or Sunday, which allows you to modify your authentication system so that it prevents each and every user from being able to log on on Saturdays and Sundays, thus allowing users to log on only on the working days. Later, you can always drop this constraint by issuing the following statement:

```
ALTER TABLE logons DROP CONSTRAINT log_time_day;
```

Turning back to the ALTER TABLE statement shown in the preceding page, note the use of the format 'Day' specified as the second parameter of the TO_CHAR function. This format tells the TO_CHAR function to convert a date stored in the log_time field to a day of the week. Then, you use the NOT IN operator to exclude Saturdays and Sundays from the list of allowed days.

Bear in mind that in this case Oracle uses case-sensitive matching. So, if you have specified 'Day' as the second argument of the TO_CHAR function, then you have to specify the days of the week in the expression list to the right of the NOT IN operator like this: 'Saturday', 'Sunday'. It would be 'SATURDAY', 'SUNDAY' if you have specified 'DAY' as the second parameter of TO_CHAR.

Now that you have modified all the required database structures as needed, you can proceed with the example whose intent is to illustrate how to create a transaction by executing a DML statement in the OCI_DEFAULT mode and then how to implicitly end that transaction by executing the subsequent statement in the OCI_COMMIT_ON_SUCCESS mode.

In reality, of course, you might want to have more than just two statements in a transaction. To accomplish this, you might execute all of the statements (except for the last one) that you want to group into a single transaction in the OCI_DEFAULT mode, and then execute the last statement in the OCI_COMMIT_ON_SUCCESS mode to close the transaction.

Graphically, it might look like the following:

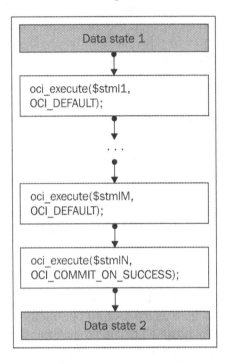

The following script demonstrates how the architecture shown in the figure can be implemented in PHP. Note that unlike the login function discussed in the *An Example of When to Use a Stored Subprogram* section in Chapter 3, the login function shown below stops execution and returns false when it fails to insert an audit record into the logons table. This makes sense, since you now insert a new record into the logons table not only to save the information about a logon, but to check if the inserted data adhere to the business rule, which says that no row in the logons table can contain a date whose day of the week is Saturday or Sunday in the log_time column.

```php
<?php
  //File: userLoginTrans.php
  function login($usr, $pswd) {
  if(!$rsConnection = oci_connect('usr', 'usr', '//localhost/orcl')) {
      $err = oci_error();
      trigger_error('Could not establish a connection: ' .
                              $err['message'], E_USER_ERROR);
  };
  $query = "SELECT full_name, num_logons FROM accounts
                  WHERE usr_id = :userid AND pswd = :passwd";
```

```
    $stmt = oci_parse($rsConnection,$query);
    oci_bind_by_name($stmt, ':userid', $usr);
    oci_bind_by_name($stmt, ':passwd', $pswd);
    if (!oci_execute($stmt)) {
     $err = oci_error($stmt);
     trigger_error('Query failed: ' . $err['message'], E_USER_ERROR);
    }
    if (!$arr = oci_fetch_array($stmt, OCI_ASSOC)) {
      print "Wrong user/password combination";
      return false;
    }
    $num_logons=$arr['NUM_LOGONS']+1;
    oci_free_statement($stmt);
    $query = "UPDATE accounts SET num_logons = num_logons + 1";
    $stmt = oci_parse($rsConnection,$query);
    if (!oci_execute($stmt, OCI_DEFAULT)) {
     $err = oci_error($stmt);
     trigger_error('Update failed: '
                                . $err['message'], E_USER_WARNING);
     return false;
    }
    oci_free_statement($stmt);
    $query = "INSERT INTO logons VALUES (:userid, SYSDATE)";
    $stmt = oci_parse($rsConnection,$query);
    oci_bind_by_name($stmt, ':userid', $usr);
    if (!oci_execute($stmt, OCI_COMMIT_ON_SUCCESS)) {
     $err = oci_error($stmt);
     trigger_error('Insertion failed: ' . $err['message'],
                                          E_USER_WARNING);
     if ($err['code']=='02290'){
       print "You cannot connect on Saturday or Sunday";
      }
     return false;
    }
    print "Hello, ".$arr['FULL_NAME']."<br/>";
    print "You have visited us ".$num_logons." time(s)";
    session_start();
    $_SESSION['user']=$usr;
    return true;
  }
?>
```

As mentioned earlier, the num_logons column in the logons table holds the number of successful logons for each user account. In the script, you define the UPDATE statement that will increase the value of the num_logons field in the record representing the user whose credentials are being used for authentication.

By executing the statement in the OCI_DEFAULT mode, you create a new transaction. This makes sense, since you may need to roll back the changes made by this UPDATE operation if the subsequent insert into the logons table fails.

If the UPDATE operation fails, you exit the login function, returning false to the calling script. This tells the calling script that the authentication has failed.

Next, you define the INSERT statement that is executed once a user has been successfully authenticated and the counter of his or her successful logons has been incremented.

Executing the INSERT statement in the OCI_COMMIT_ON_SUCCESS mode in the script guarantees that the transaction will be committed on success or rolled back on failure, which means that either both the changes made by the INSERT and the effects of the UPDATE statement become permanent or both are undone.

If you recall, the oci_error function returns an associative array of two elements, namely, code, which contains the Oracle error code, and message, which contains the message string describing the error. In this particular example, you check to see if the Oracle error code is equal to 02290. If so, this indicates that a check constraint violation error occurred. Since you have only one check constraint defined on the logons table (the one that prevents inserting new rows into the logons table on Saturdays and Sundays), you may inform the user that he or she cannot connect on Saturday and Sunday.

In this example, if the INSERT fails, you exit the login function with false, thus telling the calling script that the authentication has failed. In the case of successful authentication, you take appropriate actions, such as displaying a welcome message and creating a new session.

Now, to see the newly created login function in action, you might use the following simple script:

```php
<?php
//File: testLoginTrans.php
require_once "userLoginTrans.php";
if (login('bob','pswd')) {
  if (isset($_SESSION['user'])) {
    print '<p>'.'Your account name: '.$_SESSION['user'].'</p>';
  } else {
    print '<p>'.'Session variable representing the account name
```

```
                                                        is not set'.'</p>';
      }
    }else {
       print '<p>'.'Authentication failed'.'</p>';
    }
  ?>
```

If you run the `testLoginTrans.php` script shown in the above listing on Saturday or Sunday, you should see the following output:

```
You cannot connect on Saturday or Sunday

Authentication failed
```

On a working day, however, the output should be as follows:

```
Hello, Bob Robinson
You have visited us 1 time(s)

Your account name: bob
```

Each subsequent execution of the `testLoginTrans.php` script on a working day should increase the number of Bob Robinson's visits. However, if you execute the script on Saturday or Sunday, it will not increase that number. This proves that everything works as expected.

Moving Transactional Code to the Database

Now that you have a working transactional solution implemented mainly in PHP, it is time to think of how to minimize the amount of PHP programming, moving some of the business logic of the application to the database.

Using Triggers

To start with, you might define a BEFORE INSERT trigger on the `logons` table that will automatically update the `accounts` table, increasing the value of the `num_logons` field in the appropriate row. Doing so eliminates the need to invoke this UPDATE operation from PHP code.

The following SQL statement is used to cerate the trigger. You can run this statement from SQL*Plus when connected as `usr/usr`.

```
CREATE OR REPLACE TRIGGER logons_insert
   BEFORE INSERT
   ON logons
   FOR EACH ROW
BEGIN
```

```
    UPDATE accounts
    SET num_logons = num_logons + 1
    WHERE usr_id = :new.usr_id;
END;
/
```

Once you have created the `logons_insert` trigger shown above, you should remove the following lines of code from the `login` function in the `userLoginTrans.php` script shown in the preceding section:

```
$query = "UPDATE accounts SET num_logons = num_logons + 1";
$stmt = oci_parse($rsConnection,$query);
if (!oci_execute($stmt, OCI_DEFAULT)) {
 $err = oci_error($stmt);
 trigger_error('Update failed: ' . $err['message'],
                                        E_USER_WARNING);
 return false;
}
oci_free_statement($stmt);
```

It is important to note that the above modification in the `login` function does not require a change in the existing code that employs this function. So, to test the updated `login` function, you can still run the `testLoginTrans.php` script shown in the preceding section, which would produce the same results as before.

Dealing with Statement-Level Rollbacks

Looking through the code of the updated `login` function, you may notice that it does not execute any statement in the OCI_DEFAULT mode and so doesn't create a transaction. Instead, it executes the INSERT statement in the OCI_COMMIT_ON_SUCCESS mode, which means that any error discovered during the INSERT statement execution will cause all the effects of the INSERT to be rolled back. If the INSERT completes successfully, its effects are automatically committed.

So far, so good. But what happens if the UPDATE statement invoked from the trigger fails? Will it cause the INSERT to roll back? One simple test is to temporarily modify the UPDATE statement in the `logons_insert` trigger so that the UPDATE operation always fails, and then run the `testLoginTrans.php` script from the *Controlling Transactions from PHP* section to see what happens.

To re-create the trigger so that the UPDATE always fails, you can use the SQL statement shown below:

```
CREATE OR REPLACE TRIGGER logons_insert
    BEFORE INSERT
    ON logons
```

```
     FOR EACH ROW
BEGIN
  UPDATE accounts
  SET num_logons = num_logons + 'str'
  WHERE usr_id = :new.usr_id;
END;
/
```

It is important to note that although the UPDATE statement in the trigger will always fail, the trigger itself should be successfully compiled.

Now, if you try to run the testLoginTrans.php script, you should see the following output:

Authentication failed

As you can see, the authentication has failed. To make sure that the INSERT into the logons table has failed as well, you might count the number of rows in this table before the execution of testLoginTrans.php and after that. This can be done with the help of the following SQL statement issued from SQL*Plus when connected as usr/usr:

```
SELECT count(*) FROM logons;
```

You should see that the number of rows in the logons table remains the same after the execution of the testLoginTrans.php script. This proves that a failure to update the logons table from the logons_insert BEFORE INSERT trigger defined on the accounts table causes the INSERT statement to be rolled back as well.

 Generally, if an error occurs during the execution of a trigger, this rolls back all the effects of the operation that caused the trigger to fire. This is due to a so-called statement-level rollback—any error raised during the statement execution causes all the effects of the statement to roll back.

The above is not always true, however: for example, the logons_insert trigger may be implemented in a way in which it will not roll back the INSERT statement when the UPDATE performed from the trigger fails. Consider the logons_insert trigger shown below:

```
CREATE OR REPLACE TRIGGER logons_insert
    BEFORE INSERT
    ON logons
    FOR EACH ROW
BEGIN
    UPDATE accounts
```

```
      SET num_logons = num_logons + 'str'
      WHERE usr_id = :new.usr_id;
  EXCEPTION
    WHEN OTHERS THEN
        NULL;
  END;
  /
```

Now, if you run the `testLoginTrans.php` script, you should see the following:

Hello, Bob Robinson
You have visited us 3 time(s)

Your account name: bob

Then, if you run the script again, you should see that the number of logons displayed by the script remains the same. However, if you check the number of rows in the `logons` table as discussed earlier in this section, you should notice that a subsequent execution of the `testLoginTrans.php` script increases that number.

This indicates that although the UPDATE performed from the trigger fails, the INSERT is completed successfully. This is so because the `logons_insert` trigger shown above silently ignores any error raised during its execution—you have specified NULL in the WHEN OTHERS section, which is the only exception handler in the exception-handling part of the trigger.

 In most cases, using the above technique is not recommended since it changes the expected behavior of the database. The reasonable assumption is that if during execution an SQL statement causes an error, any effects of that statement are automatically undone.

That is why, rather then specifying a NULL in an exception handler, you should write the code that will take appropriate actions in response to an error. For example, you might make use of the RAISE_APPLICATION_ERROR procedure to issue a user-defined ORA-error. The following example shows how the `logons_insert` trigger could be modified to call RAISE_APPLICATION_ERROR from the exception handler.

```
  CREATE OR REPLACE TRIGGER logons_insert
      BEFORE INSERT
      ON logons
      FOR EACH ROW
  BEGIN
    UPDATE accounts
    SET num_logons = num_logons + 'str'
    WHERE usr_id = :new.usr_id;
```

```
EXCEPTION
  WHEN OTHERS THEN
  RAISE_APPLICATION_ERROR(-20000, 'Failed to update the counter');
END;
/
```

In the above trigger, the exception handler explicitly calls the
RAISE_APPLICATION_ERROR procedure to issue a user-defined ORA-error.

 If you have the display_errors parameter set to On in the php.ini
configuration file, the userLoginTrans.php script discussed in the
Controlling Transactions from PHP section will display the error message
specified as the second parameter in the RAISE_APPLICATION_ERROR
procedure.

Now, if you execute the testLoginTrans.php script, you should see the
following output:

Authentication failed

And the number of rows in the logons table should remain the same, which means
that the failure to update the accounts table in the trigger causes not only the
UPDATE to roll back, but also the INSERT to do so.

Before you leave this example, make sure to re-create the logons_insert trigger so
that the SET clause of the UPDATE statement looks as follows:

```
SET num_logons = num_logons + 1
```

Transaction Isolation Considerations

When a transaction modifies a table row of a database, Oracle holds that row with a
lock until the transaction is committed or rolled back. The purpose of doing this is to
prevent two concurrent transactions from modifying the same row.

It is important to note here that locked rows can still be read by both the transaction
that updates the rows and any other transaction. The difference between the two is
that the transaction holding locks on the rows can see the changes immediately after
the execution of the statement affecting the rows, whereas any other transaction
cannot see those changes until the transaction that made them is committed.

While the locking mechanisms used in Oracle are discussed in detail in Oracle
documentation (chapter *Data Concurrency and Consistency* in the *Oracle Database
Concepts* manual), this section gives a brief overview of how transaction isolation
works in PHP/Oracle applications.

What OCI8 Connection Function to Choose

If you recall from Chapter 2, section *OCI8 Functions for Connecting to Oracle*, the OCI8 PHP extension offers three different functions when it comes to establishing a connection to an Oracle database. These are the `oci_connect`, `oci_new_connect`, and `oci_pconnect` functions. These functions differ only in the type of connections they establish to the database.

Both `oci_connect` and `oci_pconnect` use a database connection cache, thus eliminating the cost of opening a database connection on every request. The difference between the two is that the connections created by `oci_connect` are released when the script execution ends, while `oci_pconnect`'s connections persist across script executions.

Unlike `oci_connect` and `oci_pconnect`, the `oci_new_connect` function doesn't use a connection cache, always returning a fresh new connection. You use this function when you need to create two or more concurrent transactions within a script. The following example shows the `oci_new_connect` function in action.

In the following script, note the use of the `oci_new_connect` function to create a concurrent transaction. While you create the first connection in the script by `oci_connect`, you use `oci_new_connect` to create a fresh new connection.

```php
<?php
//File: newConns.php
function select_emp_job ($conn, $jobno) {
    $query = "SELECT employee_id, first_name, last_name, salary
                        FROM employees WHERE job_id =:jobid";
    $stmt = oci_parse($conn,$query);
    oci_bind_by_name($stmt, ':jobid', $jobno);
    if (!oci_execute($stmt, OCI_DEFAULT)) {
      $err = oci_error($stmt);
      trigger_error('Query failed: '
                                . $err['message'], E_USER_ERROR);
    };
    print '<table border="1">';
    while ($emp = oci_fetch_array($stmt, OCI_ASSOC)) {
        print '<tr>';
        print '<td>'.$emp['EMPLOYEE_ID'].'</td>';
        print '<td>'.$emp['FIRST_NAME'].' '.$emp['LAST_NAME'].
                                        '</td>';
        print '<td>'.$emp['SALARY'].'</td>';
        print '</tr>';
    }
    print '</table>';
```

```
    }
    if(!$conn1 = oci_connect('hr', 'hr', '//localhost/orcl')) {
        $err = oci_error();
        trigger_error('Could not establish a connection: '
                                    . $err['message'], E_USER_ERROR);
    };
    if(!$conn2 = oci_new_connect('hr', 'hr', '//localhost/orcl')) {
        $err = oci_error();
        trigger_error('Could not establish a connection: '
                                    . $err['message'], E_USER_ERROR);
    };
    $jobno = 'AD_VP';
    $query = "UPDATE employees SET salary = 18000 WHERE job_id=:jobid";
    $stmt = oci_parse($conn1,$query);
    oci_bind_by_name($stmt, ':jobid', $jobno);
    if (!oci_execute($stmt, OCI_DEFAULT)) {
      $err = oci_error($stmt);
      trigger_error('Query failed: ' . $err['message'], E_USER_ERROR);
    };
    print "<h2>Transaction isolation testing!</h2>";
    print "<h4>Transaction A on conn1:</h4>";
    print "<p>(results after the update and before
                                    the commit on conn1)</p>";
    select_emp_job($conn1, $jobno);
    print "<h4>Transaction B on conn2:</h4>";
    print "<p>(results after the update and before
                                    the commit on conn1)</p>";
    select_emp_job($conn2, $jobno);

    if (!oci_commit($conn1)) {
       $err = oci_error($conn1);
       trigger_error('Failed to commit transaction: '
                                .$err['message'], E_USER_ERROR);
    }
    print "<h4>Transaction B on conn2:</h4>";
    print "<p>(results after the update and after
                                    the commit on conn1)</p>";
    select_emp_job($conn2, $jobno);
    $query = "UPDATE employees SET salary = 17000 WHERE job_id=:jobid";
    $stmt = oci_parse($conn1,$query);
    oci_bind_by_name($stmt, ':jobid', $jobno);
    if (!oci_execute($stmt)) {
      $err = oci_error($stmt);
      trigger_error('Query failed: ' . $err['message'], E_USER_ERROR);
    };
?>
```

The following figure illustrates the output of this script. As you can see from the figure, the changes made by the UPDATE operation performed within the transaction on the conn1 database connection can be seen within that transaction immediately after the UPDATE takes place, and cannot be seen from the concurrent transaction on the conn2 connection until the first transaction is committed.

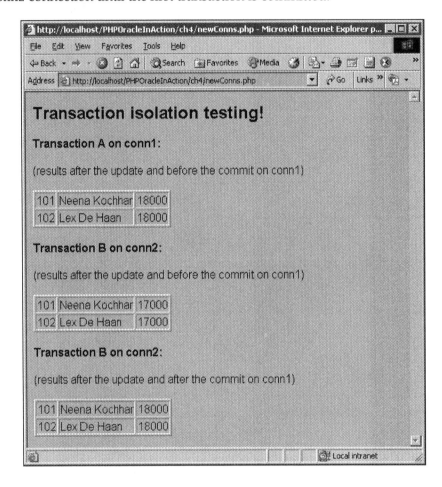

Turning back to the code for the newConns.php script discussed here, note that all the SQL statements used in this script are executed in the OCI_DEFAULT mode. This guarantees that the transactions are committed immediately.

Note that you create the first connection in this script with oci_connect. Since it's the first connection, the connection cache associated with the script is empty and so oci_connect will establish a fresh new connection to the database.

You have to create concurrent transactions on transactionally isolated connections. While the first connection in the script can be created by oci_connect, you have to use oci_new_connect to create a subsequent, transactionally isolated connection within that script.

Then, to create a fresh, new, transactionally isolated connection in the script, you call oci_new_connect.

By executing the UPDATE statement in the OCI_DEFAULT mode on the conn1 connection, you create a transaction on this connection.

After the UPDATE has been executed, the effects of this operation can be seen for any other operation performed within the same transaction. To prove this point, you select the rows affected by the UPDATE within the same transaction, before it is committed. As seen from the previous figure, a SELECT returns the new values of the rows being updated.

However, you still will see the original values of the rows being updated when performing a SELECT within a concurrent transaction. This is because simultaneous transactions are isolated from the updates made by other uncommitted transactions. Once the transaction is committed, all its effects can be seen from the other transactions.

Finally, with the help of this UPDATE, you restore the original values of the updated rows.

Concurrent Update Issues

As a developer, you have two primary concerns when designing an application that will modify database data in a multi-user environment:

- To ensure the integrity and consistency of the data
- To ensure that performance will not be hindered by locking issues

While Oracle provides a broad set of features that can help you accomplish the above goals, it is your responsibility to make the correct use of these features. The following sections focus on some concurrent update issues that may be encountered in multi-user environments when using transactions incorrectly.

Locking Issues

As mentioned earlier, Oracle puts a lock on a row being updated so that the other transactions cannot modify that row until the transaction updating it ends. While the purpose of doing this is to guarantee the integrity of the data accessed in a multi-user environment, this may add significant overhead in a badly designed application.

Let's take a look at a simple example that illustrates how a badly designed script performing long-running operations may cause locking issues when used in a multi-user environment. The updateSleep.php script shown in the following listing performs the following steps:

- Creates a transaction
- Updates some rows in the employees table
- Delays execution for 20 seconds
- Rolls back the transaction

Delaying the execution with the help of the sleep function in this example allows you to simulate a computationally expensive operation.

```php
<?php
//File: updateSleep.php
if(!$dbConn = oci_connect('hr', 'hr', '//localhost/orcl')) {
    $err = oci_error();
    trigger_error('Could not establish a connection: ' .
                        $err['message'], E_USER_ERROR);
};
$jobno = 'AD_VP';
$query = "
 UPDATE employees
 SET salary = salary*1.1
 WHERE job_id=:jobid";
$stmt = oci_parse($dbConn,$query);
oci_bind_by_name($stmt, ':jobid', $jobno);
if (!oci_execute($stmt, OCI_DEFAULT)) {
  $err = oci_error($stmt);
  trigger_error('Query failed: ' . $err['message'], E_USER_ERROR);
};
$updrows = oci_num_rows($stmt);
print 'You just updated '.$updrows. ' row(s)'.'<br/>';
sleep(20);
oci_rollback($dbConn);
print 'Transaction is rolled back';
?>
```

In this script, you execute the UPDATE statement in the OCI_DEFAULT mode, thus instructing Oracle to create a transaction.

Next, you use the sleep function to delay the execution for 20 seconds, thus simulating a computationally expensive operation.

Finally, you explicitly roll back the transaction with oci_rollback. Actually, this step is optional because transactions are automatically rolled back when the script ends.

Now, if you run the updateSleep.php script discussed here, it will update all the Administration Vice President records in the employees table, block these records for 20 seconds and then roll the transaction back.

If, within that 20 second delay, you try to update the same records from another script or, say, from SQL*Plus, you will be blocked until the updateSleep.php script releases the locks on these records.

The moral of this example is that if your script has to perform a long-running operation in a high-traffic multi-user environment, it is always a good idea to close all the active transactions within the script before beginning to process that operation.

Lost Updates

The preceding example demonstrated how a badly designed transactional application may lock database resources for long periods of time, preventing other concurrent transactions from accessing those resources in a timely manner. However, note that using a non-blocking approach while modifying database data in a multi-user environment, may cause another issue—lost updates. To understand what a lost update problem is, consider the steps that an interactive application usually performs when it comes to modifying information stored in a database:

- Selects the data from the database
- Displays the data to the user
- Waits for feedback from the user
- Updates the data in the database

It should be fairly obvious from the above scenario that while the application waits for feedback from the user, another user may change the data. Then, if the first user proceeds to update the data, the changes made by the second user will be lost.

This may be better understood with the help of an example. Let's look at the `updateQuickForm.php` script that implements the above steps using PEAR's `HTML_QuickForm` package. When you run the script, it performs the following steps:

- Updates two rows in the `employees` table
- Produces the form asking the user to commit or roll back the changes
- Ends execution, rolling back the changes

On the form that the script produced, the user can choose either commit or roll back and then click the **Submit** button. Once the user clicks **Submit**, it invokes the script again, which this time performs the following steps:

- Updates the same two rows in the `employees` table
- Commits or rolls back the changes depending on the user's choice
- Ends execution

The following figure shows the form produced by the script.

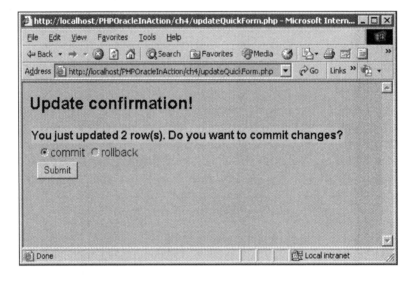

However, before you run the `updateQuickForm.php` script, make sure you install the `HTML_QuickForm` PEAR package. Since the `HTML_QuickForm` depends on another package, called `HTML_Common`, you first have to install the latter. Given that you have the PEAR Installer installed and configured, you might issue the following command to download and install the `HTML_Common` package:

```
$ pear install HTML_Common
```

Once `HTML_Common` is installed, you can download and install the `HTML_QuickForm` package as follows:

```
$ pear install HTML_QuickForm
```

With all that done, you can run the `updateQuickForm.php` script whose code is shown below:

```php
<?php
//File: updateQuickForm.php
require_once 'HTML/QuickForm.php';
if(!$dbConn = oci_connect('hr', 'hr', '//localhost/orcl')) {
    $err = oci_error();
    trigger_error('Could not establish a connection: ' .
                        $err['message'], E_USER_ERROR);
};
$jobno = 'AD_VP';
$query = "
 UPDATE employees
 SET salary = salary*1.1
 WHERE job_id=:jobid";
$stmt = oci_parse($dbConn,$query);
oci_bind_by_name($stmt, ':jobid', $jobno);
if (!oci_execute($stmt, OCI_DEFAULT)) {
  $err = oci_error($stmt);
  trigger_error('Query failed: ' . $err['message'], E_USER_ERROR);
};
print '<h2>Update confirmation!</h2>';
$updrows = oci_num_rows($stmt);
$frm=new HTML_QuickForm('frm1', 'POST');
$frm->addElement('header','msg1','You just updated '.$updrows. '
                        row(s). Do you want to commit changes?');
$grp[] =& HTML_QuickForm::createElement('radio', null,
                                        null,'commit', 'C');
$grp[] =& HTML_QuickForm::createElement('radio', null,
                                        null,'rollback', 'R');
$frm->addGroup($grp, 'trans');
$frm->setDefaults(array('trans' => 'C'));
$frm->addElement('submit','submit','Submit');
if(isset($_POST['submit'])) {
  if ($_POST['trans']=='C'){
      oci_commit($dbConn);
      print 'Transaction committed';
  } elseif ($_POST['trans']=='R'){
      oci_rollback($dbConn);
```

```
        print 'Transaction rolled back';
    } else {
    $frm->display();
    }
  } else {
    $frm->display();
  }
?>
```

Looking at the form shown in the previous figure, you may think that once the script has updated two rows in the `employees` table, it waits for user feedback, keeping the transaction active. In fact, it works in a different way.

When you run the script, it actually updates two rows in the `employees` table, but then it rolls back the transaction. Doing so allows you to count the number of rows affected by the `UPDATE`, giving that information to the user. Once the user has selected either **commit** or **rollback** and then pressed the **Submit** button, the script performs the same `UPDATE` operation again, either committing the effects of the `UPDATE` or rolling them back, depending on the user's choice.

The advantage of the above technique is that the rows being processed are not blocked while the user is deciding which radio button to select: **commit** or **rollback**, thus allowing other transactions to operate on these rows during this time. However, this may cause another problem—a lost update, as outlined earlier in this section.

To prevent a lost update problem, you might use an optimistic locking strategy, making sure that the values of the fields being updated have not changed since the user began working with them.

Autonomous Transactions

Continuing with the preceding example, you might want to record attempts made to update the rows of the `employees` table. To accomplish this, you will need to create a table to hold audit records as well as a `BEFORE UPDATE` trigger on the `employees` table, which will insert a record into the audit table whenever someone updates a row in `employees` table.

To set up the above data structures, you can execute the following SQL statement:

```
CONN usr/usr

CREATE TABLE emp_updates(
    emp_id NUMBER(6),
    job_id VARCHAR2(10),
    timedate DATE);
```

```
CONN /AS SYSDBA

GRANT INSERT on usr.emp_updates TO hr;

CONN hr/hr

CREATE OR REPLACE TRIGGER emp_updates_trigger
   BEFORE UPDATE
   ON employees
   FOR EACH ROW
BEGIN
   INSERT INTO usr.emp_updates VALUES (:new.employee_id, :new.job_id,
SYSDATE);
EXCEPTION
   WHEN OTHERS THEN
      RAISE_APPLICATION_ERROR(-20001, 'An error raised in the trigger');
END;
/
```

With that done, you may run the `updateQuickForm.php` script discussed in the preceding section to check if your auditing mechanism works as expected. In the form generated by the script, choose **rollback** and then click **Submit**. Now, if you count the number of rows in the `emp_updates` table as follows:

```
CONN usr/usr;
SELECT * FROM emp_updates;
```

you should see that the `emp_updates` table still contains no rows:

no rows selected

This indicates that when you roll back an UPDATE operation, it rolls back its audit record as well. It is the expected behavior, since you cannot roll back some effects of a transaction—you can either commit all effects of it or roll them all back.

An attempt to commit only the INSERT statement performed within the trigger will fail because no transaction control statements are allowed in a trigger. So, if you try to recreate the `emp_updates_trigger` trigger as follows:

```
CREATE OR REPLACE TRIGGER emp_updates_trigger
   BEFORE UPDATE
   ON employees
   FOR EACH ROW
BEGIN
   INSERT INTO usr.emp_updates VALUES (:new.employee_id,
                                       :new.job_id, SYSDATE);
   COMMIT;
EXCEPTION
```

```
    WHEN OTHERS THEN
        ROLLBACK;
END;
/
```

You will get the following errors when running the `updateQuickForm.php` script:

```
Warning: oci_execute() [function.oci-execute] :ORA-04092: cannot
ROLLBACK in a trigger ORA-06512: at "HR.EMP_UPDATES_TRIGGER", line
6 ORA-04092: cannot COMMIT in a trigger ORA-04088: error during
execution of trigger 'HR.EMP_UPDATES_TRIGGER'
```

```
Fatal error: Query failed: ORA-04092: cannot ROLLBACK in a trigger
ORA-06512: at "HR.EMP_UPDATES_TRIGGER", line 6 ORA-04092: cannot
COMMIT in a trigger ORA-04088: error during execution of trigger 'HR.
EMP_UPDATES_TRIGGER'
```

 The above error messages will be displayed only if you have the `display_errors` parameter set to `On` in `php.ini`.

One way to solve the above problem is to make use of an autonomous transaction.

 An autonomous transaction is a transaction within another transaction. Being totally independent of the calling transaction, an autonomous transaction lets you perform SQL operations and then either commit or roll back them, without committing or rolling back the calling transaction.

Employing an autonomous transaction in this example will allow you to commit the `INSERT` performed within the `emp_updates_trigger` trigger independently of the transaction created in the `updateQuickForm.php` script, thus creating a record in the `emp_updates` table even if the effects of the `UPDATE` operation that fired the trigger are rolled back.

The following example shows how to recreate the `emp_updates_trigger` trigger so that it uses an autonomous transaction.

```
CREATE OR REPLACE TRIGGER emp_updates_trigger
    BEFORE UPDATE
    ON employees
    FOR EACH ROW
DECLARE
  PRAGMA AUTONOMOUS_TRANSACTION;
BEGIN
    INSERT INTO usr.emp_updates VALUES (:new.employee_id,
                                        :new.job_id, SYSDATE);
```

```
    COMMIT;
EXCEPTION
  WHEN OTHERS THEN
     ROLLBACK;
END;
/
```

The above example shows an autonomous transaction implemented in a database trigger. Using an autonomous transaction here ensures that an audit record will be created in the emp_updates table, regardless of whether an UPDATE operation on the employees table is committed or rolled back.

To test the newly created trigger, run the updateQuickForm.php script again and submit the form produced by the script, having the **rollback** radio button selected. Then, select the emp_updates again as follows:

```
SELECT * FROM emp_updates;
```

This time, you should see results that might look like the following:

```
EMP_ID JOB_ID      TIMEDATE
------- ----------- ---------
    101 AD_VP       29-MAY-06
    102 AD_VP       29-MAY-06
    101 AD_VP       29-MAY-06
    102 AD_VP       29-MAY-06
```

Note that although you attempted to update only two rows in the employees table, four audit records have been inserted into the emp_updates table. Recall that the updateQuickForm.php script actually performs the UPDATE twice—first, in order to count the number of rows to be updated, and then, to actually update these rows.

Summary

Some operations performed against a database make sense only when grouped together. A classic example involves a transfer of funds between two bank accounts. The only way to perform such an operation safely is to use a transaction. Using transactions lets you group SQL statements together into logical, indivisible units of work, each of which can be either all committed or all rolled back.

In this chapter you learned when and how to use transactions in PHP/Oracle applications. The discussion began with a brief overview of Oracle transactions and why you may want to use them in PHP applications built on top of Oracle. Then, it explained how to organize a PHP/Oracle application to effectively control transactions, focusing on the benefits from moving the business logic of a transactional application from PHP to the database. You learned which OCI8 connection function to choose when it comes to using transactions, and how to create simultaneous transactions within the same script. Finally, you saw how to call an independent transaction from within another transaction and looked at the situation where it might be desired.

5
Object-Oriented Approach

Developing a serious PHP application that interacts with Oracle may require writing hundreds or even thousands of lines of code. No doubt, at some point in coding, you will start looking for a way to effectively group and organize your code, so that well-designed pieces of already written code can be reused over and over in your application development.

From the examples discussed in the previous chapters, you learned about two powerful ways to reuse the previously written codes in PHP. Specifically, you saw how to use functions and how to take advantage of putting reusable code into separate files, which can then be included in other scripts. When used together, these methods can be very efficient when developing small and midsize applications. However, while developing complex PHP/Oracle applications, you might want to take advantage of a more powerful way to obtain reusability, namely object-oriented programming.

This chapter examines the object-oriented approach for developing PHP/Oracle applications, as an efficient means to reduce the development time and complexity, and increase the maintainability and flexibility of your applications. The material in the chapter not only covers PHP 5's major object-oriented features required to build an efficient object-oriented PHP application interacting with Oracle, but also discusses some Oracle's native object-relational features that make it possible for you to organize data into object structures at the database level.

Implementing PHP Classes to Interact with Oracle

Before you start developing object-oriented solutions with PHP 5, it is important to understand that its object model provides more features than PHP 4's object model. Like most object-oriented languages, PHP 5 allows the developer to take advantage of interfaces, abstract classes, private/public/protected access modifiers, static members and methods, exception handling, and other features that were not available in PHP 4. But perhaps the most important thing to note about the object-oriented improvements of PHP 5 is that objects are now referenced by handle, and not by value.

In the following sections, you will learn how to create a simple PHP class to interact with Oracle and then how that class can be modified and reused in different scripts.

Building Blocks of Applications

As you no doubt know, the fundamental building block in any object-oriented language is a structure called a class.

 A class is a template for an object. It describes the data and behavior of its instances (objects). During run time, an application can create as many instances of a single class as necessary.

The following diagram conceptually depicts the structure of a class.

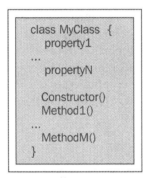

You might find it handy to think of an object-oriented application as a building made of blocks, where classes are those blocks. However, it is important to note that all blocks in this case are exchangeable. What this means is that if you are not satisfied with the implementation of a certain class, you can use a relevant class that has the same Application Programming Interface (API) but a different implementation instead. This allows you to increase the reusability and maintainability of your application, without increasing the complexity.

The intent of the example discussed in this section is to illustrate how you can rewrite the implementation of a class so that this doesn't require a change in the existing code that employs this class. In particular, you'll see how a custom PHP 4 class designed to interact with Oracle can be rewritten to use the new object-oriented features available in PHP 5.

Creating a Custom PHP Class from Scratch

To proceed with the example, you first need to create a PHP 4 class interacting with Oracle. Consider the following dbConn4 class:

```php
<?php
//File: dbConn4.php
class dbConn4 {
  var $user;
  var $pswd;
  var $db;
  var $conn;
  var $query;
  var $row;
  var $exec_mode;
  function dbConn4($user, $pswd, $db,
                   $exec_mode= OCI_COMMIT_ON_SUCCESS)
  {
    $this->user = $user;
    $this->pswd = $pswd;
    $this->db = $db;
    $this->exec_mode = $exec_mode;
    $this->GetConn ();
  }
  function GetConn()
  {
   if(!$this->conn = OCILogon($this->user, $this->pswd, $this->db))
     {
       $err = OCIError();
       trigger_error('Failed to establish a connection: ' .
                                          $err['message']);
     }
  }
  function query($sql)
  {
    if(!$this->query = OCIParse($this->conn, $sql)) {
      $err = OCIError($this->conn);
      trigger_error('Failed to parse SQL query: ' .
                    $err['message']);
      return false;
    }
    else if(!OCIExecute($this->query, $this->exec_mode)) {
      $err = OCIError($this->query);
      trigger_error('Failed to execute SQL query: ' .
                    $err['message']);
```

```
            return false;
            }
        return true;
        }
        function fetch()
        {
            if(!OCIFetchInto($this->query, $this->row, OCI_ASSOC)){
                return false;
                }
            return $this->row;
        }
    }
?>
```

In the above script, to define a class, you use the `class` keyword followed by the class name. Then, within curly braces, you define class properties and methods. Since this class is designed to work under both PHP 4 and PHP 5, all the class properties are defined with the `var` keyword. Declaring a property with `var` makes it publicly readable and writable. In PHP 5, you would use the `public` keyword instead.

In PHP 4, you define the class constructor as a function with the same name as the class itself. This still works in PHP 5 for backward compatibility. However, in PHP 5, it's recommended that you use __construct as the constructor name.

In the above example, the class constructor is used to set the member variables of a class instance to the values passed to the constructor as parameters. Note the use of the self-referencing variable `$this` that is used here to access the member variables of the current class instance.

Within class methods, you can use `$this`, the special variable that points to the current instance of a class. This variable is created automatically during the execution of any object's method and can be used to access both member variables of the current instance and its methods.

Then, you call the `GetConn` method from within the constructor to obtain a connection to the database. You reference the method using the `$this` variable. In this example, the `GetConn` method is supposed to be called from within the constructor only. In PHP 5, you would declare this method as private.

To obtain a connection to the database in this example, you use the `OCILogon` function. In PHP 5, you would use the `oci_connect` function instead.

The `query` method defined here takes an SQL string as the parameter and then parses and executes the query. It returns true on success or false on failure. This method is supposed to be called from outside an object. So, in PHP 5, you would declare it as public.

Finally, you define the `fetch` method. You will call this method to fetch the results retrieved by a SELECT statement that has been executed with the `query` method.

Testing the Newly Created Class

Once written, the `dbConn4` class discussed in the preceding section can be used in applications in order to establish a connection to an Oracle database and then issue queries against it as needed. To see this class in action, you might use the following PHP script. Assuming that you have saved the `dbConn4` class as the `dbConn4.php` file, save the following script as `select.php`:

```php
<?php
//File: select.php
require_once 'dbConn4.php';
require_once 'hrCred.php';
$db = new dbConn4($user, $pswd, $conn);
$sql="SELECT FIRST_NAME, LAST_NAME FROM employees";
if($db->query($sql)){
  print 'Employee Names: ' . '<br />';
  while ($row = $db->fetch()) {
     print $row['FIRST_NAME'] . ' ';
     print $row['LAST_NAME'] . '<br />';
   }
  }
?>
```

The above `select.php` script employs the `employees` table from the `hr/hr` demonstration schema. So, before you can execute this script, you must create the `hrCred.php` file that contains all the information required to establish a connection to your Oracle database using the HR account. The `hrCred.php` file should look as shown below (note that the connection string may vary depending on your configuration):

```php
<?php
//File: hrCred.php
$user="hr";
$pswd="hr";
$conn=" (DESCRIPTION=
        (ADDRESS_LIST=
          (ADDRESS=(PROTOCOL=TCP)(HOST=localhost)(PORT=1521))
          )
```

```
        (CONNECT_DATA=(SID=orcl)(SERVER=DEDICATED))
    )";
?>
```

Once you have created the `hrCred.php` script, you can execute the `select.php` script. As a result, it should output the names of employees from the `employees` table in the `hr/hr` demonstration schema.

Taking Advantage of PHP 5's Object-Oriented Features

Turning back to the `dbConn4` class, you may have noticed that it was written for PHP 4. Of course, it still can be used in new applications written for PHP 5. However, to take advantage of the new object-oriented features available in PHP 5, you might want to rewrite this class as follows:

```php
<?php
//File: dbConn5.php
class dbConn5 {
    private $user;
    private $pswd;
    private $db;
    private $conn;
    private $query;
    private $row;
    private $exec_mode;
    public function __construct($user, $pswd, $db,
                            $exec_mode= OCI_COMMIT_ON_SUCCESS)
    {
        $this->user = $user;
        $this->pswd = $pswd;
        $this->db = $db;
        $this->exec_mode = $exec_mode;
        $this->GetConn();
    }
    private function GetConn()
    {
    if(!$this->conn = oci_connect($this->user, $this->pswd,
                                            $this->db))
        {
            $err = oci_error();
            trigger_error('Failed to establish a connection: ' .
                                            $err['message']);
        }
```

```php
    }
    public function query($sql)
    {
      if(!$this->query = oci_parse($this->conn, $sql)) {
          $err = oci_error($this->conn);
          trigger_error('Failed to execute SQL query: ' .
                                            $err['message']);
          return false;
      }
      else if(!oci_execute($this->query, $this->exec_mode)) {
          $err = oci_error($this->query);
          trigger_error('Failed to execute SQL query: ' .
                                            $err['message']);
          return false;
        }
      return true;
    }
    public function fetch()
    {
      if($this->row=oci_fetch_assoc($this->query)){
        return $this->row;
        }
      else {
        return false;
        }
    }
  }
?>
```

As you can see, the implementation of the class has been improved to conform to the new standards of PHP 5. For instance, the above class takes advantage of encapsulation that is accomplished in PHP 5—like most other object-oriented languages—by means of access modifiers, namely public, protected, and private. The idea behind encapsulation is to enable the developer to design the classes that reveal only the important members and methods and hide the internals. For instance, the GetConn method in the dbConn5 class is declared with the private modifier because this method is supposed to be called only from inside the constructor when a new instance of the class is initialized; therefore, there is no need to allow client code to access this method directly.

Since the implementation of the newly created dbConn5 class is different from the one used in dbConn4, you may be asking yourself: "Does that mean we need to rewrite the client code that uses the dbConn4 class as well?" The answer is obvious: you don't need to rewrite client code that uses the dbConn4 class since you have neither changed the Application Programming Interface (API) of the class nor, more importantly, its functionality. Thus, all you need to do in order to make the select.php script work with dbConn5 is simply replace all the references to dbConn4 with references to dbConn5 throughout the script.

Functionality and Implementation

As you learned from the preceding example, you can easily replace one class with another in a calling script given that both the classes deliver the same API and the same functionality. Practically, this means that you can improve the implementation of the class that is used in existing applications until this changes the API of that class or its functionality. Of course, you can still extend the API of the class with some new public methods in order to add new functionality that might be employed in new applications using the class. However, in this case you must ensure that the new class still works with old clients.

Essentially, the above technique lets you improve object code without having to rewrite any client code. However, it is worth remembering that sometimes it is very hard to retain the functionality of the class when rewriting its implementation. Bear in mind that the implementation in essence forms the functionality. In some situations, like the one discussed in the previous section, you can rewrite the implementation of the class so that this doesn't change its functionality. However, in other situations, rewriting the implementation of the class, results in a change in the functionality provided by the class.

Imagine what would happen if you decided to use the oci_new_connect function in place of oci_connect in the GetConn method of the dbConn5 class. As you might recall from Chapter 4 *Transactions*, this would allow you to establish distinctly new connections to the database within a script using the class, and thereby separate transactions. In this case, you could apply commits and rollbacks to the specified connection only.

By contrast, using oci_connect assumes that commits and rollbacks are applied to all open transactions in the page. This is because oci_connect doesn't establish a new connection if you have already established a connection with the same parameters. Instead, it returns the identifier of the already opened connection.

The following script will generate different results depending on which connection function you use in the dbConn5 class.

```php
<?php
  //File: testDbConn.php
  require_once 'dbConn5.php';
  require_once 'hrCred.php';
```

```
$exec_mode=OCI_DEFAULT;
$job_id='FI_MGR';
$db = new dbConn5($user, $pswd, $conn, $exec_mode);
$sql="UPDATE employees SET salary = salary*1.1
                        WHERE job_id='".$job_id."'";
if(!$db->query($sql)){
  print 'Failed to update the employees table';
}
$newDb = new dbConn5($user, $pswd, $conn, $exec_mode);
$sql="SELECT last_name, salary FROM employees
                        WHERE job_id='".$job_id."'";
if($newDb->query($sql)){
  print '<table>';
  while ($row = $newDb->fetch()) {
      print '<tr>';
      print '<td>'.$row['LAST_NAME'].'</td>';
      print '<td>'.$row['SALARY'].'</td >';
      print '</tr>';
  }
  print '</table>';
}
?>
```

If you run the `testDbConn.php` script shown above, it should produce the
following output:

Greenberg 13200

In this example, you don't need to worry about setting Greenberg's salary
to its original value. When the script execution ends, the transaction
is automatically rolled back. This is because you execute the UPDATE
operation in OCI_DEFAULT mode and then you don't commit the opened
transaction explicitly.

Now, if you replace the `oci_connect` function in the GetConn method of the
dbConn5 class with the `oci_new_connect` function, the `testDbConn.php` script will
produce the following result:

Greenberg 12000

So, if you make such a replacement in the dbConn5 class — oci_new_connect in place
of oci_connect — then you will no longer be able to use the dbConn5 class in place
of dbConn4 in any application; you won't be able to use the dbConn5 class in the
applications that are designed to work with transactions, assuming that connections
are shared at the page level.

As you can see, having two classes that have the same API doesn't automatically mean that these classes provide the same functionality. Thus, care must be taken when you are replacing one class with another in existing applications.

Reusability

Once a class has been written and debugged, you can then reuse it over and over in new projects. In the *Building Blocks of Applications* section earlier in this chapter, you learned how to use the dbConn5 class in a script that selects data from the database.

In fact, you are not limited to a SELECT operation and can use the query method of the dbConn5 class to perform any SQL statement against the database. For instance, you might use the following script to insert a row into the departments table under the hr/hr database schema:

```php
<?php
//File: insert.php
require_once 'dbConn5.php';
require_once 'hrCred.php';
$db = new dbConn5($user, $pswd, $conn);
$sql="INSERT INTO departments VALUES(320, 'DB design',
                                      null, 1700)";
if($db->query($sql)){
    print 'data have been submitted';
    }
else {
    print 'failed to submit data';
    }
?>
```

This example shows the simplest way in which you can take advantage of code reuse. Specifically, it demonstrates how to reuse an existing class to solve a similar problem in another script. Similarly, you might use the query method to perform DDL operations against the database.

In the *Extending Existing Classes* and *Interaction between Objects* sections, later in this chapter, you will learn about more ways to achieve code reuse in object-oriented PHP applications.

Handling Exceptions

For handling errors, PHP 5 offers a new mechanism that is completely different from that in PHP 4. In PHP 5, you can create and throw an instance of the built-in Exception class in response to an error that has occurred in your object code.

Throwing an exception terminates method execution and makes the appropriate `Exception` instance available to the calling code. To be able to handle an exception thrown from inside an object's method, the calling code must call that method inside a `try` block. It also must have an appropriate `catch` block to handle the exception thrown. It might look like the following figure.

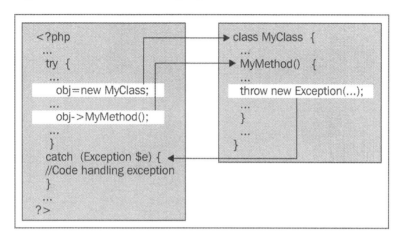

Modifying an Existing Class to use Exceptions

Now that you have a rough idea of how PHP 5's exceptions work in an object-oriented environment, it is time to look at an example of how exceptions can be used. Turning back to the dbConn5 class discussed in the *Taking Advantage of PHP 5's Object-Oriented Features* section earlier, you might rewrite it to support PHP 5's new exception model as shown below:

```php
<?php
//File: dbConn5e.php
class dbConn5e {
    private $user;
    private $pswd;
    private $db;
    private $conn;
    private $query;
    private $row;
    private $exec_mode;
    public function __construct($user, $pswd, $db,
                                $exec_mode= OCI_COMMIT_ON_SUCCESS)
    {
        $this->user = $user;
        $this->pswd = $pswd;
        $this->db = $db;
```

```
        $this->exec_mode = $exec_mode;
        $this->GetConn();
    }
    private function GetConn()
    {
    if(!$this->conn = oci_connect($this->user, $this->pswd,
                                                    $this->db))
        {
          $err = oci_error();
           throw new Exception('Could not establish a connection: ' .
                              $err['message']);
         }
    }
    public function query($sql)
    {
      if(!$this->query = oci_parse($this->conn, $sql)) {
          $err = oci_error($this->conn);
           throw new Exception('Failed to execute SQL query: ' .
                              $err['message']);
       }
      else if(!oci_execute($this->query, $this->exec_mode)) {
          $err = oci_error($this->query);
           throw new Exception('Failed to execute SQL query: ' .
                              $err['message']);
        }
      return true;
    }
    public function fetch()
    {
      if($this->row=oci_fetch_assoc($this->query)){
         return $this->row;
        }
      else {
         return false;
        }
    }
  }
?>
```

In the above class, you obtain the error as an associative array, with the help of the
`oci_error` function, just as you did in the preceding examples earlier in this book.
Then, you assign the error message to the exception object thrown here.

As you can see, the dbConn5e class no longer uses the trigger_error function that you saw in the dbConn5 class discussed earlier. Instead, when something goes wrong, the code in the dbConn5e class throws an exception using the throw new Exception syntax. As previously mentioned, when an exception is thrown, it becomes available to the client context. On the client side, you should place any code that might throw an exception inside the try block. When you have defined the try block, you must then define at least one catch block, which will be used to handle thrown exceptions. So, client code no longer needs to check the return value of a called method to see whether an error has occurred during the execution of the method — the code within a catch block takes care of the thrown exception.

Note that the fetch method of the dbConn5e class still returns false on failure to obtain the next row from the result data, rather than generating an exception. This makes sense, since generating an exception just because all the retrieved rows have been fetched might not seem appropriate.

Now that you have written the dbConn5e class, you might want to write a script to test that class. The following select_e.php script makes use of the newly created dbConn5e class.

```php
<?php
//File: select_e.php
require_once 'dbConn5e.php';
require_once 'hrCred.php';
try {
$db = new dbConn5e($user, $pswd, $conn);
$sql="SELECT last_name FROM employees";
$db->query($sql);
print 'Employee Name: ' . '<br />';
while ($row = $db->fetch()) {
    print $row['LAST_NAME'] . '<br />';
  }
}
  catch (Exception $e) {
    print $e->getMessage();
    exit();
}
?>
```

In the select_e.php script shown in the listing, you no longer need to check whether the query method of dbConn5 has returned true. Instead, you simply wrap the code that might throw an exception in the try block. Then, you define the catch block to handle the thrown exceptions. The script will simply print the appropriate error message when an exception is thrown.

Distinguishing between Different Error Types

In a real-world application you might want your application to distinguish between the different error types in the catch block. One way to do this is to use the user-defined exception flag that can be passed as an optional parameter to the Exception constructor.

The dbConn5e2 class shown below is a revision of the dbConn5e class discussed in the preceding section. The new dbConn5e2 class can throw exceptions that will differ by error type.

```php
<?php
//File: dbConn5e2.php
class dbConn5e2 {
  private $user;
  private $pswd;
  private $db;
  private $conn;
  private $query;
  private $row;
  private $exec_mode;
  const CONNECTION_ERROR = 1;
  const SQLEXECUTION_ERROR = 2;
  function __construct($user, $pswd, $db)
  {
    $this->user = $user;
    $this->pswd = $pswd;
    $this->db = $db;
    $this->exec_mode = $exec_mode;
    $this->GetConn();
  }
  function GetConn()
  {
  if(!$this->conn = oci_connect($this->user, $this->pswd,
                                            $this->db))
    {
      $err = oci_error();
       throw new Exception('Could not establish a connection: '
                  . $err['message'], self::CONNECTION_ERROR);
      }
  }
  function query($sql)
  {
    if(!$this->query = oci_parse($this->conn, $sql)) {
        $err = oci_error($this->conn);
```

```
            throw new Exception('Failed to execute SQL query: '
                        . $err['message'], self::SQLEXECUTION_ERROR);
        }
        else if(!oci_execute($this->query, $this->exec_mode)) {
            $err = oci_error($this->query);
                throw new Exception('Failed to execute SQL query: '
                        . $err['message'], self::SQLEXECUTION_ERROR);
        }
        return true;
    }
    function fetch()
    {
        if($this->row=oci_fetch_assoc($this->query)){
            return $this->row;
        }
            else {
            return false;
        }
    }
    }
?>
```

Now, you can improve the `catch` block in the client code so that it recognizes different error categories. In the `select_e2.php` script shown below, a failure to connect to the database results in a fatal error, which means the script will terminate. On the other hand, failure to perform a query against the database leads only to generation of the appropriate warning message and execution continues after the `catch` block.

```php
<?php
//File: select_e2.php
require_once 'dbConn5e2.php';
require_once 'hrCred.php';
try {
$db = new dbConn5e2($user, $pswd, $conn);
$sql="SELECT last_name FROM employees";
$db->query($sql);
 print 'Employee Name: ' . '<br />';
 while ($row = $db->fetch()) {
     print $row['ENAME'] . '<br />';
  }
}
 catch (Exception $e) {
   if ($e->getCode() == dbConn5e2::CONNECTION_ERROR) {
       die($e->getMessage());
```

```
        }
        else if ($e->getCode() == dbConn5e2::SQLEXECUTION_ERROR) {
            print $e->getMessage();
        }
    }
    //Continue execution
?>
```

It is interesting to note that using user-defined exception codes is not the only way to separate different types of exceptions in your application. Alternatively, you might define subclasses of the built-in Exception class and then use multiple catch blocks to catch different classes of exceptions. For information on this subject, refer to PHP documentation: *Language Reference*, chapter *Exceptions*.

Are Exceptions Necessarily Errors?

It is important to understand that exceptions are not necessarily errors. Whether or not an exception represents an error is determined by the application that employs the class in which the exception occurred. In other words, if an exception has been thrown, it is up to the client code to decide what to do.

For example, imagine an application that requires the user to log in using a logon page. How would you like such an application to behave if a user mistypes when entering his or her credentials? Obviously, it would be a bad idea in such a case to throw an exception that will terminate the execution. Instead, you most probably might want the application to generate a warning message and then allow the user to enter his or her credentials again.

Extending Existing Classes

In the *Implementing PHP Classes to Interact with Oracle* section earlier in this chapter, you saw an example of how to build a new class from scratch and how to reuse it then in different scripts. However, in most cases, you don't need to create a new class from scratch; instead, you may choose an existing class, say, a predefined PHP class, or a class from the PEAR library, and then customize it as needed.

This section gives an example of how the Auth class from the Auth PEAR package can be extended to better suit your needs. But first, to give you an idea of how the Auth class works and when you might need it, this section provides an example of using that class itself.

This section uses the PEAR::Auth class to illustrate an object-oriented approach when it comes to using and customizing classes from open-source libraries, or built-in PHP classes. For a detailed discussion of security issues, see Chapter 6 *Security*.

Using Standard Classes

Before you can start working with PEAR::Auth class, you have to download and install the Auth PEAR package. This can be done with the help of the PEAR Installer. Assuming that you have PEAR installed in your PHP installation, run the following command from the command line:

```
$ pear install Auth
```

 PEAR::Auth can optionally use a number of packages that provide access to various storage containers holding authentication data. In the example provided in this section, the Auth object uses the DB abstraction layer to store the login data. This means that you must have the DB PEAR package installed before proceeding to this example.

PEAR::Auth in Action

Once you have installed the Auth package, you can use the Auth class in your applications. The testAuth.php script shown below is an example of the Auth class in action.

```php
<?php
//File: testAuth.php
require_once "Auth.php";

$auth_opts = array(
  'dsn'=>'oci8://usr:usr@localhost:1521/orcl',
  'table'=>'accounts',
  'usernamecol'=>'usr_id',
  'passwordcol'=>'pswd',
  'db_fields' => '*',
  'cryptType'=>'none'
);
$auth_opts['usernamecol'] = strtoupper($auth_opts['usernamecol']);
$auth_opts['passwordcol'] = strtoupper($auth_opts['passwordcol']);
$a = new Auth('DB', $auth_opts);
$a->setIdle(5);
$a->setExpire(15);
```

```
    $a->start();
    if ($a->getAuth()) {
      print "<h2>Hello, ".$a->getAuthData('FULL_NAME')."!</h2><br/>";
    } else {
      exit;
    }
  ?>
```

Now, let's discuss the code used in the above script.

With the help of the `require_once` PHP command, you make your script aware of the `Auth` class. It is assumed that you have the `Auth` package installed.

In the array of options passed to the storage container, you specify the DSN (data source name) holding information required to obtain a database connection with `PEAR::DB`, the name of the database table holding the authorization data, the names of the columns where the username and password are stored, other fields to be fetched from the row containing the specified username and password, and password encryption type.

 The `testAuth.php` script discussed in this example queries the `accounts` table from the `usr/usr` database schema. So, it is assumed that you have that table created as described in the *An Example of When to Use a Stored Subprogram* section in Chapter 3 *Data Processing*.

As you might recall from Chapter 1 *Getting Started with PHP and Oracle*, Oracle returns all field names in the result set in uppercase. That is why you must make sure that the names of the `username` and `password` columns are specified in uppercase.

In this example, you pass `DB` as the first parameter to the `Auth` constructor, which means that the `Auth` object will use the `PEAR::DB` abstraction layer for database access. As the second parameter passed to the `Auth` constructor, you use an array of the database connection options.

With the help of the `setIdle` method of `Auth`, you set the maximum allowable idle time, in seconds, before the user is automatically logged out. In this example, you set the idle time to 5 seconds, which is good only for testing of course.

Using the setExpire method, you set the expiration time, in seconds, for the PHP session that holds the authentication data. In this example, you set the expiration time to 15 seconds, which is good only for testing.

Next, you call the start method of the Auth object to set up the PHP session that will hold the authentication information. This session has the predefined name _authsession. Once the _authsession session is established, it will exist until it expires or the specified amount of idle time has passed.

 The Auth class provides the logout method to explicitly destroy all the data associated with the _authsession session, thus giving the user a logout option. For simplicity, the logout method is not employed in this example.

Then, you call the getAuth method to check if the user has been authenticated. If so, the script produces a welcome message containing the full name of the authenticated user. Otherwise, the exit command is invoked, terminating further processing.

 Actually, getAuth calls another of Auth's methods, namely checkAuth, that simply checks if there is a valid _authsession session.

In this example, you call the getAuthData method, passing, as the parameter, the name of the field containing the full name of the authenticated user. In fact, FULL_NAME is a column in the accounts table holding the authorization data. You can access FULL_NAME here because you have enabled fetching all the columns of the accounts table by setting the db_fields option to *, in the array of options passed to the storage container.

Securing Pages with PEAR::Auth

Now that you have an idea of how the testAuth.php script works, it is time to put it into practice with an example. The appPage.php script discussed later in this section includes testAuth.php so that only the users who have been authenticated can access the page produced by appPage.php. The first time you run the appPage.php script, it displays a login form, which you must fill in with a valid username and password.

This login form is shown in the following figure:

This login form appears whenever an unauthenticated user attempts to run the appPage.php script discussed later in this section.

Once you have entered valid credentials in the form shown in the previous figure, you can access the page produced by the appPage.php script. The page looks like the following:

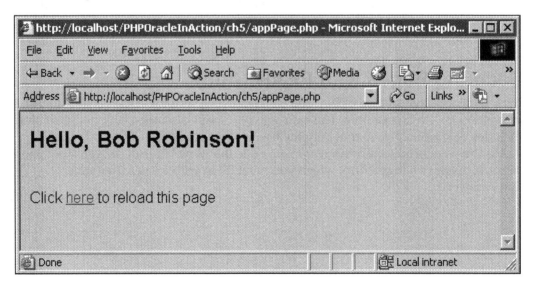

This page is an example of a secure page. This page appears only if the `getAuth` method of `Auth` returns true, which means that the user has been successfully authenticated and the `_authsession` session containing the authentication information is still valid.

> To be successfully authenticated, you must enter a valid username/ password pair stored in the `accounts` table in the `usr/usr` database schema. Provided that you have performed all of the SQL statements shown in the *An Example of When to Use a Stored Subprogram* section in Chapter 3, you should have the `accounts` table containing only one record—the one that represents the Bob Robinson's account with `bob` as the username and `pswd` as the password.

Upon successful authentication, the `appPage.php` script produces a simple page that contains a link to this same page itself (to `appPage.php` actually). When you click that link, the `appPage.php` script invokes `testAuth.php` again to make sure that the authentication session is still valid. If the session has expired or the amount of idle time has passed, the user will be asked to log in again.

The following listing shows the source code for the `appPage.php` script:

```php
<?php
//File: appPage.php
require_once "testAuth.php";
$thisPage='"'."appPage.php".'"';
print "Click <a href=".$thisPage.">here</a> to reload this page";
?>
```

By including `testAuth.php`, you make sure that the authentication mechanism implemented in this script will be invoked each time `appPage.php` is executed. If authentication fails, `testAuth.php` returns the user to the login form and stops further processing, and so `appPage.php` does not output anything.

The message produced by the `appPage.php` script includes a link to `appPage.php` itself. However, in a real-world application, it might be a link to another page of the application.

> A real-world application normally has more than one page to be secured. To use the secure mechanism discussed here in a multi-page application, you simply include `testAuth.php` at the beginning of each script producing a page that you want to secure. This will prevent unauthenticated users from accessing the secure pages of the application.

Customizing Standard Classes

Whether you use a built-in PHP class or a PEAR class, you can always customize the class you're using so that it best suits your needs. For example, you might want to build a new class on an existing one so that the new class shares the properties and the behavior of the base class, extending its functionality by adding new member variables and/or methods. Such a relationship between classes is called inheritance.

> Inheritance is a relationship between classes where one class (child/subclass) inherits attributes and behavior from another (parent/superclass). Child classes can override inherited methods with new ones, thus allowing for customizing the parent class to address a specific problem. So, inheritance provides a powerful way to achieve code reuse in an object-oriented paradigm. A class, once written and debugged, can be reused over and over as the basis for another class.

Customizing PEAR::Auth

Turning back to the PEAR::Auth class discussed in the preceding section, you might extend that class so that the derived class, say, MyAuthOrcl, inherits all the properties and methods of the Auth parent class and additionally encapsulates some functionality you repeatedly implement in the code that employs PEAR::Auth, thus making that code more readable and clearer.

The following diagram gives a conceptual depiction of the inheritance relationship between the Auth class and the MyAuthOrcl class that extends Auth.

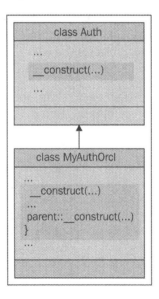

The following listing shows the code for the MyAuthOrcl class extending PEAR::
Auth. It is important to note that the new class inherits all of the properties and
method of the PEAR::Auth class. It simply overrides the parent constructor and adds
a new protected member variable, namely $auth_default_options.

```php
<?php
  //File: MyAuthOrcl.php
  require_once 'Auth.php';
  class MyAuthOrcl extends Auth
  {
   protected $auth_default_options = array(
       'cryptType'=>'none',
   );
   public function __construct ($arr)
   {
    $auth_options = array_merge($this->auth_default_options, $arr);
    $auth_options['usernamecol'] =
                 strtoupper($auth_options['usernamecol']);
    $auth_options['passwordcol'] =
                 strtoupper($auth_options['passwordcol']);
    parent::__construct('DB',$auth_options);
   }
  }
?>
```

You must always include the file containing the class you are using in the script. In
this particular example, you include Auth.php because you use the Auth class as the
parent class for the MyAuthOrcl class defined here.

You use the extends keyword to define a class based upon another class. In this
example, you build the MyAuthOrcl class upon the PEAR::Auth class.

Next, you define the member variable $auth_default_options to hold an array
of default options passed to the storage container. You should add an option to this
array only if you want to replace the option's default value used in the Auth class
with a new one.

In PEAR::Auth, the cryptType option passed to the storage container is set to md5
by default. Here, you define the new default value for the cryptType option,
namely none.

In this example, the derived class overrides the parent constructor. In the same way,
you would override any other method of the parent class.

In the constructor, you merge the elements of the array passed to the constructor and
the elements of the array defined in the $auth_default_options member variable.

In this example, you call the `strtoupper` function from inside the class constructor. By doing this, you eliminate the need to call this function from within the calling code.

In the last code line in the overriding constructor, you call the parent constructor from within the overriding constructor using the `parent` keyword followed by the scope resolution operator `::`, and then by the `__construct` keyword.

> Unlike most other object-oriented languages, PHP doesn't automatically call the parent constructor when running an overriding constructor of the subclass. So, you have to explicitly call the parent constructor from within an overriding constructor of the subclass to ensure you get a complete and correct instance of the class.

In the same way—using the `parent::` syntax—you can refer to any other public or protected member variable or method of a base class from within its subclasses.

> At the time of this writing, the `PEAR::Auth` class did not employ PHP 5's new visibility keywords when defining its member variables and methods. This means that all the member variables and methods of `PEAR::Auth` had public visibility and so they could be overridden in subclasses.

Building More Compact Client Code

Now that you have the `MyAuthOrcl` class, it's time to put it into action. However, to make the client code employing the newly created class more compact, you might want to place the array of options passed to the storage container in a separate file. The following listing shows the `connOptions.php` file containing that array.

```php
<?php
//File: connOptions.php
$auth_opts = array(
  'dsn'=>'oci8://usr:usr@localhost:1521/orcl',
  'table'=>'accounts',
  'usernamecol'=>'usr_id',
  'passwordcol'=>'pswd',
  'db_fields' => '*'
);
?>
```

Once you have created the connOptions.php file, you can include it into the scripts that use the MyAuthOrcl class, as shown below.

```php
<?php
//File: testMyAuthOrcl.php
require_once "MyAuthOrcl.php";
require_once "connOptions.php";
$a = new MyAuthOrcl($auth_opts);
$a->setIdle(5);
$a->setExpire(15);
$a->start();
if ($a->getAuth()) {
 print "<h2>Hello, ".$a->getAuthData('FULL_NAME')."!</h2><br/>";
} else {
 exit;
}
?>
```

As you can see from the listing, the testMyAuthOrcl.php script provides the same functionality as the testAuth.php discussed in the *PEAR::Auth in Action* section earlier, and requires less code. It is important to realize that the MyAuthOrcl class has all the data and methods of the PEAR::Auth class, extending its functionality a little.

You can test the newly created testMyAuthOrcl.php script with the help of the appPage.php script discussed in the *Securing Pages with PEAR::Auth* section earlier. However, before you do that, make sure to replace testAuth.php, included with the require_once command at the beginning of the appPage.php script, with testMyAuthOrcl.php.

The updated appPage.php page, when executed, should produce the same page as shown in the figure in the *Securing Pages with PEAR:: Auth* section. Further testing should indicate that the sample works as before and the changes made do not affect the application behavior from the user's point of view.

Interactions between Objects

In the preceding section, you looked at inheritance—a way to build new classes upon existing ones, thus allowing you to reuse and extend what has already been defined and debugged.

This section looks at code reuse through two powerful methods commonly used in object-oriented programming, namely composition and aggregation.

Composition

Using the functionality of an object from within another object allows you to leverage existing functionality, rather than creating it from scratch. One way to accomplish such an interaction is through composition.

> Composition takes place when one object contains another object, meaning that the owning object is responsible for creating the contained object, and once the owner is destroyed, the contained object is destroyed as well.

The best way to understand how composition works in PHP is by example. Imagine that you want to replace the default login form used in the MyAuthOrcl class discussed in the preceding section with a custom one. To achieve this goal, you might design a login function responsible for creating and displaying a custom login form, and then pass the name of that function to the Auth class constructor as the third parameter. Recall that you call the Auth class constructor from within the MyAuthOrcl constructor.

A custom login form designed with the help of the PEAR::HTML_QuickForm class might look like the following figure:

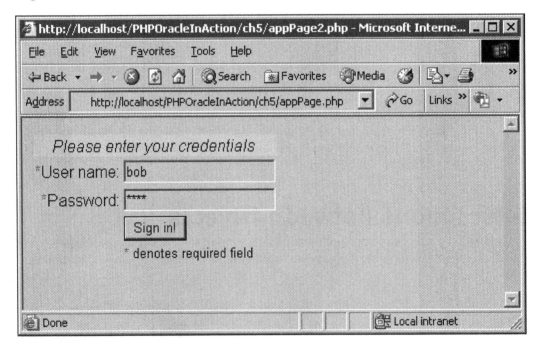

The following listing shows the code for the revision of the MyAuthOrcl class, which creates and uses an instance of the PEAR::HTML_QuickForm class to build and display a custom login form.

```php
<?php
//File: MyAuthOrcl_CustForm.php
require_once 'HTML/QuickForm.php';
//Obtain the Auth class so it can be extended
require_once 'Auth.php';
class MyAuthOrcl_CustForm extends Auth
{
 protected $auth_default_options = array(
      'cryptType'=>'none',
  );
 public function __construct ($arr)
 {
  function login_function($username, $status)
   {
    $headerTemplate  = '<tr><td style="background-color:
              #dddddd;" align="center" colspan="2"><font
                face="Arial"><i>{header}</i></font></td></tr>';
    $elementTemplate  = '<tr><td align="right"><font
              face="Arial"><!-- BEGIN required --><span
                style="color: #ff0000">*</span>';
    $elementTemplate  .= '<!-- END required -->
            {label}</font></td><td align="left">{element}</td></tr>';
    $form=new HTML_QuickForm('login', 'POST');
    $renderer = $form->defaultRenderer();
    $renderer->setHeaderTemplate($headerTemplate);
    $renderer->setElementTemplate($elementTemplate);
    $header='Please enter your credentials';
    switch ($status) {
     case -1: $header='You have been idle for too long.
                Please login again.';
              break;
     case -2: $header='Session expired. Please login again.';
              break;
     case -3: $header='You entered wrong data. Please try again.';
              break;
    }
    $form->addElement('header',null,$header );
    $form->addElement('text','username','User name:');
    $form->addRule('username','The username field is
              required!','required', null, 'client');
```

```
        $form->addElement('password','password','Password:');
        $form->addRule('password','The password field is
                required!','required', null, 'client');
        $form->addElement('submit','submit','Sign in!');
        $form->display();
    }
    $auth_options = array_merge($this->auth_default_options, $arr);
    $auth_options['usernamecol'] =
                strtoupper($auth_options['usernamecol']);
    $auth_options['passwordcol'] =
                strtoupper($auth_options['passwordcol']);
    parent::__construct('DB',$auth_options, 'login_function');
    }
}
?>
```

In this example, you create an instance of the PEAR::HTML_QuickForm class from within the login_function defined inside the constructor of the MyAuthOrcl_CustForm class. The HTML_QuickForm object created here is referenced only within that function and cannot be referenced by external code.

> Alternatively, the custom function passed to the Auth constructor might be defined in the client code, rather than in the MyAuthOrcl_CustForm class constructor. However, encapsulating it in the class constructor allows for building more compact and clearer client code.

Now, to put the new MyAuthOrcl_CustForm class into action, all you need to do is revise the testMyAuthOrcl.php script discussed in the *Building More Compact Client Code* section earlier, so that the revision, say, testMyAuthOrcl_CustForm. php script, includes the MyAuthOrcl_CustForm.php file with the require_once command, instead of the MyAuthOrcl.php file, and creates the new MyAuthOrcl_ CustForm object instead of the MyAuthOrcl one. Next, in the appPage.php script discussed in the *Securing Pages with PEAR::Auth* section, you need to include the testMyAuthOrcl_CustForm.php file instead of the testMyAuthOrcl.php.

With that done, you can run the appPage.php script to test the newly created MyAuthOrcl_CustForm class. Besides the new look of the login form, the sample should behave as before.

Aggregation

Aggregation is another powerful way for objects to interact with each other. Unlike composition, aggregation does not imply ownership—several objects may share a single object at the same time.

Aggregation takes place when one object uses another one, taking a reference to it as a parameter passed to the constructor or any other method. So, in aggregation the object does not create another object, and the aggregated object is not necessarily destroyed when the object that uses it is destroyed.

To understand better how aggregation works, let's look at an example of it in action. Looking through the PEAR documentation on the Auth class, you may notice that you are allowed to specify an existing DB object with the dsn option instead of a DSN string when using the DB abstraction layer to store the login data.

The following example shows how the MyAuthOrcl class discussed in the *Customizing PEAR::Auth* section earlier in this chapter might use an instance of PEAR::DB, taking a reference to it as a parameter passed to the constructor. It is important to note that, to accomplish this, no change is required in the MyAuthOrcl class code. In the code that uses that class, you simply have to set the dsn parameter, which is passed within an array to the class constructor, to a reference of DB object.

The following listing contains a revision of the testMyAuthOrcl.php script discussed in the *Building More Compact Client Code* section earlier. The testMyAuthOrcl_DB.php script shown in the listing illustrates a situation in which a MyAuthOrcl object aggregates a PEAR:DB object.

```php
<?php
//File: testMyAuthOrcl_DB.php
require_once "MyAuthOrcl.php";
require_once "connOptions.php";
require_once 'DB.php';
$dbh = DB::connect($auth_opts['dsn']);
if(DB::isError($dbh)) {
    die($dbh->getMessage());
}
$auth_opts['dsn'] = $dbh;
$a = new MyAuthOrcl($auth_opts);
$a->setIdle(5);
$a->setExpire(10);
$a->start();
if ($a->getAuth()) {
  print '<font face="Arial">';
  print "<h2>Hello, ".$a->getAuthData('FULL_NAME')."!</h2><br/>";
  print '</font>';
} else {
 exit;
}
?>
```

As in the preceding examples, to test the testMyAuthOrcl_DB.php script shown in the listing, you can still use the appPage.php script, having included testMyAuthOrcl_DB.php with require_once, of course. Again, from the user's standpoint, the changes made should not affect the sample behavior.

Now that you have seen how an object can aggregate another object, it is time to look at a more complicated example of object aggregation. The following listing shows how the MyAuthOrcl_dbConn5 class derived from the PEAR::Auth class could be modified to aggregate an instance of the dbConn5 class discussed in the *Implementing PHP Classes to Interact with Oracle* section earlier in this chapter.

```php
<?php
//File: MyAuthOrcl_dbConn5.php
require_once 'HTML/QuickForm.php';
require_once 'Auth.php';
class MyAuthOrcl_dbConn5 extends Auth
{
 protected $auth_default_options = array(
      'cryptType'=>'none',
 );
 private $dbConn = null;
 public function __construct ($arr, $conn)
 {
  $this->dbConn=$conn;
  function login_function($username, $status)
  {
     ...
     // Here is the body of the login_function function as
                                    shown in listing 5.16
     ...
  }
  $auth_options = array_merge($this->auth_default_options, $arr);
  $auth_options['usernamecol'] =
                     strtoupper($auth_options['usernamecol']);
  $auth_options['passwordcol'] =
                     strtoupper($auth_options['passwordcol']);
  parent::__construct('DB',$auth_options, 'login_function');
 }
 public function login()
 {
    function defaultLoginCallback($username, $authObj)
    {
     $query="INSERT INTO logons
                 VALUES ("."'".$username."'",".".SYSDATE)";
```

```
        if(!$authObj->dbConn->query($query)){
            print "Failed to create an audit record";
        }
    };
    if ($this->loginCallback==''){
        $this->setLoginCallback('defaultLoginCallback');
    }
    return parent::login();
  }
 }
?>
```

In this example, you define the dbConn member variable to hold a reference to a dbConn5 object. Since the client code that will use the MyAuthOrcl_dbConn5 class is not supposed to initialize this member variable directly, you define it as private.

Then, you define the MyAuthOrcl_dbConn5 class constructor so that it takes a reference to a dbConn5 object as the second parameter. In the constructor, you initialize the dbConn member variable to the value returned in the second constructor parameter.

In this example, you override the login method that the MyAuthOrcl_dbConn5 class inherits from the Auth class.

Looking through the documentation on the PEAR::Auth class, you may notice that it doesn't contain a section on the login method. So, you might be asking yourself, how would I know that the PEAR::Auth class includes a login method at all? Well, the best way to understand how an existing class works and what member variables and methods it contains is by stepping through its source code, if it is available, of course. In this particular example, it is highly recommended that you examine the source code for the PEAR::Auth class, which can be found in the pear/Auth.php source file.

Within the login method, you define the defaultLoginCallback function. Later in the login method, you set the loginCallback member variable to the name of this function. By doing this, you instruct the MyAuthOrcl_dbConn5 object to call the defaultLoginCallback function every time a user is successfully authenticated.

Within the defaultLoginCallback function, you define the INSERT statement that, when executed, inserts an audit record into the logons table.

Again, it is assumed that you have the `logons` table as described in the *An Example of When to Use a Stored Subprogram* section in Chapter 3 *Data Processing*. Then, you use the `dbConn5`'s `query` method to execute the `INSERT` statement.

Next, you check to see if the `loginCallback` member variable has been set in the client code. If so, your `MyAuthOrcl_dbConn5` object will invoke the specified function every time a user is successfully authenticated.

If the `loginCallback` member variable has not been set in the client code, you set it to `defaultLoginCallback`.

As you can see, the mechanism used here allows the client code to override the default function invoked when a user is successfully authenticated.

Finally, you explicitly call `Auth`'s `login` method. This ensures that the overriding method, in addition to the custom code you defined in this method, will execute the code defined in the overridden method.

Now that you have an idea of how the `MyAuthOrcl_dbConn5` class works, it is time to put it into action. The `testMyAuthOrcl_dbConn5.php` script shown below makes use of the `MyAuthOrcl_dbConn5` class.

```php
<?php
//File: testMyAuthOrcl_dbConn5.php
require_once "MyAuthOrcl_dbConn5.php";
require_once "connOptions.php";
require_once "dbConn5.php";
$db = new dbConn5('usr', 'usr', '//localhost/orcl');
$a = new MyAuthOrcl_dbConn5($auth_opts, $db);
$a->setIdle(5);
$a->setExpire(10);
$a->start();
if ($a->getAuth()) {
  print '<font face="Arial">';
  print "<h2>Hello, ".$a->getAuthData('FULL_NAME')."!</h2><br/>";
  print '</font>';
} else {
  exit;
}
?>
```

Again, to test the script shown in the listing, you can use the `appPage.php` script, this time having included `testMyAuthOrcl_dbConn5.php` with `require_once`. Besides the fact that information about successful logons will be stored in the `logons` table, the updated sample should behave as in the preceding examples.

Event-Driven Communication

In the preceding section, you saw how you can take advantage of an event-driven model when developing object code. In particular, you saw an example of the class that allows for registering a custom function with an instance of that class, so that this function is invoked whenever a certain event occurs.

Graphically, an event-driven communication might look like that shown in the following diagram:

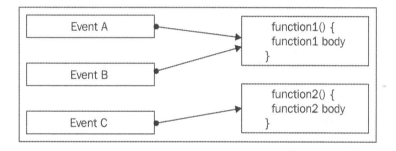

In the preceding example, you learned that the `PEAR::Auth` class allows you to define a custom function that will be invoked automatically whenever a user is successfully authenticated.

However, looking through the `Auth.php` source file, you may notice that the `Auth` class also allows you to define a custom function that will be invoked automatically whenever an authentication process fails. This comes in handy when you need to record every login attempt, whether it is successful or not.

To start with, you have to create a database table that will be used to store audit records. To do this, you might connect to the database as `usr/usr` from SQL*Plus and then issue the `CREATE TABLE` statement shown below:

```
CREATE TABLE log_attempts (
    usrname     VARCHAR2(10),
    success     NUMBER(1),
    log_time    DATE
);
```

Once the `log_attempts` table has been created, you can modify the `testMyAuthOrcl_dbConn5.php` file discussed in the preceding section as shown below:

```php
<?php
//File: testMyAuthOrcl_Events.php
require_once "MyAuthOrcl_dbConn5.php";
require_once "connOptions.php";
require_once "dbConn5.php";
function loginCallback_function($username, $authObj)
{
  if ($authObj->getAuth()){
    $auth=1;
  } else {
    $auth=0;
  }
  $query="INSERT INTO log_attempts
              VALUES ("."'".$username."'",".".$auth.", SYSDATE)";
  if (!$authObj->dbConn->query($query)){
    print "Failed to create an audit record";
  }
}

$db = new dbConn5('usr', 'usr', '//localhost/orcl');
$a = new MyAuthOrcl_dbConn5($auth_opts, $db);
$a->setLoginCallback('loginCallback_function');
$a->setFailedLoginCallback('loginCallback_function');
$a->setIdle(5);
$a->setExpire(10);
$a->start();
if ($a->getAuth()) {
  print '<font face="Arial">';
  print "<h2>Hello, ".$a->getAuthData('FULL_NAME')."!</h2><br/>";
  print '</font>';
} else {
 exit;
}
?>
```

As you can see in the code for the `testMyAuthOrcl_Events.php` script, the `loginCallback_function` function is created, and then is registered to be called whenever a login attempt occurs, regardless of whether that attempt is successful or not. To achieve this goal, you set both the `loginCallback` and `failedLoginCallback` member variables of `MyAuthOrcl_ dbConn5` to the same value, namely `loginCallback_function`.

As a result, you have two different types of events, which are generated by the `MyAuthOrcl_dbConn5` object on login and logout operations respectively, bound to the single event handler. In the event handler `loginCallback_function` function, you call the `query` method of the `dbConn5` aggregated object to insert an audit record into the `log_attempts` table.

Using Oracle Object-Relational Features

So far, you have looked at the features that can help you take advantage of the object-oriented model at the PHP side of your PHP/Oracle application. This section briefly touches upon the Oracle object-relational features, providing some examples that should help you better understand how these features can be used to develop effective PHP/Oracle applications. For detailed information about Oracle object-relational features, see Oracle documentation: *Application Developer's Guide - Object-Relational Features*.

Using Oracle Object Types

As an alternative to creating relational tables and views, Oracle allows you to define tables and views based on user-defined object types, making it easier for you to model real-world entities and relationships between them.

Turning back to the example discussed in the *Using Transactions in PHP/Oracle Applications* section in Chapter 4, let's look at how you might reorganize the database data used by the example into Oracle objects, moving some of the business logic of the example into the methods of those objects. This section discusses how to create and populate with data the `jobs_obj_table` object table, which will be used in this example instead of the `jobs` relational table. In the following section, you will see how to define the `emp_t` object type with the `newsalary` member function and then define the `emps_obj_table` object table based on that type.

The following listing shows how to create the `jobs_obj_table` object table based on the `job_t` user-defined object type. You can run the SQL statements shown in the listing from SQL*Plus.

```
CONN usr/usr
CREATE OR REPLACE TYPE job_t AS OBJECT(
  job_id              VARCHAR2(10),
  job_title           VARCHAR2(35),
  min_salary          NUMBER(6),
  max_salary          NUMBER(6)
);
/
```

In this code we define an object type, which, in Oracle, is a kind of datatype. Once an Oracle object type is defined, you can declare variables of that type in PL/SQL programs or define a table column of it.

By issuing the following command, you create the jobs_obj_table object table of the job_t type defined above:

```
CREATE TABLE jobs_obj_table OF job_t;
```

You cannot declare a primary key when defining an object type. But you can always add the primary key to an object table by using the ALTER TABLE statement with the ADD PRIMARY KEY clause, as demonstrated in the following example:

```
ALTER TABLE jobs_obj_table ADD PRIMARY KEY (job_id);
```

An object table can be populated with data in the same way as a relational table. In this example, you populate the jobs_obj_table object table with the data retrieved from the jobs table located in the default hr/hr database schema:

```
CONN /AS SYSDBA
GRANT SELECT on hr.jobs TO usr;
CONN usr/usr
INSERT INTO jobs_obj_table SELECT * FROM hr.jobs;
```

Implementing Business Logic with Methods of Oracle Objects

Optionally, you can declare methods in an object type definition. Using object methods allows you to encapsulate some of the business logic of your application along with the data, thus providing another way of moving data processing to the data.

The following listing comprises of a set of SQL statements and shows how you can define an object type with a member function. Specifically, it shows how to define the emp_t object type with the newsalary member function that calculates the new salary for the current employee record based upon the factor passed to the function as the parameter and the current salary. If the new salary exceeds the maximum allowable salary defined in the jobs_obj_table table for the particular title, the newsalary function triggers an error.

```
CONN usr/usr

CREATE OR REPLACE TYPE emp_t AS OBJECT(
  empno   VARCHAR2(6),
  name    VARCHAR2(30),
  job_ref REF job_t,
  salary  NUMBER,
```

```
MEMBER FUNCTION newsalary(inc_sal NUMBER) RETURN NUMBER DETERMINISTIC
);
/

CREATE OR REPLACE TYPE BODY emp_t IS
MEMBER FUNCTION newsalary(inc_sal NUMBER) RETURN NUMBER IS
 job_obj job_t;
 maxsal NUMBER;
BEGIN
 UTL_REF.SELECT_OBJECT(self.job_ref,job_obj);
 maxsal:=job_obj.max_salary;
 IF (inc_sal*self.salary > maxsal) THEN
   RAISE_APPLICATION_ERROR(-20000, 'New salary exceeds the maximum
                             allowable salary');
 END IF;
 RETURN inc_sal*self.salary;
END;
END;
/

CREATE TABLE emps_obj_table OF emp_t;

ALTER TABLE emps_obj_table ADD PRIMARY KEY (empno);

CONN /AS SYSDBA

GRANT SELECT on hr.employees TO usr;

CONN usr/usr

INSERT INTO emps_obj_table(empno, name, salary, job_ref)
SELECT employee_id, last_name, salary, (SELECT REF(j) FROM
            jobs_obj_table j WHERE j.job_id=e.job_id)
            FROM hr.employees e;
```

Once you have executed all the SQL statements shown in the above listing, you should have the emps_obj_table object table created and populated with the emp_t objects generated from the relational data retrieved from the hr.employees table.

You select the data stored in an object table in the same way you would do it when dealing with a relational table—with the help of the SELECT statement. In the following example, you select all the records representing stock managers in the emps_obj_table object table, using the DEREF SQL function to retrieve the corresponding job_t objects from the jobs_obj_table object table created in the preceding section.

```
SELECT empno, name, DEREF(job_ref).job_id as job_id, salary FROM
            emps_obj_table WHERE DEREF(job_ref).job_id ='ST_MAN';
```

This should produce the following output:

```
EMPNO   NAME                            JOB_ID          SALARY
------  ------------------------------  ----------      ----------
120     Weiss                           ST_MAN          8000
121     Fripp                           ST_MAN          8200
122     Kaufling                        ST_MAN          7900
123     Vollman                         ST_MAN          6500
124     Mourgos                         ST_MAN          5800
```

To update the data stored in an object table, you use an UPDATE statement, as with a relational table. In the following example, you're attempting to increase stock managers' salaries by 10 percent, calling the newsalary member function of the emp_t object type from within the SET clause of the UPDATE statement.

```
UPDATE emps_obj_table e
SET salary=e.newsalary(1.1)
WHERE DEREF(job_ref).job_id ='ST_MAN';
```

The UPDATE operation should fail with the following error message:

```
ERROR at line 2:
ORA-20000: New salary exceeds the maximum allowable salary
ORA-06512: at "USR.EMP_T", line 9
```

The fact is that not all records representing stock managers can be updated with this UPDATE operation. Looking through the current stock the managers' salaries, you may notice that some of them will exceed the maximum allowed value specified for the stock manager in the jobs table, when giving a 10 percent raise. When it happens, the newsalary member function generates an error and so the UPDATE operation is aborted.

However, you should have no problem when giving a 10 percent raise to administration vice presidents. Before updating their records, however, you might select them as follows:

```
SELECT empno, name, DEREF(job_ref).job_id as job_id, salary FROM
        emps_obj_table WHERE DEREF(job_ref).job_id ='AD_VP';
```

This should produce the following output:

```
EMPNO   NAME                            JOB_ID          SALARY
------  ------------------------------  ----------      ----------
101     Kochhar                         AD_VP           17000
102     De Haan                         AD_VP           17000
```

To perform the UPDATE, you might issue the following statement:

```
UPDATE emps_obj_table e
SET salary=e.newsalary(1.1)
WHERE DEREF(job_ref).job_id ='AD_VP';

2 rows updated.
```

Now, if you select the administration vice presidents' records again, you should see the following results:

EMPNO	NAME	JOB_ID	SALARY
101	Kochhar	AD_VP	18700
102	De Haan	AD_VP	18700

Finally, don't forget to roll back the changes made by this UPDATE operation by issuing the ROLLBACK statement:

```
ROLLBACK;
```

Using Oracle Objects to Simplify Application Creation

Now that you have a rough idea of how object-relational features work in Oracle, it is time to look at an example of how you can benefit from using them in your PHP/Oracle applications.

The updateWithObjects.php script shown below issues an UPDATE operation against the emps_obj_table table defined in the preceding section. Since the emps_obj_table table is an object, SQL operations issued against it deal with objects, rather than relational rows. In this particular example, the UPDATE operation, when executed, modifies emp_t objects rather than just relational rows stored in the emps_obj_table table.

```php
<?php
  //File: updateWithObjects.php
  if(!$dbConn = oci_connect('usr', 'usr', '//localhost/orcl')) {
      $err = oci_error();
      trigger_error('Could not establish a connection: ' .
                              $err['message'], E_USER_ERROR);
  };
  $jobno = 'ST_MAN';
  $query = "
  UPDATE emps_obj_table e
  SET salary=e.newsalary(1.1)
```

```
     WHERE DEREF(job_ref).job_id =:jobid;
     $stmt = oci_parse($dbConn,$query);
     oci_bind_by_name($stmt, ':jobid', $jobno);
     if (!oci_execute($stmt, OCI_COMMIT_ON_SUCCESS)) {
       $err = oci_error($stmt);
       trigger_error('Query failed: ' . $err['message'], E_USER_ERROR);
     };
     print "Transaction is committed";
?>
```

 The above script is a revision of the script originally shown in the *Using Transactions in PHP/Oracle Applications* section in Chapter 4, and then improved as discussed in the *Structuring a PHP/Oracle Application to Control Transactions* section. This example illustrates how organizing database data into Oracle objects can make it easier for you to write PHP code manipulating that data.

In this example, you call the newsalary member function of the emp_t object type to calculate the value for the salary attribute of the emp_t instance that is currently being invoked. If the new salary exceeds the maximum salary defined for the specified job title in the jobs table, the newsalary function triggers an error and so all the effects of the UPDATE operation are rolled back. If it happens, the UPDATE operation updates no rows, as discussed in the preceding example.

Summary

Using object-oriented design principles to organize your applications can help you build re-usable, maintainable, and well-structured solutions. With classes as building blocks of your application, you can focus on the specifics of the application rather than on what is going on "under the hood".

In this chapter, you saw methods for code reuse when building object-oriented PHP applications on top of Oracle. In particular, you saw how to build a new class from scratch and how to build a child class upon an existing one, customizing the parent class to address a specific problem. You also learned how to use the try/catch/throw exception-handling paradigm in object-oriented PHP applications.

Finally, you learned that Oracle objects, like PHP objects, make it possible to encapsulate operations along with the data, thus allowing you to take advantage of reusing business logic implemented with object's methods.

6
Security

The main reason for setting up security in your PHP/Oracle application is to protect it against unauthorized access or alteration of the data.

In the preceding chapter, you learned how to build an authentication system in PHP using the `Auth` class from the PEAR library. You also saw several examples of how this class might be extended to suit the needs of a particular application. However, it is important to realize that implementing an authentication system is only the first step in building a secure application. Once a user is successfully authenticated, your application should determine whether that user is authorized to access the requested database resources, thus defining different levels of permissions for different users. It is always a good idea to implement authorization within the database as it guarantees that no one will be able to bypass the application's security, even if the connecting to the database is made directly.

This chapter discusses how to effectively use the security features of both PHP and Oracle together, examining the fundamental aspects of building a secure PHP/Oracle application. In particular, you will learn how to:

- Separate security management and data
- Implement an authentication/authorization system
- Hash sensitive data
- Implement fine-grained access using database views
- Mask column values returned to the application
- Use Oracle Virtual Private Database (VPD) technology

Securing PHP/Oracle Applications

In this section, you will learn how to build a simple secure PHP/Oracle application. The intent of this example is to demonstrate how to use simple security mechanisms available in PHP and Oracle in a complementary way in order to protect sensitive data from unauthorized disclosure and prevent data from unauthorized modification or destruction of data.

In particular, you will see how to organize data structures within the database to ensure a secure access to the application data stored in the database, and how to build secure PHP scripts through which application users will access that data.

An important point to note here is that the example discussed in this section uses only those Oracle database features that are available in any of Oracle the database editions, including Oracle Database Express Edition.

Another point to note about the example discussed here is that, in order to follow it, you do not necessarily need to have the samples from the previous chapters built. You simply will need to borrow the `testAuth.php` script described in the *PEAR:: Auth in Action* section in Chapter 5 and the `usr.acoounts` table created as described in the *An Example of When to Use a Stored Subprogram* section in Chapter 3, before proceeding to the sample.

Authenticating Users

In the *Using Standard Classes* section in Chapter 5, you saw an example of an authentication system built using the `Auth` package from the PEAR library. In particular, you saw how the `PEAR::Auth` class can be used to build secure pages in your PHP/Oracle application, preventing unauthenticated users from accessing secure information. The following steps outline how it works:

- Users cannot access any secure application page until they log in. Users log in through a login form, supplying a valid username/password pair maintained in the database.

- Once logged in, the user gains access to secure pages. He or she doesn't need to supply his or her credentials again when moving from one secure page to another. Before a secure page is displayed, a check of whether a session with valid authentication information exists takes place.

- An authenticated user is automatically logged out when the session holding the authentication information expires or the specified amount of idle time has passed, whichever is soonest.

In a real-world application, in addition to this functionality, you would, no doubt, implement the logout functionality based on the `logout` method of the `PEAR::Auth` class, providing a way for users to log out.

For simplicity, the example discussed in Chapter 5, on its secure page, displays a hello message including the name of the authenticated user and some text applicable to all application users. Regardless of the credentials being used by the end users to get authenticated, the application connects all users to the single database schema. The following diagram offers a high-level view of that interaction.

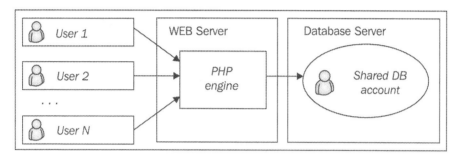

As you can see from the figure, you don't need to create a database account for each application user just to make it possible for him or her to access the data stored in the database—all application users are associated with the same single database account.

Being commonly used in database-driven web applications, this all-to-one type of mapping will be used in all the examples discussed throughout this chapter. The next sections examine how the authentication system discussed here can be improved for better security.

Separating Security Management and Data

In the example discussed in the *Using Standard Classes* section in Chapter 5, the application uses the same database schema to connect to the database and to hold the database tables queried from the application. However, from a security standpoint, using the same single database schema in this case is definitely not the best way to go.

The fact is that when connecting to a database schema, the user obtains full access to all the database objects belonging to that schema. In practice, this means that after a connection to the database is established the application can not only issue SELECT statements against the database objects it works with, but also issue DML (INSERT, UPDATE, DELETE) and DDL (DROP TABLE, for example) statements against those objects, thus creating a potential security issue. Such issues can be resolved by using database schemas as discussed in the following sections.

Using Two Database Schemas to Improve Security

To improve security, you might create another database schema to be used only for establishing connections, and then give only SELECT privileges on the database objects that your application queries to that schema.

As an example of where this technique might be useful, let's turn back to the example discussed in the *PEAR::Auth in Action* section in the preceding chapter. Looking through the testAuth.php script shown in the listing, you may notice that it authenticates users against the accounts table, which in turn is created as described in the *An Example of When to Use a Stored Subprogram* section in Chapter 3. Since the testAuth.php script connects to the database through the same database schema where the accounts table resides, this represents a weak spot in the application's defense.

Before you proceed with this example, make sure that you have the accounts table installed in your database. To do this, issue the following SELECT statement from SQL*Plus when connected as usr/usr:

```
SELECT * FROM accounts;
```

If you have performed the SQL statements shown in the *An Example of When to Use a Stored Subprogram* section in Chapter 3, you should receive results that might look as follows:

USR_ID	FULL_NAME	PSWD	NUM_LOGONS
bob	Bob Robinson	pswd	32

 The num_logons column was added to the accounts table when performing SQL statements shown in the *Controlling Transactions from PHP* section in Chapter 4. For the example discussed in this section, it does not matter if your accounts table contains the num_logons column or not.

If you still don't have the accounts table, you need to create it now, using the appropriate statements from the *An Example of When to Use a Stored Subprogram* section in Chapter 3.

Once you have that set up, you can create a new database schema through which the testAuth.php script will connect to the database. Then, you can grant the SELECT privileges on the accounts table to the newly created schema. The following SQL statements are required to perform these tasks.

```
CONN /AS sysdba
```

Using this SQL statement, you create a new database schema that will be used by the application to connect to the database.

```
CREATE USER app_conn IDENTIFIED BY appconn;
```

Once a database schema is created, you should grant all the required privileges to it. When granting privileges, you should always remember the least privilege principle, which implies that users should be given only the minimum privileges required to do their job and nothing else.

 To make managing and controlling privileges easier, Oracle uses roles, combining related privileges into groups. In addition to predefined roles available in Oracle, you can create and then employ your own roles, grouping privileges as needed.

In this example, you grant only the default CONNECT role to the newly created schema, thus allowing users accessing only this account to connect to the database:

```
GRANT CONNECT TO app_conn;
```

 Starting with Oracle Database 10g Release 2, the CONNECT role has only the CREATE SESSION privilege—the minimum required to establish a connection to the database. Other privileges, such as CREATE TABLE and CREATE VIEW, were removed from the CONNECT role for security reasons.

Next, you grant the SELECT privilege on the usr.accounts table to the app_conn schema, so that the application users using app_conn schema to connect to the database will be able to view data stored in this table, but not alter it.

```
GRANT SELECT ON usr.accounts TO app_conn;
```

Now that you have the app_conn schema set up and granted the CONNECT role, you can use this schema instead of usr in your application in order to connect to the database. So, you should revoke the CONNECT role from the usr schema for security reasons.

```
REVOKE CONNECT FROM usr;
```

Once you have performed all the SQL statements discussed above, you need to slightly modify the testAuth.php script discussed in the *PEAR::Auth in Action* section in Chapter 5 to use the newly created app_conn database schema instead of usr.

In fact, all you need to modify is the array of options passed to the storage container of the `Auth` object, as shown below:

```
$auth_opts = array(
  'dsn'=>'oci8://app_conn:appconn@localhost:1521/orcl',
  'table'=>'usr.accounts',
  'usernamecol'=>'usr_id',
  'passwordcol'=>'pswd',
  'db_fields' => '*',
  'cryptType'=>'none'
);
```

Once you've done that, you can then test the updated authentication system. To do this, you might run the `appPage.php` script discussed in the *Securing Pages with PEAR::Auth* section in the preceding chapter. When testing the sample, you should note that while the above changes improve the security of the authentication scheme used here, from the user's point of view, the sample behaves as before.

Using Three Database Schemas to Improve Security

Having two database schemas—one for establishing connections and the other for holding database resources used by the application—is undoubtedly a good idea from the point of view of security. This way the schema used for establishing a connection to the database has no rights to modify the data accessed by the application. However, it is still not an optimal security solution—everyone who can obtain the database connection credentials embedded in the application source code will be able to issue a `SELECT` query against the `usr.accounts` table, thus obtaining access to all application users' accounts stored in this table.

One possible solution to this problem is to create another database schema that will serve as an intermediate point of connection between the above two schemas. In this schema, you might create a set of stored procedures providing secure access to database resources. Graphically, it might look like the following figure.

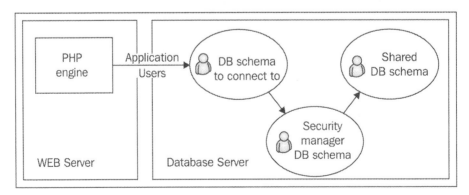

Using the security solution shown in the figure, you restrict access to database data by allowing users to manipulate it only through the stored procedures that in turn have a restricted set of privileges on the data they manipulate. Residing in a separate database schema, these stored procedures are used to safely access resources stored in another schema. For better security, the schema used for establishing connections has only the rights to execute these stored procedures but not to create or alter them.

You need to execute the following SQL statements to create a new database schema for holding stored procedures that will be used to safely access database data.

```
CONN /AS sysdba
```

Next, you create the `sec_adm` database schema that will be used to perform the security related tasks:

```
CREATE USER sec_adm IDENTIFIED BY secadm;
```

You grant the RESOURCE role to the newly created schema so that you can create database resources in it. Note that you should not grant the CONNECT role to this schema because your application will use only the `app_conn` schema to connect to the database:

```
GRANT RESOURCE TO sec_adm;
```

To be able to view the `usr.accounts` table from `sec_adm`, you grant the SELECT privilege on this table to `sec_adm`:

```
GRANT SELECT ON usr.accounts TO sec_adm;
```

Since the SELECT privilege on `usr.accounts` table granted to the `app_conn` schema is no longer needed, you should revoke it.

```
REVOKE SELECT ON usr.accounts FROM app_conn;
```

Employing PL/SQL Packages and Table Functions to Securely Access Database Data

After you have created a single database schema for performing security-related tasks, the next step is to create appropriate database objects in that schema. In this example, you might create a single stored function that will take a user name as the parameter and then return the corresponding row from the `usr.accounts` table if any.

The following listing shows how to create the `sec_pkg` PL/SQL package containing the `f_auth` function that will be used to securely access the `usr.accounts` table.

```
CONN /AS sysdba

CREATE OR REPLACE PACKAGE sec_adm.sec_pkg IS
 TYPE acc_rec_typ IS RECORD (
 USR_ID      VARCHAR2(10),
 FULL_NAME   VARCHAR2(20),
 PSWD        VARCHAR2(10),
 NUM_LOGONS  NUMBER(38));
 TYPE acc_rec_set IS TABLE OF acc_rec_typ;
 FUNCTION f_auth(usrid VARCHAR2) RETURN acc_rec_set PIPELINED;
 END sec_pkg;
 /

CREATE OR REPLACE PACKAGE BODY sec_adm.sec_pkg IS
FUNCTION f_auth(usrid VARCHAR2)
RETURN acc_rec_set PIPELINED IS
 acc_rec acc_rec_typ;
BEGIN
 SELECT * INTO acc_rec FROM usr.accounts WHERE usr_id=usrid;
 PIPE ROW(acc_rec);
 RETURN;
END;
END sec_pkg;
 /
```

Now let's discuss the statements in the above listing, step by step.

As you might recall from the preceding section, the `sec_adm` database schema is granted only the RESOURCE role. Therefore, you cannot connect to the `sec_adm` database schema directly, because it lacks the CREATE SESSION privilege required for this operation. In this example, you connect to the database as `sysdba` and then create the desired database objects in `sec_adm`.

With the help of the CREATE PACKAGE statement shown in the above listing, you create a new PL/SQL package specification, declaring types, variables, and subprograms that can be referenced from both inside the package and outside it. Note that in this example you create a package specification from outside the database schema to which that package will belong. That is why in this case, the parameter of the CREATE PACKAGE statement must contain that schema name followed by the package name.

In the *Performing Authorization Based on the User Identity* section later in this chapter, you will see how package variables can be used to hold authentication information during a database session.

In the package specification, you first define the `acc_rec_typ` user-defined record type, which should reflect the structure of a `usr.accounts` table row. To see the exact structure of the `usr.accounts` table, you might issue the following SQL statement from SQL*Plus when connected as `sysdba`:

```
DESC usr.accounts
```

If you have performed the SQL statements described in the *An Example of When to Use a Stored Subprogram* section in Chapter 3, as well as the statements in the *Controlling Transactions from PHP* section in Chapter 4, then the above statement should produce the following results:

```
Name                                     Null?     Type
---------------------------------------- --------- ------------
USR_ID                                   NOT NULL  VARCHAR2(10)
FULL_NAME                                          VARCHAR2(20)
PSWD                                     NOT NULL  VARCHAR2(10)
NUM_LOGONS                                         NUMBER(38)
```

If you did not perform the SQL statements from the *Controlling Transactions from PHP* section in Chapter 4, you will not see `num_logons` field in the above output. If so, you must not include this field in the `acc_rec_typ` record type either.

Next, you declare the `acc_rec_set` table type of `acc_rec_typ`. You will use this type as the return type of the `f_auth` package function declared in the next line.

The `f_auth` function will be called from outside the package. Note the use of the `PIPELINED` keyword when declaring the `f_auth` function. By declaring a function as `PIPELINED`, you specify that this function will return a collection of rows like a database table or view when queried.

Pipelined functions, also known as pipelined table functions, may come in very handy when you need to protect sensitive database data from unauthorized access. Unlike regular database tables and views that may be queried with `SELECT` statements containing no `WHERE` clause, and, thus, returning all the rows from the queried object, a table function can be organized so that it never returns all the rows from the table or view queried inside the function. For more information on pipelined functions, refer to Oracle documentation: *Tuning PL/SQL Applications for Performance* chapter in the *Oracle Database PL/SQL User's Guide and Reference* book.

Next, you use the CREATE PACKAGE BODY statement to define the sec_pkg package body, in which you define the code for the f_auth function declared in the package specification.

You begin creating the f_auth function by declaring its header, as defined earlier in the package specification. In this example, the f_auth function takes only one parameter, namely usrid, and then returns the corresponding row from the usr.accounts table if the SELECT statement executed within this function finds one.

Then, you define the acc_rec variable of the acc_rec_typ type declared earlier in the package specification. This variable will be used to hold the row retrieved by the SELECT statement.

Next, you query the usr.accounts table to obtain the row whose usr_id field value is equal to the value of the parameter passed to the f_auth function. It is important to note that since the usr_id column in the usr.accounts table is the primary key column, the SELECT statement used here cannot return more than one row. Otherwise, you would have to process the retrieved rows individually in a loop.

Now, look at the following statement. With it, you might create the sec_pkg.f_auth function so that it could theoretically return more than one row to the caller:

```
CREATE OR REPLACE PACKAGE BODY sec_adm.sec_pkg IS
FUNCTION f_auth(usrid VARCHAR2)
RETURN acc_rec_set PIPELINED IS
BEGIN
  FOR acc_rec IN (SELECT * FROM usr.accounts WHERE usr_id=usrid)
  LOOP
    PIPE ROW(acc_rec);
  END LOOP;
  RETURN;
END;
END sec_pkg;
/
```

In this particular example, the sec_pkg.f_auth function will always return either one row or none, regardless of whether you perform the SELECT operation in a loop or not. This is because a given username cannot be associated with more than one row in the usr.accounts table.

You use the PIPE ROW statement to pipeline the row retrieved out of the f_auth function to the caller. Once an appropriate row has been pipelined, you use the RETURN statement to end the execution of the function and return control to the caller.

Using the %ROWTYPE Attribute

As an alternative to using a user-defined record when defining the `acc_rec_typ` type in the `sec_pkg` package discussed in the preceding example, you might define that type as `usr.accounts%ROWTYPE`, which could save you the trouble of needing to know whether the `usr.accounts` table contains the `num_logons` column.

The problem with this approach in this example is that you're using the `%ROWTYPE` attribute with the `accounts` table that resides in the `usr` database schema, while the `sec_pkg` PL/SQL package, which employs `%ROWTYPE`, resides in a different schema, namely `sec_adm`. Looking through the *%ROWTYPE Attribute* section in the *PL/SQL User's Guide and Reference* Oracle documentation book, you may notice that the syntax of the `%ROWTYPE` attribute does not imply specifying a database schema name in front of the table (or view) name used with the attribute.

> Actually, you can still do so. However, there is no guarantee that this will work as expected. In this particular example, using `usr.accounts%ROWTYPE` instead of the user-defined record may result in a runtime error when the `sec_pkg.f_auth` function is invoked.

One way to solve this problem is to define a view on the `usr.accounts` table in the `sec_adm` schema, and then use the name of that view with `%ROWTYPE` to declare a record type representing a row in the `usr.accounts` table. From a security perspective, it is important that the newly created view, while having the same structure as the `usr.accounts` base table, selects no rows from this table. This can be achieved by specifying, say, 1=0 in the `WHERE` clause of the view's defining query.

The following listing shows how to create a view on the `usr.accounts` table in the `sec_adm` schema, and then rewrite the `sec_pkg` package created as described in the preceding section so that it uses the name of the newly created view with `%ROWTYPE` when declaring a record type representing a row in the `usr.accounts` table.

```
CONN /AS sysdba

CREATE VIEW sec_adm.accounts_empty_v AS
SELECT * FROM usr.accounts WHERE 1=0;

CREATE OR REPLACE PACKAGE sec_adm.sec_pkg IS
 TYPE acc_rec_set IS TABLE OF accounts_empty_v%ROWTYPE ;
 FUNCTION f_auth(usrid VARCHAR2) RETURN acc_rec_set PIPELINED;
 END sec_pkg;
/

CREATE OR REPLACE PACKAGE BODY sec_adm.sec_pkg IS
FUNCTION f_auth(usrid VARCHAR2)
RETURN acc_rec_set PIPELINED IS
```

```
   acc_rec accounts_empty_v%ROWTYPE;
BEGIN
   SELECT * INTO acc_rec FROM usr.accounts WHERE usr_id=usrid;
   PIPE ROW(acc_rec);
   RETURN;
END;
END sec_pkg;
/
```

By issuing the CREATE VIEW statement in the above listing, you create an empty view whose structure is the same as the structure of the usr.accounts table. It is important to understand that the only goal of this view is to provide information about the usr.accounts table's structure, rather than providing information stored in the table. So, you specify 1=0 in the WHERE clause of the view's query to make sure that it returns no rows from the base table and, thus, the view is empty.

Another good thing, from a security standpoint, is that you don't have to grant any privileges on the accounts_empty_v view to the app_conn schema through which your application establishes connections to the database. This is because you reference the accounts_empty_v view within the sec_pkg package, which belongs to the same database schema as the view.

In the package specification, you declare a table type of accounts_empty_v%ROWTYPE. Note the use of the accounts_empty_v view that was created earlier in this listing. The table type declared here will be used as the return type of the f_auth package function.

Next, you declare the acc_rec variable of accounts_empty_v%ROWTYPE. You will then use this variable to hold the account information retrieved from the usr.accounts table.

Then you define the SELECT statement that queries the usr.accounts table, inserting appropriate account data into the acc_rec variable.

Now that you have examined the sec_pkg package's code and learned how login credentials are processed within the f_auth function defined in the package, you might want to look at how the example will use it in the authentication process.

However, before you start using the f_auth function defined in the sec_pkg package, you need to grant the EXECUTE privilege on the sec_pkg package to the app_conn database schema so that the f_auth function can be executed from within the applications connecting to the database through that schema. This can be done with the following SQL statement:

```
CONN /AS sysdba

GRANT EXECUTE ON sec_adm.sec_pkg TO app_conn;
```

It is important to understand that the EXECUTE privilege on a package allows the schema that is granted it only to execute subprograms from the package, not to alter or drop it.

Once you've done all that, you can turn back to the testAuth.php script, making it work with the sec_adm.f_auth function rather than with the usr.accounts table directly.

One problem here is that you cannot simply specify sec_adm.f_auth instead of usr.accounts as the value for the table parameter in the array of options passed to the storage container of the Auth object. This is because the sec_adm.f_function takes the parameter, which is passed to the function when the user submits the login form.

Building a Custom Storage Container for the PEAR::Auth Class

A simple, yet effective solution to the above problem is to create a custom storage container for the Auth class that would work with a table function rather than with a regular database table or view.

In the spirit of code reuse, you don't have to write a storage container from scratch. Instead, you might take advantage of an existing one, customizing it as needed. The Auth PEAR package ships with a number of storage containers, which are implemented as classes and stored in single files in the /Auth/Container directory located within the PEAR directory. It is important to note that the /Auth/Container directory is hard-coded into the Auth class. Therefore, if you want to create a custom storage container, you have to store it in this directory.

As you may recall from Chapter 5 *Object-Oriented Approach*, PHP allows you to extend existing classes by adding new methods and properties and overriding the existing ones. In this example, you need to extend the class that implements the DB container used by PEAR::Auth, so that the new class can work with a table function that takes a user ID as the parameter, rather than working with a regular table or view.

Examining the files in the /Auth/Container directory, you may find that the DB container is implemented as the Auth_Container_DB class and resides in the Auth/Container/DB.php file. Now, to build a custom class upon Auth_Container_DB, create a new file, say, DB_func.php, in the Auth/Container directory and insert the following code

```php
<?php
//File: DB_func.php
```

```
require_once 'Auth/Container/DB.php';
class Auth_Container_DB_func extends Auth_Container_DB
{
  function fetchData($username, $password,
                     $isChallengeResponse=false){
    $this->options['table']="TABLE(".
                  $this->options['table']."('".$username."'))";
    return parent::fetchData($username, $password,
                     $isChallengeResponse=false);
  }
}
?>
```

In the above script, you include the `Auth/Container/DB.php` file because it contains the `Auth_Container_DB` class that acts as the parent class for the `Auth_Container_DB_func` class defined in this script.

Next, you begin the class definition, specifying that the newly created class is built upon `Auth_Container_DB`.

The only parent class method you override in the `Auth_Container_DB_func` class is the `fetchData` method. This method is invoked immediately after a user submits the login form, using the given username to fetch the corresponding authentication information from the database.

Within the `fetchData` method, you override the `table` parameter in the array of options passed to the container. In the new value of the `table` parameter, you include the old value of the parameter, which in turn includes the name of the `sec_adm.f_auth` function, and specify the `username` variable as the function's input argument, which in turn is an input parameter of the `fetchData` method.

Once the `table` parameter is set up to the new value, you call the `fetchData` method of the parent class.

Testing the Authentication System

Now it's time to put the newly created authentication system into action. Note that the `testAuth.php` script shown below, which was originally discussed in the *PEAR:: Auth in Action* section in Chapter 5, is modified to support user authentication against the `sec_adm.sec_pkg.f_auth` table function rather than the `usr.accounts` table.

```
<?php
//File: testAuth.php
require_once "Auth.php";
$auth_opts = array(
```

```
    'dsn'=>'oci8://app_conn:appconn@localhost:1521/orcl',
    'table'=>"sec_adm.sec_pkg.f_auth",
    'usernamecol'=>'usr_id',
    'passwordcol'=>'pswd',
    'db_fields' => '*',
    'cryptType'=>'none'
);
$auth_opts['usernamecol'] = strtoupper($auth_opts['usernamecol']);
$auth_opts['passwordcol'] = strtoupper($auth_opts['passwordcol']);
$a = new Auth('DB_func', $auth_opts);
$a->setExpire(5);
$a->start();
if ($a->getAuth()) {
  print '<font face="Arial">';
  print "<h2>Hello, ".$a->getAuthData('FULL_NAME')."!</h2><br/>";
  print '</font>';
} else {
  exit;
}
?>
```

In the above script, you specify a table function as the value of the table parameter in the array of options passed to the storage container in the same way you would specify a regular table. In this example, to reference the f_auth function, you use dot notation, specifying the database schema and then the package to which this function belongs.

By specifying DB_func as the first parameter of the Auth's constructor, you tell the Auth object to use the DB_func storage container discussed in the preceding section.

After you have updated the testAuth.php script as shown above, you can run the appPage.php script discussed in the *Securing Pages with PEAR::Auth* section in Chapter 5 to test the authentication system developed in this section. As in the example from Chapter 5, you may use the bob/pswd username/password combination to get authenticated.

After successful authentication, you will see the secure page produced by the appPage.php script. You may reload this page several times by clicking the **here** link on it until the authentication session expires (for testing purposes, it is set to 5 seconds in this example). When this happens, you are redirected to the login page again.

As you may conclude, from the end-user point of view, the updated example discussed here behaves exactly like the sample discussed in Chapter 5. What this means in practice is that you can apply security techniques discussed in this section not only when developing a new application but also when improving the security of an existing application.

Performing Authorization Based on the User Identity

Now that you have an authentication system installed and working, it's time to think about authorization. So far, all application users in the example discussed here are associated with the same database schema and, once successfully authenticated, have the same privileges to access the data stored in the database. Going one step further, you might implement an authorization schema so that a given user has access only to certain database resources.

Graphically, it would look like the following figure:.

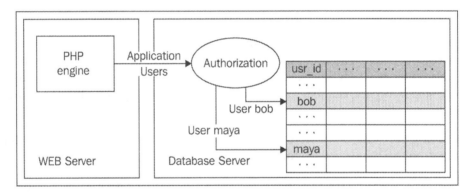

The diagram in the figure shows authentication in action. Once a user is authenticated, he or she is authorized to access only his or her own record in the table holding authentication information. In a real-world situation, you probably will want to authorize the user to access not only his or her account record but also the related records in another table or tables.

One way to achieve this functionality is to store information about an authenticated user in the database session and then use this information when performing authorization checks. It is interesting to note that a database session is created when a user connects to the database and ends when the user disconnects (explicitly or implicitly).

Using Sessions to Hold Information about the Authenticated User

As you may recall from Chapter 4, if you're establishing a connection to the database from PHP with the oci_connect function, then the connection is automatically closed when the script ends. The fact is that the DB storage container, which is used by the PEAR::Auth object in the sample discussed here, uses the oci_connect function in the long run to connect to the database. What this means is that once the script that performs authentication ends, the database connection used by that script and, thus, the corresponding database session are closed as well.

On the other hand, the _authsession PHP session, which is set up by the PEAR::Auth object to hold the authentication information once a user is successfully authenticated, exists until it expires or the specified amount of idle time has passed.

To handle this problem, you have to transmit the information about the current authenticated user to the database before performing any database-related operations from within PHP. In particular, you have to set appropriate database session variables to the values held in the corresponding variables of the _authsession PHP session, prior to issuing any queries against the database within a script.

 The same technique is used when implementing row-level security with Virtual Private Database (VPD). You will see this in action in the *Using VPD to Implement Row-Level Security* section later in this chapter.

Holding a User's Information in Package Variables

The easiest way to pass a user's information to the database is to use PL/SQL packages. The fact is that the state of a package persists for the lifetime of a database session (unless you marked that package SERIALLY_REUSABLE). Moreover, the state of a package is private to each database session, which makes it possible for you to use package variables for keeping information about the current user.

Later in this section we look at how to create two PL/SQL packages that will be used to transmit and hold information about the current authenticated user in the database session. The idea is to have one package to hold the user information and the other to manipulate the variables from the first package, setting them to appropriate values and getting them when necessary.

The fact is that the EXECUTE privilege granted on a package to a database schema permits the users connected to the database through that schema to execute any public subprograms in the package and access any public package variables. You cannot grant EXECUTE privilege for a certain subprogram or variable in a package.

Thus, this separation of the packages allows for better security. This is because you have to grant the EXECUTE privilege only on the package containing the 'setter' and 'getter' methods to the schema used for establishing connections to the database, while the package holding user information in its package variables will be inaccessible from that schema. This ensures that the only way for users to pass authentication information to the database is to use the 'setter' package procedures.

You start by creating the sec_adm.app_cxt_pkg package as follows:

```
CONN /as sysdba
CREATE OR REPLACE PACKAGE sec_adm.app_cxt_pkg IS
  userid VARCHAR2(40);
END;
/
```

In this simple case, you define the sec_adm.app_cxt_pkg package containing only one variable, userid, which will hold the name of the application user being connected. Since you are not going to grant any privileges on the sec_adm.app_cxt_pkg package to any other database schema, the userid package variable can be referenced only within database objects belonging to the sec_adm schema.

Next, you create the sec_adm.set_cxt_pkg package as follows:

```
CREATE OR REPLACE PACKAGE sec_adm.set_cxt_pkg IS
  FUNCTION get_userid RETURN VARCHAR2;
  PROCEDURE set_userid(usrid VARCHAR2);
END;
/
```

In the above package, you declare the 'getter' function and the 'setter' procedure, which are then defined in the package body. Note that the function takes no parameter, while the procedure takes only one parameter, namely userid.

Then you create the package body for the sec_adm.set_cxt_pkg package:

```
CREATE OR REPLACE PACKAGE BODY sec_adm.set_cxt_pkg IS
  FUNCTION get_userid RETURN VARCHAR2
  AS
  BEGIN
```

```
    RETURN app_cxt_pkg.userid;
  END;
  PROCEDURE set_userid(usrid VARCHAR2)
  AS
  BEGIN
   IF (SYS_CONTEXT('USERENV', 'IP_ADDRESS') = '127.0.0.1')
   THEN
     app_cxt_pkg.userid:=usrid;
   END IF;
  END;
  END;
  /
```

The get_userid package function used here simply returns the value of the app_
cxt_pkg.userid package variable.

In this example, the app_cxt_pkg.userid package variable is set to the value passed
to the set_cxt_pkg.set_userid procedure as the parameter only if the web/PHP
server through which the user is being connected to the database resides on the same
machine as the database server. To obtain the IP address of the web/PHP server,
you use the SYS_CONTEXT function with the built-in USERENV namespace as the first
parameter and IP_ADDRESS as the second parameter, which is associated with the
USERENV namespace.

 If your web/PHP server and database server reside on different
machines, you have to specify the actual IP address of the web/PHP
server here, rather than specifying 127.0.0.1.

Performing this additional security check for callers of the
set_cxt_pkg.set_userid procedure allows you to make sure that only
users connected through a certain web/PHP server pass authorization.

 Checking the IP address at this stage is definitely a good idea. However,
in a real-world situation, you should not rely on a single check—after all,
IP addresses can be spoofed. It is good practice to check a combination
of things when making access-control decisions. For example, you might
check whether the request occurs during normal operating hours, thus
ensuring timely access to the database resources.

Finally, you grant the EXECUTE privilege on the sec_adm.set_cxt_pkg package
to the app_conn schema, thus making it possible for applications connecting to
the database through this schema to call the set_userid procedure and the
get_userid function.

```
    GRANT EXECUTE ON sec_adm.set_cxt_pkg TO app_conn;
```

Once you have created packages to hold and manipulate information about the current authenticated user, the next step is to set up database objects that will use these packages to provide secure access to protected resources.

Protecting Resources Based on Information about the Authenticated User

To be in line with the least privilege principle, which implies that each user should be given only the minimum privileges required to do his or her job and nothing else, you might implement an authorization system so that each user can see only the set of records related to his or her account record in the usr.account table. In the simplest case, you might authorize an authenticated user to access only the record representing his or her account.

Using the following statements, you create a view on a table function that will take the sec_adm.set_cxt_pkg.get_userid getter function as the parameter and retrieve the corresponding row from the usr.accounts table.

```
CONN /as sysdba
CREATE OR REPLACE VIEW sec_adm.accounts_v AS
SELECT usr_id, full_name
FROM TABLE(sec_adm.sec_pkg.f_auth(sec_adm.set_cxt_pkg.get_userid));
GRANT SELECT ON sec_adm.accounts_v TO app_conn;
```

You don't have to include all the columns from the base table when creating a view. In this example, you exclude the pswd column from the select list of the view's defining query.

As you can see, the sec_adm.accounts_v view discussed here is based on a table function, rather than a regular table. Specifically, it is based on the sec_adm.sec_pkg.f_auth table function discussed in the preceding section, which returns a row from the usr.accounts table based on the username passed in as the parameter.

Since the sec_adm.accounts_v view is supposed to contain the usr.accounts table's row representing the current authenticated user, it would be a good idea to insert a couple of new records into the usr.accounts table, before you proceed to testing the view.

You could insert rows into usr.accounts as shown below:

```
INSERT INTO usr.accounts (usr_id, full_name, pswd) VALUES
    ('maya', 'Maya Silver', 'mayapwd');
INSERT INTO usr.accounts (usr_id, full_name, pswd) VALUES
    ('john', 'John Stevenson', 'johnpwd');
COMMIT;
```

With that done, you can turn back to the `testAuth.php` script discussed in the *Testing the Authentication System* section earlier in this chapter. The `testAuthor.php` script shown below is a version of `testAuth.php` revised to use authorization based on the name of the current authenticated user.

```php
<?php
//File: testAuthor.php
require_once "Auth.php";
require_once "DB.php";
$auth_opts = array(
 'dsn'=>'oci8://app_conn:appconn@localhost:1521/orcl',
 'table'=>"sec_adm.sec_pkg.f_auth",
 'usernamecol'=>'usr_id',
 'passwordcol'=>'pswd',
 'db_fields' => '*',
 'cryptType'=>'none'
);
$dbh = DB::connect($auth_opts['dsn']);
if(DB::isError($dbh)) {
    die($dbh->getMessage());
}
$auth_opts['dsn'] = $dbh;
$auth_opts['usernamecol'] = strtoupper($auth_opts['usernamecol']);
$auth_opts['passwordcol'] = strtoupper($auth_opts['passwordcol']);
$a = new Auth('DB_func', $auth_opts);
$a->setExpire(5);
$a->start();
if ($a->getAuth()) {
  $username= $a->getUsername();
  $rslt =$dbh->query("BEGIN sec_adm.set_cxt_pkg.set_
userid('".$username."'); END;");
    if (PEAR::isError($rslt)) {
    print $rslt->getMessage();
  }
  print '<font face="Arial">';
  print "<h2>Hello, ".$a->getAuthData('FULL_NAME')."!</h2><br/>";
  print '</font>';
} else {
  exit;
}
?>
```

In the above script, you establish a connection to the database using the connect method of the PEAR::DB class, passing the DSN string defined in the array of options to be passed to the storage container used by the Auth object.

In the DSN string used here, you specify an existing instance of PEAR::DB with the dsn parameter instead of a DSN string.

In this example, you use the getUsername method of the Auth object to obtain the name of the current authenticated user.

Next, you set the sec_adm.set_cxt_pkg.userid package variable to the name of the authenticated user obtained by the getUsername method.

It is interesting to note that the script doesn't stop its execution on failure to set the sec_adm.set_cxt_pkg.userid package variable. This makes sense here, since having the sec_adm.set_cxt_pkg.userid package variable undefined simply means that the sec_adm.accounts_v view defined at the beginning of this section contains no record, and, thus, the user will see no account information on the secure page shown in the following figure:

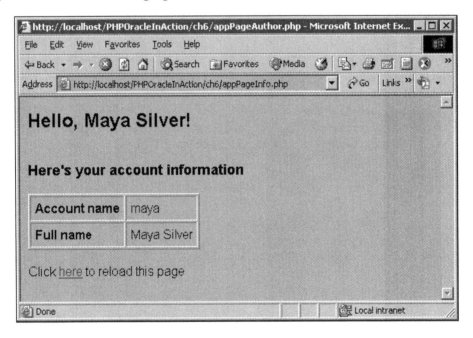

This secure page displays account information of the current authenticated user. Information is displayed only if the user has been successfully authenticated and the sec_adm.set_cxt_pkg.userid package variable has been successfully set to the user's account name.

To see the page shown in the figure, you should run the appPageInfo.php script shown next, and then enter maya/mayapwd as the username/password combination on the login page.

```php
<?php
  //File: appPageInfo.php
  require_once "testAuthor.php";
  $thisPage='"'."appPageInfo.php".'"';
  $rslt =$dbh->query('SELECT * FROM sec_adm.accounts_v');
  if (PEAR::isError($rslt)) {
    print $rslt->getMessage();
  }
  print '<font face="Arial">';
  print "<h3>Here's your account information</h3>";
  $row = $rslt->fetchRow(DB_FETCHMODE_ASSOC);
  print '<table border="1" cellpadding="5">';
  print '<tr>';
  print '<td><b>Account name</b></td><td>'.$row['USR_ID'].'</td>';
  print '</tr>';
  print '<tr>';
  print '<td><b>Full name</b></td><td>'.$row['FULL_NAME'].'</td >';
  print '</tr>';
  print '</table>';
  print '<br/>';
  print "Click <a href=".$thisPage.">here</a> to reload this page";
  print '</font>';
?>
```

Let's walk through exactly what the above script does.

Including testAuthor.php at the beginning of the appPageInfo.php script guarantees that only an authenticated user will see the page produced by appPageInfo.php.

Note the use of the $dbh variable representing the PEAR::DB instance created in the testAuthor.php script discussed earlier in this section. So, you don't need to create another instance of PEAR::DB because testAutor.php has been included in the script.

Then, you fetch the results of the query issued earlier. In this example, you specify DB_FETCHMODE_ASSOC as the fetch mode, which tells the fetchRow method of PEAR::DB to return results as an associative array.

For testing purposes, you include here the link to the same page. In a real-world application, it would be a link to another secure page of the application.

Hashing

It is critical that sensitive data is securely sent over the network. For example, it is always a good idea to transmit user passwords over the network in a secure manner, rather than transmitting them in clear text. One way to achieve this is by using hashing.

 Hashing is the process of converting a plaintext string of variable length to a fixed-length string, a hash value, which serves as a digital "fingerprint" of the input string. If two hash values generated with the same hashing algorithm are different, this automatically means that the two input strings are different as well. Hashing is a one-way process—theoretically, it is impossible to determine the original string based on its hash value.

The following sections demonstrate how to add another level of security to the sample application discussed in the preceding sections by hashing user passwords. So, you will see how an existing authentication system can be modified to take advantage of hashing.

Hashing Passwords

Turning back to the testAuthor.php script discussed in the *Protecting Resources Based on Information about the Authenticated User* section earlier, you may notice that the cryptType parameter in the array of options is set to none, meaning that the storage container used by the Auth object will use no hashing algorithm when processing the password entered by a user, implying that the password retrieved from the database is in plain-text format as well.

Now, to start using hashed passwords in the sample application discussed in the previous section, you have to perform the following two general steps:

- Make sure that the database sends hashed passwords instead of plain-text passwords when passing account data to the testAuthor.php script.
- Modify the testAuthor.php script so that the Auth object hashes passwords entered via the login form.

The easiest way to make sure that the database sends password hashes when passing account data to the testAuthor.php script would be to store password hashes in the usr.accounts table, rather than storing actual passwords in clear text in this table.

However, since hashed data cannot be returned to its original state, in some situations you might want to still store user passwords in clear text, while hashing a password just before sending the user account record to which that password belongs to over the network. For example, you might want your application to support forgotten passwords functionality, sending a user his or her forgotten password via email once he or she has successfully answered a secure question.

The following figure illustrates the process of hashing a user password stored in the database in plain-text format, before sending it to the PHP script running on the web/PHP server for further processing.

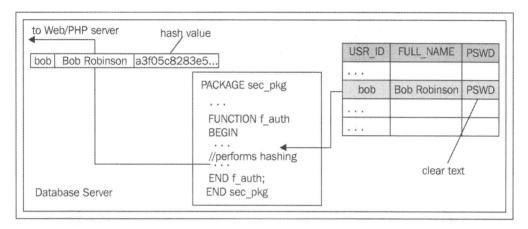

The figure depicts the process of hashing a password stored in plain-text format. The f_auth function from the sec_adm package retrieves appropriate account data from the usr.accounts table and then hashes the password in the retrieved data. Finally, it sends the updated account data to the authAuth.php script.

As you can see from the figure, in the f_auth package function you hash only the password—the rest of the account data is sent to the web/PHP server unhashed.

Before you can implement the functionality shown in the previous figure, you first have to decide which hashing algorithm to choose.

As for the Oracle Database 10g Release 2, it supports several industry standard hashing algorithms, including MD4, MD5, and SHA-1. As for the PEAR::Auth package Release: 1.3.0, it uses MD5 hashing algorithm by default. Alternatively, PEAR::Auth allows you to employ any other hash function available in PHP. For example, you might use the sha1 hash function to take advantage of the SHA-1 hashing algorithm that produces a 160-bit hash.

While MD5 and SHA-1 hashing algorithms are implemented in individual PHP functions, called md5 and sha1 respectively, PHP doesn't provide a single function implementing the MD4 algorithm. To produce an MD4 hash value in PHP, you should use the hash function, specifying md4 as the first parameter and a string to be hashed as the second one. This makes using MD4 with PEAR::Auth a little tricky. Another reason not to employ MD4 is that this hashing algorithm is less secure than its successor MD5.

So, you might consider using either MD5 or SHA-1 in the example discussed here. The following table briefly summarizes these two hashing algorithms.

Hashing algorithm	Description
MD5 (Message-Digest algorithm 5)	MD5 hashing algorithm is defined in the RFC 1321 document. This algorithm produces a 128-bit hash value and is widely used to hash passwords.
SHA-1 (Secure Hash Algorithm)	SHA-1 hashing algorithm is defined in RFC 3174. It produces a 160-bit hash value. Oracle recommends using this algorithm rather than using its less secure predecessor, MD5.

The choice of the algorithm to be used is up to you. While the example in the next section uses the MD5 hashing algorithm, you could easily use SHA-1 instead.

Modifying an Authentication System to Use Hashing

Now that you have a rough idea of how hashing might be used to secure passwords in the sample application discussed in this chapter, it's time to see how to put this into action.

By executing the SQL following statements you set up database objects so that the authentication system used in the sample application uses password hashes rather than plain text passwords.

You start by altering the usr.accounts table. In particular, you enlarge the pswd column in the usr.accounts table so that it can store hash values.

You may be wondering why you need to do that—after all, you are not going to replace clear text passwords stored in this column with password hashes. Yes, you are not going to do that. However, you might refer to the *Separating Security Management and Data* section, where you use the structure of the sec_adm. accounts_empty_v view based on the usr.accounts table when creating a record with the account data, which is then sent to the testAuth.php script for further processing.

So, you have to make sure that the `pswd` column in the `sec_adm.accounts_empty_v` view could be used to hold a hashing value. The only way to achieve this is to alter the base table.

```
CONN /as sysdba
ALTER TABLE usr.accounts
MODIFY (pswd VARCHAR2(40));
```

After you have altered the structure of the `usr.accounts` table by issuing the above statement, the structure of the `sec_adm.accounts_empty_v` view based on that table is altered automatically. Since the `sec_adm.sec_pkg` package contains a reference to the `sec_adm.accounts_empty_v` view, the package needs to be recompiled to pick up the changes made.

Then, you recompile the package by simply recreating it.

```
CREATE OR REPLACE PACKAGE sec_adm.sec_pkg IS
 TYPE acc_rec_set IS TABLE OF accounts_empty_v%ROWTYPE ;
 FUNCTION f_auth(usrid VARCHAR2) RETURN acc_rec_set PIPELINED;
 END sec_pkg;
/
```

Before you can start using the `DBMS_CRYPTO` package in your PL/SQL subprograms, you have to grant the `EXECUTE` privilege on this package to the database schema under which those subprograms are created.

In this particular example, you grant the `EXECUTE` privilege on `DBMS_CRYPTO` package to the `sec_adm` schema. This is because the `f_auth` function from the `sec_adm.sec_pkg` package will use `DBMS_CRYPTO`.

```
GRANT EXECUTE ON dbms_crypto TO sec_adm;
```

Next, you recreate the `sec_pkg` package body in order to recreate the `f_auth` package function so that it hashes the password before sending account data to the `testAuthor.php` script for further processing.

```
CREATE OR REPLACE PACKAGE BODY sec_adm.sec_pkg IS
FUNCTION f_auth(usrid VARCHAR2)
RETURN acc_rec_set PIPELINED IS
 acc_rec accounts_empty_v%ROWTYPE;
BEGIN
 SELECT * INTO acc_rec FROM usr.accounts WHERE usr_id=usrid;
 acc_rec.pswd := DBMS_CRYPTO.HASH (
 UTL_I18N.STRING_TO_RAW (acc_rec.pswd, 'AL32UTF8'),
 DBMS_CRYPTO.HASH_MD5);
 acc_rec.pswd:=NLS_LOWER(acc_rec.pswd);
 PIPE ROW(acc_rec);
```

```
    RETURN;
  END;
END sec_pkg;
/
```

In the f_auth function, note the use of the HASH function from the DBMS_CRYPTO package. This function either takes a RAW or LOB value as a parameter and returns the hashed value computed using the hashing algorithm specified with the constant passed to the HASH function as the second parameter.

Since the HASH function can take only a RAW or LOB value as the parameter to be hashed, rather than taking a VARCHAR2 value, you first have to convert a VARCHAR2 to a RAW before passing it to the function. In this example, you use the UTL_I18N. STRING_TO_RAW function to convert a password stored in the database in clear text as VARCHAR2 to a RAW value.

In this example, you specify the DBMS_CRYPTO.HASH_MD5 package constant as the second parameter of the HASH function. This tells the HASH function to compute a hash value using the MD5 hashing algorithm.

 If you want to use SHA-1 hashing algorithm rather than MD5, you must specify the DBMS_CRYPTO.HASH_SH1 package constant instead.

Finally, you convert the hash value returned by the HASH function to lowercase. This is because the HASH function returns a hash value in uppercase, but the md5 PHP function, which is used by the PEAR::Auth class to hash a password entered via the login form, returns a hash value in lowercase.

Now, to make sure that everything works as expected, you might perform the following quick test from SQL*Plus when connected as sysdba:

```
SELECT * FROM TABLE(sec_adm.sec_pkg.f_auth('bob'));
```

The results should look as follows:

USR_ID LOGONS	FULL_NAME	PSWD	NUM_
bob	Bob Robinson	a3f05c8283e5350106829f855c93c07d	32

As you can see, the `pswd` column in the output contains a hash value rather than a plain text. This means that a user password, being a sensitive part of the account data, will be sent to the web/PHP server processing the `testAuthor.php` script, as a 32-character string of random-looking hexadecimal digits.

Now, you can test the updated authentication system by running the `appPageInfo.php` script discussed in the *Performing Authorization Based on the User Identity* section earlier in this chapter. Before you can do that, however, you have to turn back to the `testAuthor.php` source code and set the `cryptType` parameter in the array of options to `md5`, as shown below:

```
'cryptType'=>'md5'
```

 Alternatively, you might simply remove this parameter from the array. The fact is that `PEAR::Auth` uses the MD5 hashing algorithm by default, when it comes to passwords. However, if you have decided to use the SHA-1 hashing algorithm, you must explicitly set the `cryptType` parameter to `sha1`.

It is important to note that the hashing mechanism employed here works behind the scenes. From the end user standpoint, the sample application behaves as before.

Setting Up Fine-Grained Access with Database Views

There may be situations where you need to remove access to a certain column within the table because that column contains sensitive data. In such situations, using views is definitely the best way to go.

Your first step is to create a view that selects all the columns from the underlying table except the one you want to make inaccessible.

Then, you grant the `SELECT` privilege on that view to your users, instead of granting this privilege on the underlying table.

The following figure gives a graphical depiction of this solution.

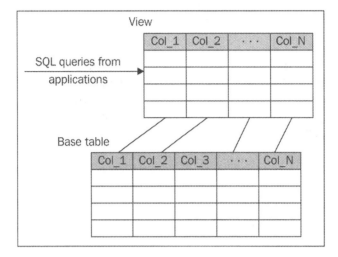

As you can see from the figure, the simple technique based on using views allows you to restrict access to sensitive data within tables, without the need to reconstruct existing database objects.

 It is interesting to note that views can also be used to restrict access to certain rows in their base tables. To achieve this, you define the WHERE clause in the view's defining query so that the view displays only allowable rows of the base table or tables.

The examples provided in the following sections demonstrate how views can be used when implementing fine-grained access for each application user in a PHP/Oracle application that uses a single database schema on behalf of all users. The first example will show using views for column-level security. Then, you will see an example of implementing value-based security with views.

Implementing Column-Level Security with Views

For the purpose of the example discussed in this section, let's say that the usr. accounts table used in the previous examples contains records representing sales representatives working for your firm. Suppose you store all the orders placed by the sales representatives in the orders table, which resides in the usr database schema.

With the following SQL statements, you create the `usr.orders` table and populate it with data:

```
CONN /as sysdba

CREATE TABLE usr.orders(
   ordno    NUMBER PRIMARY KEY,
   empno    VARCHAR2(40) REFERENCES usr.accounts(usr_id),
   orddate DATE,
   total    NUMBER(10,2)
);

INSERT INTO usr.orders VALUES
(1001, 'bob', '01-aug-2006', 5870.00);
INSERT INTO usr.orders VALUES
(1002, 'bob', '01-aug-2006', 12500.00);

INSERT INTO usr.orders VALUES
(1003, 'maya', '04-aug-2006', 1100.50);

INSERT INTO usr.orders VALUES
(1004, 'bob', '05-aug-2006', 10230.00);

COMMIT;
```

Now, suppose you want each sales representative to be ale to view all the orders, regardless of who placed an order, but, at the same time, you want to keep the `empno` column in the `orders` table inaccessible, so that everyone can view any order but there is no way to determine who placed it.

Next, you create a view on the `usr.orders` table created above, so that the newly created view contains only allowable columns from the base table.

```
CONN /as sysdba

CREATE OR REPLACE VIEW usr.orders_v AS
SELECT ordno, orddate, total
FROM usr.orders;

GRANT SELECT ON usr.orders_v TO app_conn;
```

In this example, for better security you create the `order` table as well as the `orders_v` view built upon this table in the `usr` database schema, and then grant `SELECT` privilege only on the view to the `app_conn` schema, which is used by application users to connect to the database.

A secure page based on the `orders_v` view created here might look like the following figure:

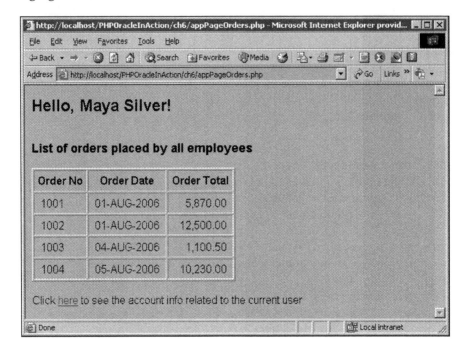

The above page can be seen by anyone who has successfully authenticated. Containing information about the orders placed by all employees, the page doesn't provide any information on who exactly placed a certain order.

To see the page shown in the figure, you might run the `appPageOrders.php` script shown below:

```php
<?php
//File: appPageOrders.php
require_once "testAuthor.php";
$infoPage='"'."appPageInfo.php".'"';
$rslt =$dbh->query("SELECT ordno, TO_CHAR(orddate,
          'DD-MON-YYYY') orddate, total FROM usr.orders_v");
if (PEAR::isError($rslt)) {
   print $rslt->getMessage();
}
print '<font face="Arial">';
print "<h3>List of orders placed by all employees</h3>";
print '<table border="1" cellpadding="5">';
print '<tr>';
print '<th>Order No</th><th>Order Date</th><th>Order Total</th>';
```

```
print '</tr>';
while($row = $rslt->fetchRow(DB_FETCHMODE_ASSOC)){
  print '<tr>';
  print '<td>'.$row['ORDNO'].'</td><td>'.$row['ORDDATE'].
          '</td><td align="right">'.number_format($row['TOTAL'],
                                              2).'</td>';
  print '</tr>';
};
print '</table>';
print '<br/>';
print "Click <a href=".$infoPage.">here</a> to see the account
                      info related to the current user";
print '</font>';
?>
```

In the above script, note the use of the TO_CHAR function to convert a DATE to VARCHAR2 in the query. You pass the date format as the second parameter to the function.

After the query has completed, you can fetch the results using one of the fetch functions available in PEAR::DB. In this example, you use the fetchRow method, which is called in a loop until there are no more rows to fetch.

Finally, you define a link to another secure page of the sample, which is produced by the appPageInfo.php script discussed in the *Protecting Resources Based on Information about the Authenticated User* section earlier in this chapter.

Masking the Column Values Returned to the Application

Using views is definitely the best way to go if you need to remove access to a certain column or columns within the underlying table. However, in some situations, making a certain column completely inaccessible may be inappropriate. Instead, you might want to mask some values within a certain column, letting a user access only those column values that he or she is authorized to access.

Using the DECODE Function

This section discusses how the built-in DECODE function can be used to implement column masking when implementing a fine-grained access with views.

Turning back to the preceding example, suppose you want to add the full_name column from the usr.accounts table to the select list of the of the orders_v view's defining query, masking the values of that column so that each user can see the employee's name only in records representing orders placed by him or her (in other words, the user will see his or her name), while the other records should contain `null` in this column.

By issuing the following SQL statements, you create the orders_decode_v view whose defining query employs the DECODE function for masking the full_name column derived from the usr.accounts table.

```
CONN /as sysdba

GRANT EXECUTE ON sec_adm.set_cxt_pkg TO usr;

CREATE OR REPLACE FUNCTION usr.f_get_userid RETURN VARCHAR2 IS
BEGIN
   RETURN sec_adm.set_cxt_pkg.get_userid;
END;
/

CREATE OR REPLACE VIEW usr.orders_decode_v AS
SELECT ordno, DECODE(empno, usr.f_get_userid, full_name, NULL)
empname, orddate, total
FROM usr.orders, usr.accounts
WHERE empno=usr_id;

GRANT SELECT ON usr.orders_decode_v TO app_conn;
```

You start by creating a function that will return the account name of the currently authenticated user held in the userid variable of the app_cxt_pkg package in the sec_adm schema.

You create this function in the usr schema so that it can be called from within the orders_decode_v view created in the same schema, when connected to the database through the app_conn schema.

As you can see, the usr.orders_decode_v view is based on two tables, namely usr.orders and usr.accounts. The DECODE function is used in the select list of the view's query to mask values of the full_name column derived from the usr.accounts table.

The following figure illustrates what a secure page based on the
`usr.orders_decode_v` view just created might look like.

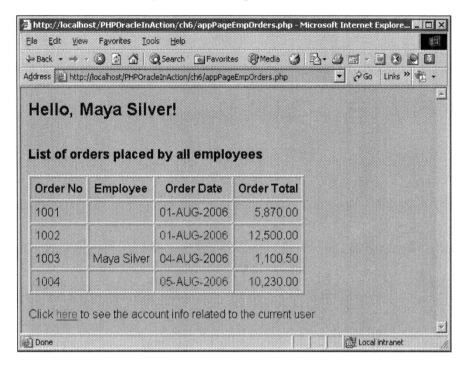

While the above page displays all the orders placed by all employees, there is no way
the user can determine who exactly placed a certain order unless he or she did it.

The following listing shows the source code for the `appPageEmpOrders.php` script
that might be used to produce the page shown in the above figure.

The page produced by this script will contain information about orders
placed by all employees, masking the values in the `empname` column
depending on the currently authenticated user.

```php
<?php
//File: appPageEmpOrders.php
require_once "testAuthor.php";
$infoPage='"'."appPageInfo.php".'"';
$rslt =$dbh->query("SELECT ordno, empname, TO_CHAR(orddate,
    'DD-MON-YYYY') orddate, total FROM usr.orders_decode_v");
if (PEAR::isError($rslt)) {
    print $rslt->getMessage();
}
```

```
    print '<font face="Arial">';
    print "<h3>List of orders placed by all employees</h3>";
    print '<table border="1" cellpadding="5">';
    print '<tr>';
    print '<th>Order No</th><th>Employee</th><th>Order Date</
th><th>Order Total</th>';
    print '</tr>';
    while($row = $rslt->fetchRow(DB_FETCHMODE_ASSOC)){
      print '<tr>';
      if (is_null($row['EMPNAME'])){$row['EMPNAME']=' ';}
      print '<td>'.$row['ORDNO'].
      '</td><td>'.$row['EMPNAME'].'</td><td>'.$row['ORDDATE'].
      '</td><td align="right">'.number_format($row['TOTAL'], 2).'</td>';
      print '</tr>';
    };
    print '</table>';
    print '<br/>';
    print "Click <a href=".$infoPage.">here</a> to see the account
                        info related to the current user";
    print '</font>';
?>
```

In the above script, you query the usr.orders_decode_v view created earlier in
this section. Note that empname in the select list of the query is an alias for the view's
select list item built on the DECODE function.

Implementing Row-Level Security with Views

In the preceding example, you saw how to restrict access to sensitive fields within
the view's record based on the user's identity, while still allowing each user to view
all records in the view. However, sometimes you might need to allow a user to view
only the records related to his or her account, completely restricting access to all
other records.

Continuing with the preceding example, suppose you want to create another page in
the sample application on which each user will see only his or her orders. To achieve
this, you first need to create another view on the usr.orders and usr.accounts
tables, defining a predicate in the view's query that will be specific to the current
user. This view will return only the records related to the currently authenticated
user's account, and eliminate all the other records.

```
CONN /as sysdba

CREATE OR REPLACE VIEW usr.orders_emp_v AS
SELECT ordno, full_name as empname, orddate, total
```

```
FROM usr.orders, usr.accounts
WHERE (empno=usr.f_get_userid) AND (empno=usr_id);

GRANT SELECT ON usr.orders_emp_v TO app_conn;
```

Note the use of an alias for the second item in the select list of the view query. Here, you use the same alias you used for the second item in the select list of the usr.orders_decode_v view created as described in the preceding section. By doing so, you eliminate the need to change a lot in the appPageEmpOrders.php script when modifying it to use the usr.orders_emp_v view instead of usr.orders_decode_v.

Unlike the usr.orders_decode_v view that uses the usr.f_get_userid PL/SQL function in the view's select list as a parameter of the DECODE function, the usr.orders_emp_v view discussed here employs this function in the WHERE clause to enforce row-level security through a predicate.

A secure page based on the usr.orders_emp_v view discussed here might look like the following figure:

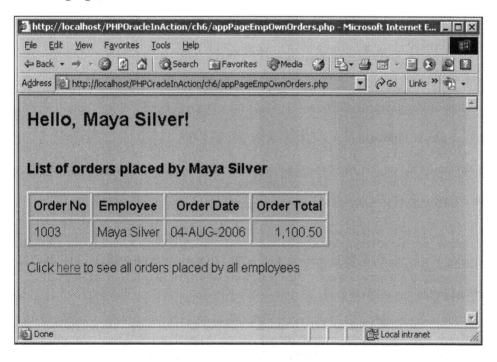

This page displays all the orders placed by the currently authenticated user (employee). By clicking the link at the bottom of the page, a user can load a page as shown in the figure in the *Using the DECODE Function* section in order to see all orders placed by all employees.

The `appPageEmpOwnOrders.php` script shown below might be used to produce a page like that shown in the previous figure.

```php
<?php
//File: appPageEmpOwnOrders.php
require_once "testAuthor.php";
$ordersPage='"'."appPageEmpOrders.php".'"';
$rslt =$dbh->query("SELECT ordno, empname, TO_CHAR(orddate,
        'DD-MON-YYYY') orddate, total FROM usr.orders_emp_v");
if (PEAR::isError($rslt)) {
   print $rslt->getMessage();
}
print '<font face="Arial">';
print "<h3>List of orders placed by
                    ".$a->getAuthData('FULL_NAME')."</h3>";
print '<table border="1" cellpadding="5">';
print '<tr>';
print '<th>Order No</th><th>Employee</th><th>Order
                    Date</th><th>Order Total</th>';
print '</tr>';
while($row = $rslt->fetchRow(DB_FETCHMODE_ASSOC)){
  print '<tr>';
  print '<td>'.$row['ORDNO'].
'</td><td>'.$row['EMPNAME'].'</td><td>'.$row['ORDDATE'].
'</td><td align="right">'.number_format($row['TOTAL'], 2).'</td>';
  print '</tr>';
};
print '</table>';
print '<br/>';
print "Click <a href=".$ordersPage.">here</a> to see all orders
                    placed by all employees";
print '</font>';
?>
```

As you can see, the query passed to PEAR::DB's `query` method here looks the same as the query in the `appPageEmpOrders.php` script discussed in the *Using the DECODE Function* section earlier. The only difference between these queries is the view specified in the FROM clause.

Since all the orders displayed on a page generated by this script are always specific to a current user, it makes sense to display a message that includes the name of that user, saying who placed the orders displayed on the page. Note the use of the `$a` variable, which contains a reference to the Auth object created during execution of the `testAuthor.php` script included at the beginning of the script. Here, you call the `getAuthData` method of Auth with FULL_NAME as the parameter to get the full name of the currently authenticated user.

Here, you display a link to the `appPageEmpOrders.php` script that produces a page displaying all orders placed by all employees and masking the `empname` column values depending on the currently authenticated user.

Using VPD to Implement Row-Level Security

Virtual Private Database (VPD) is a powerful Oracle Database security feature that allows you to implement row-level security, centralizing access security mechanisms within the database. The basic idea behind this approach is that each user, when successfully authenticated, is authorized to access only certain rows within a database table or view protected with a VPD security policy.

 The Virtual Private Database feature is available only in Oracle Database Enterprise Edition. If you're using another edition of Oracle database, consider using a view-based approach when implementing row-level security, as discussed in the preceding section.

Since a VPD policy can be applied directly to a database table and is enforced whenever data in that table is accessed (directly or indirectly), there is no way for the user to bypass security. To protect a table or view with a VPD policy, you have to perform the following general steps:

1. Create a PL/SQL function that implements the security policy.
2. Register the function created in step 1 against the table or view to be protected.

That is it. Once you have performed the above steps, the database will append a dynamic predicate generated by the function created in step 1 to the original SQL statement whenever you issue it against the protected table or view.

Turning back to the preceding example where you implemented a security solution to protect the information in the `usr.orders_emp_v` view at the row level, based on the user's identity, you might achieve the same general results using the VPD feature.

To start with, you have to recreate the `usr.orders_emp_v` view so that its defining query does not contain the `empno=usr.f_get_userid` predicate. You really don't need this predicate in the view's query because the database will automatically append a dynamic predicate to each SQL statement issued against the view once you've protected it by a VPD policy.

So, the updated view might be created as follows:

```
CONN /as sysdba

CREATE OR REPLACE VIEW usr.orders_vpd_v AS
SELECT ordno, full_name as empname, orddate, total
FROM usr.orders, usr.accounts
WHERE empno=usr_id;

GRANT SELECT ON usr.orders_vpd_v TO app_conn;
```

Here, you create the usr.orders_vpd_v view on the usr.orders and usr.accounts tables. Unlike the usr.orders_emp_v view created as described in the *Using the DECODE Function* section earlier, usr.orders_vpd_v doesn't use the empno=usr.f_get_userid predicate in the WHERE clause of the view's query. This is because the usr.orders base table containing sensitive information on orders will be protected by the VPD policy based on the PL/SQL function defined later in this section.

From a security standpoint, it would be a good idea in this example to apply a VPD policy to the usr.orders base table, rather than protecting the usr.orders_vpd_v view based on this table. Protecting the usr.orders table with a VPD policy guarantees that each user will be able to access only those order records that he or she is authorized to access, whether the user is using the usr.orders_vpd_v view for that, or accessing the usr.orders base table directly.

Therefore, the next step is to create a policy that can be applied to the usr.orders table to enforce row-level security based on the user's identity. To do this, you first need to create a PL/SQL function that implements the security policy, producing a dynamic predicate that will be appended to SELECT statements issued against the usr.orders table. You might create the following function:

```
CONN /as sysdba

CREATE OR REPLACE FUNCTION sec_adm.f_vpd_ord (D1 VARCHAR2, D2
VARCHAR2) RETURN VARCHAR2
IS
 predicate VARCHAR2(1000);
BEGIN
 predicate := 'empno = '''||sec_adm.set_cxt_pkg.get_userid||'''';
 RETURN predicate;
END;
/
```

As you can see, the sec_adm.f_vpd_ord function will generate a different predicate for each user, based on the user's identity.

Once you have created the `usr.f_vpd_ord` function, you need to register that function against the `usr.orders` table, as shown below:

```
CONNECT /AS sysdba;

BEGIN
  DBMS_RLS.ADD_POLICY ('usr', 'orders', 'ord_policy',
                        'sec_adm', 'f_vpd_ord', 'select');
END;
/

GRANT EXECUTE ON sec_adm.f_vpd_ord TO app_conn;
```

Now, whenever you query the `usr.orders` table (directly or indirectly) Oracle will append a dynamic predicate generated by the `sec_adm.f_vpd_ord` function to the original SELECT statement.

 This works regardless of the way in which you query the `usr.orders` table. Whether you query it directly, by issuing a query against that table, or indirectly, by issuing a query against a view based on this table, the database will filter the records retrieved from the `usr.orders` table, based on the security policy implemented in the `sec_adm.f_vpd_ord` function.

To make sure that everything works as expected, you might make use of the `appPageEmpOwnOrders.php` script discussed in the preceding section. Before you run this script, make sure to replace `orders_emp_v` with `orders_vpd_v` in the FROM clause of the query used in the script to retrieve information on the orders placed by the current user.

When testing the updated sample application, you should notice that employing a VPD-based mechanism to secure information on the orders stored in the `usr.orders` table makes no difference to the sample behavior. If you login as `maya/mayapwd`, you should see the same page as shown in the previous figure.

It is interesting to note that you can always drop an existing VPD policy by using the `DROP_POLICY` procedure from the `DBMS_RLS` package. For example, to drop the policy created in the preceding listing, you might issue the PL/SQL block shown below:

```
CONNECT /AS sysdba;

BEGIN
  DBMS_RLS.DROP_POLICY('usr', 'orders', 'ord_policy');
END;
/
```

Since the `usr.orders` table will be used in the examples in the following chapters, you have to perform the PL/SQL block shown in the listing before moving on.

The example discussed in this section illustrates how a VPD secure policy can be applied to `SELECT` statements issued against a certain database table. However, in a real-world situation, you might apply a VPD policy to `INSERT`, `UPDATE`, `INDEX`, and `DELETE` statements issued against a certain table or view. For more information on the Oracle VPD security feature, refer to Oracle Documentation: the *Using Virtual Private Database to Implement Application Security Policies* chapter in *Oracle Database Security Guide*.

Summary

If your application provides access to confidential information, you need to control access more carefully, employing different security mechanisms protecting your data from unauthorized access and/or modification.

In this chapter, you learned how to build secure PHP/Oracle applications using the security features of both PHP and Oracle in a complementary way. The chapter began with an example of how an easy-to-use authentication mechanism provided by the `PEAR::Auth` class could be used with Oracle database security features to secure your PHP/Oracle application. Using techniques discussed in the *Securing PHP and Oracle Applications* section in this chapter, you will be able to build a simple, yet effective security solution for your PHP/Oracle application, even if you are using Oracle Database Express Edition.

Then we looked at how to use hashing to protect end-user passwords stored in a database table in plain text format and how view-based security techniques could be used to implement column-level security and row-level security, based on the user's identity. Finally, you saw how Oracle's Virtual Private Database (VPD) feature available in the Enterprise Edition of Oracle Database might be used instead of view-based security techniques to provide access control at the row level, ensuring that each user can access only those records that he or she is authorized to access.

By now, you should have a solid understanding of how to build a secure PHP/Oracle application, using different techniques and technologies available for PHP/Oracle developers.

7
Caching

While developing a PHP/Oracle application that uses database data heavily, it makes sense to think about caching the data that is frequently moved between the database server and web server. In practice, for the purpose of increasing performance, it might be useful not only to cache database result sets on the web server, but also to hold information that is used often, which is relevant to an application, in the memory of the database server instance.

However, to effectively implement caching on the database server, you must have a good understanding of how Oracle's default caching mechanisms work. In particular, you must have a grasp of how Oracle caches the data and metadata of SQL and PL/SQL statements issued against the database.

The challenge with caching data on the web server is to know in advance the time to update the cache. Obviously, a time-triggered approach that is commonly used in caching systems is not the best strategy when it comes to implementing caching systems for applications where using up-to-date database result sets is vital. In such cases, the Oracle Database Change Notification feature, which allows for notification an application whenever a change occurs to the application data stored in the database, may come in very handy.

This chapter discusses how to effectively use the caching mechanisms available in PHP and Oracle and provides several examples of caching in action.

Caching Data with Oracle and PHP

You may achieve good performance by using several caching mechanisms available in PHP and Oracle. Certain caching mechanisms and strategies should be chosen depending on several factors, such as whether the data you're caching is fairly static and whether using up-to-date data is crucial for your application.

In the following sections, you will learn how to implement efficient caching schemas using the capabilities of both Oracle and PHP.

Caching Queries on the Database Server

The good news is that Oracle has several built-in caching mechanisms that are used by default. Nevertheless, you should have a good understanding of how these default mechanisms work to take full advantage of them.

This section discusses how Oracle processes SQL statements issued against the database, focusing on the issues related to caching.

Processing SQL Statements

Like any other computer program, an SQL statement has to be compiled (parsed) before it can be executed. When a new SQL statement is parsed, Oracle creates the parse tree and execution plan for that statement and then caches this information in the shared pool portion of the system global area (SGA) memory, as an item usually called a **shared SQL area**. Oracle reuses a shared SQL area for similar SQL statements issued against the database, thus using the cached information instead of generating it from scratch.

 The system global area (SGA), also known as the shared memory area, is a basic memory structure shared by all processes of an Oracle database instance. The SGA consists of a set of memory structures, buffers and pools, which allow for high-speed access to data and control information. For more information on the Oracle memory structures, refer to Oracle documentation: *Memory Architecture* chapter in the *Oracle Database Concepts* manual.

Once Oracle has the shared SQL area for the statement being processed, it checks the buffer cache, searching for the required data blocks.

 The buffer cache is a portion of the system global area (SGA) memory designed for caching data blocks read from and written to the database files.

Upon failure to find these blocks in the buffer cache, Oracle reads them from the appropriate database files and then loads the retrieved data blocks into the buffer cache, which is, of course, an expensive operation in terms of CPU time and physical I/Os.

The following figure depicts the process of SQL statement processing diagrammatically.

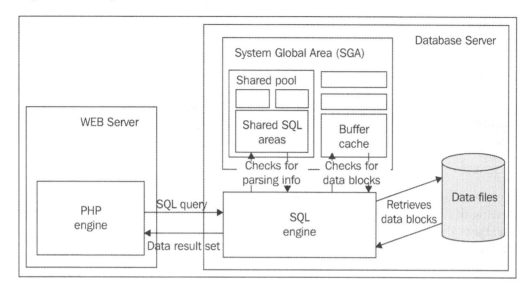

For detailed information on what happens during the execution of an SQL statement, see Oracle documentation: *SQL, PL/SQL, and Java* chapter in the *Oracle Database Concepts* manual.

It is important to understand that the parsing information held in the shared pool and the data blocks kept in the buffer cache are shared across all database sessions, regardless of the database schema under which a certain session is created, thus allowing multiple applications and multiple users to use cached data. To understand this better, consider the following example.

Suppose an application, which connects to the database using, say, usr1 database schema, issues an SQL query. The database server in turn processes the query, caching the generated execution plan and parse tree for the query in the shared pool and the data blocks retrieved from the data file or files in the buffer cache. Then, another application, when connected to the database through, say, the usr2 schema, issues the same query. This time, Oracle will not generate the execution plan and parse tree for the query again and nor will it retrieve the appropriate data blocks from the database files. Instead, it will reuse the data held in the SGA, specifically, in the shared pool and in the buffer cache, which was loaded there when processing the query issued by the first application.

When an SQL statement is issued, Oracle, checks whether the database schema, through which the application issuing the statement is connected, has privileges to access the database objects referenced in the statement.

Another important point to note here is that Oracle can reuse parsing information for similar statements. You might be wondering which statements Oracle considers to be similar when it comes to sharing parsing information. Well, Oracle will use the same shared SQL area for two SQL statements if their SQL texts are identical, including white spaces and case. Consider the following statement:

```
SELECT * FROM users WHERE usrid=:id
```

As you can see, this statement contains a placeholder in the WHERE clause, thus allowing the application to supply a particular value for the :id placeholder at run time. From the user's perspective, the above SQL string can be used to issue similar statements that differ by the user ID specified in the WHERE clause at run time. However, to Oracle, all those statements based on the above one are identical, at least at the stage of determining whether the same shared SQL area can be used for each of them.

For detailed discussion on SQL sharing criteria used by Oracle, see Oracle documentation: chapter *Memory Configuration and Use* in the *Oracle Database Performance Tuning* guide.

Using Bind Variables to Increase the Probability of Shared Pool Cache Hits

As you have no doubt guessed, an efficient way to reduce the number of parses required is to use bind variables in SQL and PL/SQL statements, rather than using string literals. What this means in practice is that you should use placeholders in SQL and PL/SQL statements to mark where actual data must be supplied at run time.

For example, Oracle will use the same parsing information for the query used in the code snippet below, regardless of the actual value of the $usrno bind variable passed to the getUser function as the parameter.

```php
<?php
function getUser($usrno)
  {
  ...
```

```
$sql = 'SELECT * FROM users WHERE usrid=:id';
$stmt = oci_parse($dbConn, $sql);
oci_bind_by_name($stmt,":id", $usrno);
if(!oci_execute($stmt))
{
 $err = oci_error($stmt);
 trigger_error($err['message'], E_USER_ERROR);
}
...
}
?>
```

When using the PEAR::DB package for interacting with the database, the above snippet might look like this:

```
<?php
function getUser($usrno)
{
...
$sql ='SELECT * FROM orders WHERE usrid=?';
$res =$db->query($sql, $usrno);
if (PEAR::isError($res)) {
    die($res->getMessage());
}
...
}
?>
```

Looking through the above snippets, you might come to the conclusion that they both issue the same SQL statement. This is not the case, however. While the first code snippet issues exactly the same query as you see in the code:

```
SELECT * FROM users WHERE usrid=:id
```

The second one, which is based on using PEAR:DB, will convert the SQL before passing it to the database, generating the following query:

```
SELECT * FROM users WHERE usrid=:bind0
```

Although the :bind0 and :id placeholders are of the same data type, they differ in name, and, therefore, Oracle cannot use the same shared SQL area when processing the above two statements.

If you are employing the PEAR::DB package to interact with Oracle, you don't have to worry about using a naming convention for placeholders; – PEAR::DB does it for you. However, when using OCI8 APIs directly, it's important that you standardize how you name placeholders in SQL statements and PL/SQL code.

As mentioned above, PEAR::DB implicitly names placeholders using the prefix bind followed by a number starting with 0. If you're using more than one bind variable in a statement, you should pass an array of the actual values for the placeholders to the query method, and PEAR::DB in turn will rename each placeholder to the appropriate name before sending the statement to the database server for processing. Take a look at the following snippet:

```php
<?php
function getUserOrders($usrno, $status)
{
...
$sql ='SELECT * FROM users WHERE (usrid=?)AND(status=?)';
$params =array($usrno, $status);
$res =$db->query($sql, $params);
if (PEAR::isError($res)) {
    die($res->getMessage());
}
...
}
?>
```

After processing the SQL in this snippet, PEAR::DB will produce the following statement:

```
SELECT * FROM users WHERE (usrid=:bind0)AND(status=:bind1);
```

It is interesting to note that the same statement will be generated by PEAR::DB even if you change the names of the $usrno and $status variables in the snippet.

Using Oracle's Application Contexts for Caching

Although Oracle automatically uses caching when processing SQL and PL/SQL statements, there is still room for improvement here. A useful technique for caching the information your application uses most often is to use application contexts. Since application contexts are held in memory, it is typically more efficient from a performance perspective to retrieve frequently queried information from an application context, rather than retrieving that information from the database tables or views.

In the preceding chapter, you saw an example of using USERENV, a built-in application context whose attributes hold information regarding a user session. Upon creating a new session, Oracle automatically fills the values of the USERENV's predefined attributes with appropriate data. In an example discussed in the preceding chapter, you checked the IP_ADDRESS attribute of USERENV to determine the IP address of the web server through which the current user was interacting with the database.

 The USERENV built-in context is an example of a local context. The attributes of USERENV provide information specific to the current database session—you cannot share this information across different sessions. If you need to share data across database sessions, you have to define a global context.

Unlike a local application context whose attributes are private to the user's session, attributes of a global context can be defined so that they are loaded in the SGA memory and thus, shared across all database sessions. Once attributes of a global context are initialized, they can be referenced in SQL as well as database tables and views.

The following figure depicts this diagrammatically. The figure illustrates that information needed to satisfy an SQL query may be stored not only in the database tables and views but also in global contexts held in the SGA memory of an Oracle database instance. The fact is that accessing data through contexts is more efficient in terms of performance compared to accessing it through tables or views.

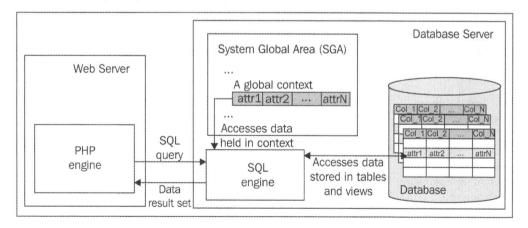

The important thing about global contexts is that you don't need to initialize their attributes each time a new session is established. You initialize them once, say, upon startup of the database server, and then reuse their values across all database sessions.

Creating a Global Application Context

Continuing with the example discussed in the preceding chapter, you might, for example, want to add some information about the most recently placed order to the page where users view their orders, so that each user can see who placed the most recent order and when it happened. Since this information is supposed to be shared across all database sessions and all users, it would be a good idea to cache it in a global context in the SGA memory.

To build the example discussed in this section, you need to have some data structures and PHP scripts defined in the preceding chapters. At a minimum, you must have created the items listed in the following table.

Data structure or PHP script	Created as described in	Comments
`usr` database schema	*An Example of When to Use a Stored Subprogram* section, Chapter 3.	This schema contains data structures storing users' data. In particular, the `accounts` and `orders` tables used in the sample reside in this schema.
`usr.accounts` database table	*An Example of When to Use a Stored Subprogram* section, Chapter 3.	This table contains records representing users of the sample application. Once you have this table created, make sure to fill it with data as discussed in the *Protecting Resources Based on Information about the Authenticated User* section in Chapter 6.
`app_conn` database schema	*Using Two Database Schemas to Improve Security* section, Chapter 6.	This schema is used for establishing connections to the database.
`sec_adm` database schema	*Using Three Database Schemas to Improve Security* section, Chapter 6.	This schema is designed to contain database objects required to perform security-related tasks.
`sec_adm. accounts_empty_v` database view	*Using the %ROWTYPE Attribute* section, Chapter 6.	This view is required for the `sec_adm. sec_pkg` package to work.

Data structure or PHP script	Created as described in	Comments
`sec_adm.sec_pkg` PL/SQL package	*Using the %ROWTYPE Attribute* section, Chapter 6.	This package is used to provide secure access to account information stored in the `usr.accounts` table. Once you have this package created, make sure to grant `EXECUTE ON sec_adm.sec_pkg` to `app_conn` as discussed in the *Using the %ROWTYPE Attribute* section, Chapter 6.
`Auth_Container_DB_func` PHP class	*Building a Custom Storage Container for the PEAR::Auth Class* section, Chapter 6.	This PHP class extends the predefined `Auth_Container_DB` class that represents the DB storage container used by the `PEAR::Auth` class.
`sec_adm.app_cxt_pkg` PL/SQL package	*Holding a User's Information in Package Variables* section, Chapter 6.	All this package contains is a package variable intended to hold the current user's name during a database session.
`sec_adm.set_cxt_pkg` PL/SQL package	*Holding a User's Information in Package Variables* section, Chapter 6.	This package contains setter and getter methods intended to manipulate the package variable defined in the `sec_adm.app_cxt_pkg` package.
`testAuthor.php` script	*Protecting Resources Based on Information about the Authenticated User* section, Chapter 6	This script is included at the beginning of each secure page in the sample application. It is responsible for authentication and authorization, preventing unauthorized access to sensitive data.
`usr.orders` database table	*Implementing Column-Level Security with Views* section, Chapter 6.	This table is used to store orders placed by the sales representatives whose records are stored in the `usr.accounts` table defined as described in the *An Example of When to Use a Stored Subprogram* section, Chapter 3.
`usr.f_get_userid` PL/SQL function	*Using the DECODE Function* section, Chapter 6.	This function returns the account name of the currently authenticated user held in the `userid` variable of the `app_cxt_pkg` package created as described in the *Holding a User's Information in Package Variables* section in Chapter 6. You use this function in the `WHERE` clause of the defining query of the `usr.orders_emp_v` view.
`usr.orders_emp_v` database view	*Implementing Row-Level security with Views* section, Chapter 6.	This view is based on the `usr.orders` and `usr.accounts` tables. It returns only records related to the account of the currently authenticated user, eliminating all other records.

As you can see, most of the items listed in the table are either data structures or PHP scripts created in Chapter 6. So, before moving on, it is highly recommended that you read Chapter 6 and build the sample application discussed in that chapter, rather than simply creating the data structures and PHP scripts listed in the table.

Once you have all these objects created, you can proceed to the sample discussed in this section. To start with, you need to create a global context. You might do that by issuing the following SQL commands from SQL*Plus:

```
CONN /as sysdba

CREATE CONTEXT cxt_ord USING sec_adm.cxt_ord_pkg ACCESSED GLOBALLY;
```

By specifying the `sec_adm.cxt_ord_pkg` in the `USING` clause of the `CREATE CONTEXT` statement, you tell Oracle that only subprograms in the `sec_adm.cxt_ord_pkg` package can be used to manipulate the attributes of the application context created here.

By including `ACCESSED GLOBALLY` clause, you specify that attributes of the application context can be shared across all database sessions.

> To be able to create an application context, the database user needs the `CREATE ANY CONTEXT` privilege. In this particular example, you create a context when connected as `sysdba`, which implies that you have this privilege by default.

Manipulating Data Held in a Global Context

Once a global context is created, you need to define the package specified in the `USING` clause of the `CREATE CONTEXT` statement to manipulate the data held in the context.

By issuing the following statements you create the `cxt_ord_pkg` package in the `sec_adm` schema to manipulate values in the `cxt_ord` global context.

```
CONN /as sysdba
```

Since the `cxt_ord_pkg.getRecentOrder` getter function declared a bit later issues a query against the `usr.accounts` and `usr.orders` tables, you first have to grant `SELECT` privileges on these tables to the `sec_adm` schema.

```
GRANT SELECT ON usr.accounts TO sec_adm;
```

If you have executed all the statements provided in the *Using Three Database Schemas to Improve Security* section in Chapter 6, the sec_adm schema already should be granted the SELECT privilege on the usr. accounts table, and so you need not execute the above GRANT statement.

Next, you grant the SELECT privilege on the usr.orders table:

```
GRANT SELECT ON usr.orders TO sec_adm;
```

The next step is to create the cxt_ord_pkg package in the sec_adm schema.

```
CREATE OR REPLACE PACKAGE sec_adm.cxt_ord_pkg
AS
TYPE ord_rec_typ IS RECORD (
  EMPNAME    VARCHAR2(20),
  ORDDATE    DATE);
  TYPE ord_rec_set IS TABLE OF ord_rec_typ;
  PROCEDURE setRecentOrder(empname VARCHAR2,orddate DATE);
  FUNCTION getRecentOrder RETURN ord_rec_set PIPELINED;
END;
/
```

In this example, you set up only two attributes for the cxt_ord global context, namely empname and orddate. So, you pass these two parameters to the setRecentOrder setter procedure.

You also declare the getRecentOrder package function that will query the cxt_ord context, retrieving information about the most recent order placed by the current user. If the cxt_ord context's attributes are not set, it retrieves this information from the usr.orders table, and then calls the setRecentOrder package procedure to set the attributes of the cxt_ord context to appropriate values.

Next, you create the body for the sec_adm.cxt_ord_pkg package:

```
CREATE OR REPLACE PACKAGE BODY sec_adm.cxt_ord_pkg IS
PROCEDURE setRecentOrder(empname VARCHAR2,orddate DATE) IS
BEGIN
  DBMS_SESSION.SET_CONTEXT(
    NAMESPACE => 'cxt_ord',
    ATTRIBUTE => 'empname',
    VALUE => empname
  );
  DBMS_SESSION.SET_CONTEXT(
    NAMESPACE => 'cxt_ord',
```

```
        ATTRIBUTE => 'orddate',
        VALUE =>      orddate
    );
END;
FUNCTION getRecentOrder RETURN ord_rec_set PIPELINED IS
 ord_rec ord_rec_typ;
BEGIN
 IF SYS_CONTEXT('cxt_ord', 'empname') IS NULL THEN
   SELECT * INTO ord_rec FROM
   (SELECT full_name as empname, orddate  FROM usr.orders, usr.accounts
WHERE empno=usr_id ORDER BY orddate DESC)
   WHERE rownum=1;
   setRecentOrder(ord_rec.empname, ord_rec.orddate);
 ELSE
   ord_rec.empname:= SYS_CONTEXT('cxt_ord', 'empname');
   ord_rec.orddate:= SYS_CONTEXT('cxt_ord', 'orddate');
 END IF;
 PIPE ROW(ord_rec);
 RETURN;
END;
END;
/
```

In the setRecentOrder procedure, you set up attributes within the context so that
their values are available for all database sessions and all database schemas. In the
getRecentOrder function, you start by checking to make sure that these values have
been set up. For simplicity, in this example you only check to see if the empname
attribute is set.

To access attributes of an application context, you use SYS_CONTEXT function,
passing the name of the context as the first parameter and the name of the attribute
as the second.

If the attributes in the context are not set, you retrieve the information about the
most recent order from the usr.orders table. Normally, it happens the first time the
getRecentOrder function is invoked.

In this example, when designing the query that will retrieve the row representing
the most recently placed order, you rely on the fact that Oracle considers a later
date greater than an earlier one. So, the query used here retrieves the first row from
the subquery that selects all order records, sorting them by the orddate column in
descending order.

Finally, you need to grant the EXECUTE privilege on sec_adm.cxt_ord_pkg TO
app_conn. This can be done as follows:

```
GRANT EXECUTE ON sec_adm.cxt_ord_pkg TO app_conn;
```

Now that you have the `sec_adm.cxt_ord_pkg` package created, you can turn back to the `appPageEmpOwnOrders.php` script created as described in the *Implementing Row-Level Security with Views* section in Chapter 6, and modify it so that the updated script produces a page that will display not only the information about the orders placed by the current user but also some information on the most recent order, whoever placed it.

The following figure illustrates what this page might look like.

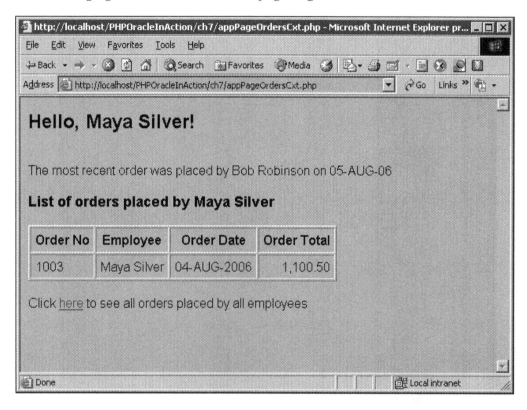

The following listing contains the source code for the `appPageEmpOwnOrders.php` script. The updated script will produce a page that might look like the previous figure:

```php
<?php
//File: appPageOrdersCxt.php
require_once "testAuthor.php";
$ordersPage='"'."appPageEmpOrders.php".'"';
$rslt =$dbh->query("SELECT * FROM
            TABLE(sec_adm.cxt_ord_pkg.getRecentOrder)");
```

```
        if (PEAR::isError($rslt)) {
           print $rslt->getMessage();
        }
        $cxt =$rslt->fetchRow(DB_FETCHMODE_ASSOC);
        print '<font face="Arial">';
        print "The most recent order was placed by ".$cxt['EMPNAME'].
                  " on ".$cxt['ORDDATE'];
        $rslt =$dbh->query("SELECT ordno, empname, TO_CHAR(orddate,
               'DD-MON-YYYY') orddate, total FROM usr.orders_emp_v");
        if (PEAR::isError($rslt)) {
           print $rslt->getMessage();
        }
        print "<h3>List of orders placed by ".
                  $a->getAuthData('FULL_NAME')."</h3>";
        print '<table border="1" cellpadding="5">';
        print '<tr>';
        print '<th>Order No</th><th>Employee</th><th>Order
               Date</th><th>Order Total</th>';
        print '</tr>';
        while($row = $rslt->fetchRow(DB_FETCHMODE_ASSOC)){
          print '<tr>';
          print '<td>'.$row['ORDNO'].
        '</td><td>'.$row['EMPNAME'].'</td><td>'.$row['ORDDATE'].
        '</td><td align="right">'.number_format($row['TOTAL'], 2).'</td>';
          print '</tr>';
        };
        print '</table>';
        print '<br/>';
        print "Click <a href=".$ordersPage.">here</a> to see all orders
               placed by all employees";
        print '</font>';
     ?>
```

In the above script, you obtain information about the most recent order. For this, you query the sec_adm.cxt_ord_pkg.getRecentOrder table function like a regular database table. This query is highlighted in the above script (see previous page).

Once you know who placed the most recent order and when it happened, you can display this information.

Next, you can use the same PEAR::DB object to obtain records representing orders placed by the current user.

Resetting Values in a Global Context

As mentioned earlier, the `sec_adm.cxt_ord_pkg.getRecentOrder` function is responsible for initializing the `cxt_ord` global context. The stage of initialization takes place when the above function is called for the first time. However, later, when a new order is submitted, you will need to reset the values in the context to appropriate values.

Since, for security reasons, the `app_conn` database schema through which the sample application connects to the database has no rights to access the `usr.orders` table, you first have to decide which mechanism to use when it comes to submitting a new order. A common approach to this problem is to create a stored subprogram through which the application will insert new records into the table.

By issuing the statements in the following listing, you create the `newOrder` procedure that will be used for inserting new records into the `usr.orders` table, and grant the `EXECUTE` privilege on this procedure to the `app_conn` schema.

```
CONN /as sysdba

CREATE OR REPLACE PROCEDURE usr.newOrder(
    ordno NUMBER,
    empno VARCHAR2,
    total NUMBER)
IS
BEGIN
    INSERT INTO usr.orders VALUES(ordno, empno, SYSDATE, total);
END;
/

GRANT EXECUTE ON usr.newOrder TO app_conn;
```

For simplicity, the procedure shown in the listing simply issues an `INSERT` statement against the `usr.orders` table.

It's interesting to note that in DML statements embedded in PL/SQL code, Oracle automatically turns the variables in the `WHERE` and `VALUES` clauses into bind variables. So, in this PL/SQL procedure you don't have to use bind variables explicitly.

Once you have the `newOrders` procedure created, you can move on to creating a script that will use this procedure to insert new rows into the `usr.orders` table.

The following figure illustrates a mock-up of the input form that might be used for entering data for a new order.

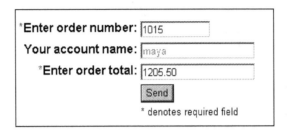

When executed, the newOrder.php script shown below produces a page containing the input form as shown in the above figure. Upon submission of the form, the script calls the newOrder procedure defined in the preceding listing, which in turn issues an INSERT statement against the orders table.

```php
<?php
//File: newOrder.php
require_once "testAuthor.php";
require_once "HTML/QuickForm.php";
$form = new HTML_QuickForm('newOrderForm');
$form->setDefaults(
    array(
    'empno' => $username
    )
);
$form->addElement('text', 'ordno', 'Enter order number:',
                array('size' => 10, 'maxlength' => 10));
$form->addElement('text', 'empno', 'Your account name:',
                array('size' => 20, 'readonly'));
$form->addElement('text', 'total', 'Enter order total:',
                array('size' => 20, 'maxlength' => 20));
$form->addElement('submit', 'submit', 'Send');
// Define validation rules
$form->addRule('ordno', 'Please enter order number', 'required',
                null, 'client');
$form->addRule('total', 'Please enter order total', 'required',
                null, 'client');
if(isset($_POST['submit'])) {
    $arr_ord =array(
                $form->getSubmitValue('ordno'),
                $form->getSubmitValue('empno'),
                $form->getSubmitValue('total')
                );
```

```
    $rslt =$dbh->query("BEGIN usr.newOrder(?,?,?); END;",$arr_ord);
    if (PEAR::isError($rslt)) {
     die($rslt->getMessage());
    }
    $f_name =$a->getAuthData('FULL_NAME');
    $rslt =$dbh->query("BEGIN sec_adm.cxt_ord_pkg.setRecentOrder(?,SYS
DATE); END;",$f_name);
    if (PEAR::isError($rslt)) {
     print $rslt->getMessage();
    }
    print "<h4>You just placed a new order!</h4>";
  } else{
  $form->display();
  }
  ?>
```

Now, let's break into the above script and look at how it works, step by step.

By including the `testAuthor.php` script discussed in the *Protecting Resources Based on Information about the Authenticated User* section in Chapter 6, you secure the page produced by the script shown in the above listing, which guarantees that only authenticated users will be able to access the input form on this page.

In this example, you create the input form for entering a new order, using the `HTML_QuickForm` PEAR package. In Chapter 5 *Object-Oriented Approach*, you saw an example of using `PEAR::HTML_QuickForm` when building a custom login form to be used with a class based on `PEAR::Auth`.

Next, you set the default value for the `empno` input element of the `HTM_QuickForm` form created.

Once the form object is created, you can add elements to the form. In particular, you add three input boxes that will be used for entering data for a new order. Note that the `empno` input box element is defined as `readonly`, which means that the user will not be able to change its default value.

Next, with the help of the `addRule` method, you add validation rules to the form. The rules specified here tell the form to verify whether the `ordno` and `total` input boxes are filled, upon submission of the form.

Then, you check to see if the form has been submitted. It is important to note that if at least one of the validation rules defined earlier in this script is not satisfied, so validation fails, the form is displayed again along with an error message.

Once the form is submitted, you can retrieve the submitted elements' values, by using the `getSubmitValue` method. In this example, you save the entered data in an array, which is then passed to the `query` method as the second parameter.

You issue the PL/SQL statement through which you call the `usr.newOrder` procedure defined as described earlier in this section. Note the use of placeholders in the parameter list of the procedure. You supply particular values to these placeholders during execution, through the `$arr_ord` array.

If the PL/SQL statement issued within the script fails, you issue an error message and stop execution with the help of the `die` function.

If the PL/SQL statement is executed successfully, you obtain the full name of the currently authenticated user. For this, you call the `getAuthData` method of the `PEAR::Auth` object created in the included `testAuthor.php` script, specifying the `FULL_NAME` as the parameter.

Then, you reset the `cxt_ord` global context created as described in the *Manipulating Data Held in a Global Context* section earlier, so that it contains information about the order that was just inserted. To do this, you issue the PL/SQL statement that calls the `setRecentOrder` setter method of the `sec_adm.cxt_ord_pkg` package created as described in the *Manipulating Data Held in a Global Context* section earlier in this chapter.

Now that you know how the `newOrder.php` script works, it is time to put it into action. When you run the script, you first will be prompted to enter a user name and password to get authenticated. You might, for example, use `maya/mayapwd` account/password combination. After you are successfully authenticated, you should see the input form for entering a new order, like the one as shown in the previous figure. In the form, simply enter the order number and total for the order and then click the **Send** button. As a result, a new record should be inserted in the `usr.orders` table and you should see a message telling you about this.

Once a new record has been inserted into the `usr.orders` table, you might run the `appPageOrdersCxt.php` script discussed in the *Manipulating Data Held in a Global Context* section again in order to make sure that everything works as expected. This time, the message displayed below the welcome message on the page should contain information about the order that was just inserted.

Caching Mechanisms Available in PHP

While holding often-used information in a global context in the SGA memory of the database instance lets you avoid repetitively querying database tables or views, caching the database result sets retrieved from the database on the web server reduces the need to even send a query to the database because many data requests may be eventually satisfied from the local cache.

 Caching database result sets on the web server makes sense when the web server and database server reside on different machines.

Choosing a Caching Strategy

Before you can start caching database result sets on the web server side, you first have to decide which caching strategy best fits your needs.

A time -triggered caching approach, which is commonly used in caching systems, implies that the cache is regenerated each time an expiry timestamp is reached. While such a caching system can be easily implemented, it is not always a satisfactory solution for those applications where using up-to-date database result sets is crucial.

In such cases, you need to employ a mechanism that will notify your application each time a change occurs to the database data the application is interested in caching, so that the application can reconcile cached, out-of-date data with the database. You can achieve this functionality with Database Change Notification, a new Oracle Database 10g Release 2 feature.

The rest of this section discusses how to implement a time triggered-caching system on the web server side with the help of the PEAR::Cache_Lite package. In the following sections, you will see how to use the Database Change Notification feature to create a notification-based caching system.

Caching Function Calls with the PEAR::Cache_Lite Package

Turning back to the appPageOrdersCxt.php script discussed earlier in this chapter, you might want to update it so that it caches the information on the orders retrieved from the database in a local cache of the web server, thus reducing the overhead associated with frequent database server requests.

One way to achieve this is to encapsulate the code responsible for retrieving information about orders from the database into a separate function and then cache the results of this function, thus taking advantage of so-called caching functions calls. For example, you might create the getEmpOrders function that will query the database and retrieve the orders for the currently authenticated user, returning this information to the caller. After you create the getEmpOrders function, you can rewrite the `appPageOrdersCxt.php` script so that it calls `getEmpOrders` and caches its results in the local cache of the web server.

This can be depicted diagrammatically, as shown in following figure

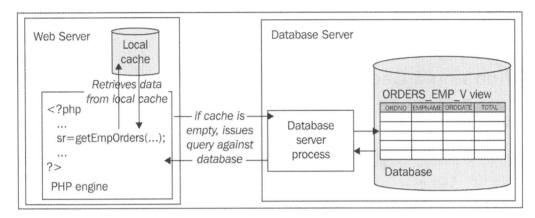

The following listing shows the source code for the script containing the `getEmpOrders` function, which returns information about the orders of the current user, whose results you are going to cache on the web server.

```php
<?php
//File: getEmpOrders.php
function getEmpOrders($dsn, $user) {
$db = DB::connect($dsn);
if(DB::isError($db)) {
    die($db->getMessage());
}
$db->setFetchMode(DB_FETCHMODE_ASSOC);
$rs =$db->getAll("SELECT ordno, empname, TO_CHAR(orddate,
          'DD-MON-YYYY') orddate, total FROM usr.orders_emp_v");
if (PEAR::isError($rs)) {
    print $rs->getMessage();
}
 return($rs);
}
?>
```

It is interesting to note that the second parameter passed to the `getEmpOrders` function is not referenced within the function code. You have to use this parameter, which contains the account name of the current user, in order to make it possible for the caching system to distinguish between the calls of `getEmpOrders` made to obtain the orders placed by different users.

In this script, by setting the fetch mode to DB_FETCHMODE_ASSOC, you tell the PEAR::
DB object to return the resulting data as an associative array.

Next, you use the getAll method to run the query and retrieve all the data as an
array, thus eliminating the need to make a separate call to a fetching method.

Now you can turn back to the appPageOrdersCxt.php script and update it to use
getEmpOrders, caching its results on the web server. The following listing contains
the source code for such a revision.

```php
<?php
//File: appPageOrdersCache.php
require_once "testAuthor.php";
require_once "getEmpOrders.php";
require_once 'Cache/Lite/Function.php';
$options = array(
  'cacheDir' => '/tmp/',
  'lifeTime' => 300
);
$ordersPage='"'."appPageEmpOrders.php".'"';
$rslt =$dbh->query("SELECT * FROM TABLE(sec_adm.cxt_ord_pkg.
getRecentOrder)");
if (PEAR::isError($rslt)) {
    print $rslt->getMessage();
}
$cxt =$rslt->fetchRow(DB_FETCHMODE_ASSOC);
print '<font face="Arial">';
print "The most recent order was placed by ".$cxt['EMPNAME']."
                        on ".$cxt['ORDDATE'];
$cache = new Cache_Lite_Function($options);
if ($rslt = $cache->call('getEmpOrders', $dbh->dsn, $username)){
  print "<h3>List of orders placed by ".
                        $a->getAuthData('FULL_NAME')."</h3>";
  print '<table border="1" cellpadding="5">';
  print '<tr>';
  print '<th>Order No</th><th>Employee</th><th>Order
                    Date</th><th>Order Total</th>';
  print '</tr>';
  foreach ($rslt as $row) {
    print '<tr>';
    print '<td>'.$row['ORDNO'].
'</td><td>'.$row['EMPNAME'].'</td><td>'.$row['ORDDATE'].
'</td><td align="right">'.number_format($row['TOTAL'], 2).'</td>';
    print '</tr>';
  };
```

```
    print '</table>';
    } else {
     print "Some problem occurred while getting orders!\n";
      $cache->drop('getEmpOrders', $dbh->dsn, $username);
    }
   print '<br/>';
   print "Click <a href=".$ordersPage.">here</a> to see all orders
                         placed by all employees";
   print '</font>';
  ?>
```

In this example, you cache results returned by the getEmpOrders function with the help of the Cache_Lite_Function class from the PEAR package. So, before you can run the script defined in the listing, you have to install the PEAR::Cache_Lite package. As usual, this can be done with the help of the PEAR Installer. Assuming PEAR is installed in your PHP installation, you can run the following command from the command line to install the PEAR::Cache_Lite package:

```
  $ pear install Cache_lite
```

The Cache/Lite/Function.php file included in the above script is created during PEAR::Cache_Lite installation. This file contains the Cache_Lite_Function class used in the script to cache getEmpOrders calls.

However, before you can create an instance of Cache_Lite_Function you have to define an array of options, which will be passed to the class constructor as the parameter. In this particular example, you set the lifeTime option to 300, which will tell the Cache_Lite_Function object to cache the results of the getEmpOrders function for 300 seconds.

Another parameter included in the array of options is cacheDir, through which you define the directory to hold cache files on the web server. In this example, you set this option to /tmp/, thus specifying the /tmp directory to be the cache directory.

 If you are a Windows user, you might want to use the %SystemDrive%\temp directory as the cache directory. In that case, you have to set cacheDir to /temp/.

Next, you call the getEmpOrders cacheable function using the call method of the Cache_Lite_Function object. The $dbh->dns and $username are the parameters passed to getEmpOrders. As mentioned earlier, the $username parameter is used only to make it possible for the Cache_Lite_Function object to distinguish between the calls of getEmpOrders made to obtain the orders placed by different users.

Next, you use the `foreach` construct to loop over the array returned by the `getEmpOrders` function.

In this example, you drop the cached data associated with the corresponding `getEmpOrders` function call with given parameters if the `call` method returns false instead of the array of orders, which in turn is returned either by the `getEmpOrders` function or from the local cache.

Updating Cached Data

Once the data has been updated in the database, it is good practice to update the cache to make sure that it does not contain out-of-date data. The problem with the caching approach used in the preceding example is that it does not provide a way to determine when the time comes to update the cache.

To solve this problem, you can make use of the `drop` method of the `Cache_Lite_Function` class, removing from the cache a specific call of the `getEmpOrders` function when the data that that call is supposed to return has been changed in the database.

So, you can now turn back to the `newOrder.php` script discussed in the *Resetting Values in a Global Context* section earlier and revise it so that it removes the set of orders placed by the current user from the cache once that user has successfully inserted a new order into the `usr.orders` table.

The following listing shows the updated `newOrder.php` script that calls the `drop` method of the `Cache_Lite_Function` object to remove the out-of-date set of orders from the cache.

```php
<?php
//File: newOrderCache.php
require_once "testAuthor.php";
require_once 'Cache/Lite/Function.php';
print '<font face="Arial">';
require_once 'HTML/QuickForm.php';
$form = new HTML_QuickForm('newOrderForm');
$form->setDefaults(
    array(
    'empno' => $username
    )
);
$form->addElement('text', 'ordno', 'Enter order number:',
                  array('size' => 10, 'maxlength' => 10));
$form->addElement('text', 'empno', 'Your account name:',
                  array('size' => 20, 'readonly'));
```

```
$form->addElement('text', 'total', 'Enter order total:',
                  array('size' => 20, 'maxlength' => 20));
$form->addElement('submit', 'submit', 'Send');
// Define validation rules
$form->addRule('ordno', 'Please enter order number',
               'required', null, 'client');
$form->addRule('total', 'Please enter order total',
               'required', null, 'client');
// Try to validate a form
if(isset($_POST['submit'])) {
    $arr_ord =array($form->getSubmitValue('ordno'),
             $form->getSubmitValue('empno'),
             $form->getSubmitValue('total')
          );
    $rslt =$dbh->query("BEGIN usr.newOrder(?,?,?); END;",$arr_ord);
    if (PEAR::isError($rslt)) {
     die($rslt->getMessage());
    }
    $f_name =$a->getAuthData('FULL_NAME');
    $rslt =$dbh->query("BEGIN sec_adm.cxt_ord_pkg.setRecentOrder(?,SY
SDATE);
                   END;",$f_name);
    if (PEAR::isError($rslt)) {
     print $rslt->getMessage();
    }
    print "<h4>You just placed a new order!</h4>";
    $options = array(
      'cacheDir' => '/tmp/'
    );
    $cache = new Cache_Lite_Function($options);
    $cache->drop('getEmpOrders', $dbh->dsn, $username);
} else{
// Output the form
$form->display();
}
 print '</font>';
?>
```

You start with including the file that contains the `Cache_Lite_Function` class upon which you then create an object within the second highlighted block in the above script.

Note that you don't specify the cache lifetime in the array of caching options highlighted in the script opposite. This is because a `Cache_Lite_Function` object doesn't need this parameter when it comes to removing a function call from the cache. Here, you specify only the cache directory to tell the `Cache_Lite_Function` object created in this script where the cache files reside.

To remove a specific function call from the cache, you must pass the same parameters to the `drop` method, called within the highlighted block opposite, as you passed to the `call` method when making that function call.

That is it. Now, the `newOrderCache.php` script will take care to remove the out-of-date data from the cache upon insertion of a new order. To make sure that it works as expected, you might perform the following steps:

- Step 1: Run the `appPageOrdersCache.php` script discussed in the *Caching Function Calls with the PEAR::Cache_Lite Package* section earlier, and when connecting, enter the `maya/mayapwd` username/password combination.

- Step 2: Check out the `/tmp` directory where the `Cache_Lite_Function` object had to create a cache file for the `getEmpOrders` function call made by the `appPageOrdersCache.php` script in Step 1. This newly created cache file might be named something like this:

  ```
  cache_7b181b55b55aee36ad5e7bd9d5a091ec_
  7fb088baee4564f0a34f41fa4223a877
  ```

- Step 3: Run the `newOrderCache.php` script discussed at the beginning of this section, and connect as `maya/mayapwd`. Through the new order form, submit a new order.

- Step 4: Check out the cache directory again. If the cache file created during execution of the `appPageOrdersCache.php` script in Step 1 has gone, then everything works as expected.

As you can see, the `newOrderCache.php` script not only provides an input form for entering a new order, but also removes the set of orders that becomes out of date upon insertion of that new order from the cache.

Implementing Notification-Based Caching

The preceding example illustrates a simple way of solving the problem of outdated data. Through the application, you automatically remove a result set from the cache upon making a change to this result set in the database. This mechanism works perfectly provided that the only way to change the data you're working with is through your application. This will most likely be the case for applications like the one discussed in the preceding chapters. After all, there is no reason to have more than one application to work with the orders stored in the usr.orders table, and have more than one input form within this application to insert new orders, right?

However, in practice you may find yourself developing an application that assumes that the data it will work with may be changed by more than one application. In such cases, you might find it useful to employ the database change notification feature, which has been available in Oracle Database since version 10g release 2.

This notification mechanism will trigger a change notification whenever a database object (table or view) holding the application data is modified. To handle notifications, you must create a notification handler, a PL/SQL stored procedure or a client-side OCI callback function, which will be executed when a change notification is issued. The notification handle is designed to invoke a PHP script that will remove the out-of-date data from the cache on the web server, depending on the information contained in the change notification message.

Graphically, this might look like the following figure:

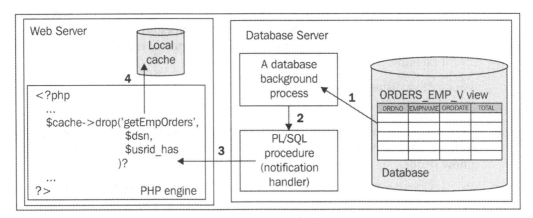

Here is the explanation of the steps in the figure:

- Step 1: When the usr.orders table is modified, Oracle automatically notifies a job queue background process about it.

- Step 2: The job queue background process in turn invokes a notification handler, which is usually a PL/SQL procedure.

- Step 3: The notification handler, when executed, invokes a PHP script, passing the information describing which set of orders must be removed from the cache.

- Step 4: The PHP script removes the specified set of orders from the local cache on the web server.

The following sections show how you can implement a caching system based on the change notification mechanism discussed here.

Using Database Change Notification

To make use of the database change notification feature, you have to perform the following two general steps:

- Step 1: Create a notification handler to be executed in response to a notification.

- Step 2: Register a query on a database object or objects for which you want to receive change notifications, so that the notification handler created in step 1 is invoked whenever a transaction changes any of these objects and commits.

The following subsections discuss how to implement these steps when developing a notification-based caching system.

 For detailed information on the database change notification feature, refer to Oracle documentation: chapter *Developing Applications with Database Change Notification* in *Oracle Database Application Developer's Guide – Fundamentals*.

Auditing Notification Messages

It is good practice to audit notification messages issued by the change notification mechanism. To achieve this, you first have to create an audit table that will hold information about issued notifications.

By issuing the following CREATE TABLE SQL statement you create the usr. ntfresults table to be used for holding information about each notification issued.

```
CONN /as sysdba

CREATE TABLE usr.ntfresults (
 ntf_date DATE,
 tbl_name VARCHAR2(60),
 emp_id VARCHAR2(40),
 rslt_msg VARCHAR2(100)
);
```

As you can see, the table is designed to hold the following information about a notification:

- The date and time the notification was issued
- The table for which the change notification was received (it's usr.orders in this example)
- The ID of the employee who placed the record
- The message describing whether the notification handler has managed to invoke the PHP script responsible for cleaning the cache

The notification handler is responsible for generating an audit record based on the notification received.

Building a PL/SQL Procedure Sending Notifications to the Web Server

Next, you might want to encapsulate the functionality associated with posting a notification to the client into a separate PL/SQL procedure, which will allow you to have a simpler and more readable notification handler.

The following listing contains the statements you have to issue in order to create the usr.postNtf PL/SQL procedure that will be called from within the notification handler and will invoke a PHP script dropping the set of orders that have become out of date, from the local cache on the web server.

```
CONN /as sysdba

GRANT EXECUTE ON dbms_crypto TO usr;

CREATE OR REPLACE PROCEDURE usr.postNtf(url IN VARCHAR2,
              sch_tbl IN VARCHAR2, usr IN VARCHAR2) IS
 req    UTL_HTTP.REQ;
 resp   UTL_HTTP.RESP;
 err_msg VARCHAR2(100);
 usr_hash VARCHAR2(40);
BEGIN
    BEGIN
     usr_hash:= DBMS_CRYPTO.HASH (
     UTL_I18N.STRING_TO_RAW (usr, 'AL32UTF8'),
     DBMS_CRYPTO.HASH_SH1);
     usr_hash:=NLS_LOWER(usr_hash);
     req := UTL_HTTP.BEGIN_REQUEST(url||usr_hash);
     resp := UTL_HTTP.GET_RESPONSE(req);
```

```
        INSERT INTO ntfresults VALUES(SYSDATE, sch_tbl,
              usr, resp.reason_phrase);
        UTL_HTTP.END_RESPONSE(resp);
      EXCEPTION WHEN OTHERS THEN
        err_msg := SUBSTR(SQLERRM, 1, 100);
        INSERT INTO ntfresults VALUES(SYSDATE, sch_tbl, usr, err_msg);
      END;
    COMMIT;
  END;
  /
```

In the above script, you start with granting the EXECUTE privilege on the DBMS_CRYPTO package to the usr database schema. You refer to this package from within the usr.postNtf procedure.

The usr.postNtf procedure created by the above CREATE PROCEDURE statement takes the following information through its parameters:

- The URL of the PHP script removing the out-of-date set of orders from the local cache on the web server.

- The name of the table (including the schema name in which this table resides) that was modified. In this example, it is the usr.orders table.

- The ID of the user who inserted a new order into the usr.orders table.

For security reasons, you hash the ID of the user before sending it as the parameter in the HTTP request issued by the UTL_HTTP.BEGIN_REQUEST function.

So, the usr.postNtf procedure uses the UTL_HTTP.BEGIN_REQUEST function to send a notification message to the client in the form of an HTTP request. And the usr_hash parameter in the request contains the hash of the ID of the user who just inserted a new record into the usr.orders table.

Then, the usr.postNtf procedure calls UTL_HTTP.GET_RESPONSE to obtain response information indicating whether the PHP script specified in the HTTP request has been successfully invoked. Actually, usr.postNtf is not interested in processing the whole response returned from the client. Instead, it obtains only a short message stored in the reason_phrase field of the RESP record, describing the status code. This message, among other pieces of information, is stored in the ntfresults table created as described in the *Auditing Notification Messages* section. However, if the UTL_HTTP package raises an error, a new record is inserted into ntfresults in the exception handler block.

Performing Configuration Steps Required for Change Notification

Now, the last thing you have to do before proceeding to the notification handler is to grant the usr schema the privileges required to work with the change notification, and alter the system to receive notifications.

Here are the SQL statements you have to execute before you can create the notification handler. Specifically, you grant the usr schema privileges required to work with notifications and alter the system to receive notifications.

```
CONNECT /AS SYSDBA;

GRANT CHANGE NOTIFICATION TO usr;

GRANT EXECUTE ON DBMS_CHANGE_NOTIFICATION TO usr;

ALTER SYSTEM SET "job_queue_processes"=2;
```

As an alternative to issuing ALTER SYSTEM, you might set the job_queue_processes parameter in the init.ora configuration file to a non-zero value to receive PL/SQL notifications.

Building the Notification Handler

As its name implies, the notification handler is used to handle notifications. By issuing the CREATE PROCEDURE statement shown below, you create the usr.orders_ntf_callback procedure that will then be used as the notification handler for the notifications issued in response to changes to the usr.orders table.

```
CONN /as sysdba

CREATE OR REPLACE PROCEDURE usr.orders_ntf_callback (ntfnds IN SYS.
CHNF$_DESC) IS
 tblname VARCHAR2(60);
 numtables NUMBER;
 event_type NUMBER;
 row_id VARCHAR2(20);
 numrows NUMBER;
 usr VARCHAR2(40);
 url VARCHAR2(256) := 'http://localhost/PHPOracleInAction/ch7/
dropCachedEmpOrders.php?par=';
BEGIN
 event_type := ntfnds.event_type;
```

```
   numtables := ntfnds.numtables;
  IF (event_type = DBMS_CHANGE_NOTIFICATION.EVENT_OBJCHANGE) THEN
   FOR i IN 1..numtables LOOP
    tblname := ntfnds.table_desc_array(i).table_name;
    IF (bitand(ntfnds.table_desc_array(i).opflags, DBMS_CHANGE_
NOTIFICATION.ALL_ROWS) = 0) THEN
      numrows := ntfnds.table_desc_array(i).numrows;
    ELSE
      numrows :=0;
    END IF;
    IF (tblname = 'USR.ORDERS') THEN
     FOR j IN 1..numrows LOOP
      row_id := ntfnds.table_desc_array(i).row_desc_array(j).row_id;
      SELECT empno INTO usr FROM usr.orders WHERE rowid = row_id;
      postNtf(url, tblname, usr);
     END LOOP;
    END IF;
   END LOOP;
  END IF;
  COMMIT;
 END;
 /
```

To figure out how the `orders_ntf_callback` notification handler created as shown above works, let's take a closer look at its code.

As you can see, the notification handler takes the `SYS.CHNF$_DESC` object as its parameter. Through this parameter, the notification system passes the information about the change that occurred.

The `url` variable declared in the `orders_ntf_callback` created above contains the URL that points to the PHP script that will be used to remove the out-of-date set of orders from the local cache on the web server. Notice that the URL specified here is not completed—it is assumed that the value of the `par` parameter will be appended to the URL during execution. If you recall from the *Building a PL/SQL Procedure Sending Notifications to the Web Server* section, the `usr.postNtf` PL/SQL procedure called from within the notification handler appends the hash value of the employee's ID to the value of the `url` variable.

Next, before proceeding with processing the notification information, you check to see whether the notification type is set to `EVENT_OBJCHANGE`, which means that the notification has been published by the database in response to changing data in an object or objects registered for notification.

The change notification mechanism discussed here also issues notifications in response to other database events, such as instance startup or instance shutdown. In this particular example, the notification handler will ignore the notifications on these events.

If the notification type is set to EVENT_OBJCHANGE, you move on to the loop iterating through the tables registered for notification in which a change occurred.

 Although this example assumes that the usr.orders table will be the only table registered for notification, using a loop here is a good idea anyway. With it, logic for processing another table can easily be added to the notification handler if needed.

Within the loop, you obtain the name of the modified table, getting the value of the table_name attribute of the so-called table change descriptor—an object holding change notification information related to a particular modified table. The SYS.CHNF$_DESC object, which is passed to the notification handler as the parameter, contains the table_desc_array attribute holding an array of table change descriptors. Again, in this particular example, this array will contain the only table descriptor—the one that corresponds to the usr.orders table.

Before obtaining the number of modified rows (actually, inserted and/or updated rows) in a given modified table, you check to see whether the ROWID information for those rows is available through the table change descriptor.

For the usr.orders table change descriptor, you begin a nested loop to step through all of the modified rows. You obtain the ROWID of each row and then you use this information in the WHERE clause of the SELECT query to obtain the value of the empno field in the modified row. Then, you invoke the postNtf procedure created as discussed in the *Building a PL/SQL Procedure Sending Notifications to the Web Server* section earlier, passing to it the following parameters: the URL defined at the beginning of the procedure, the table name obtained in the first line of the outer loop, and the empno of the modified (inserted or updated) row.

Creating a Query Registration for the Notification Handler

Once you have created a notification handler, you then have to create a query registration for it. In this example, you need to execute any query on the usr.orders table within the so-called registration block, specifying orders_ntf_callback as the notification handler.

By issuing the following PL/SQL block, you create a query registration for the notification handler defined in the preceding section.

```
CONN /as sysdba

GRANT CONNECT TO usr;

CONNECT usr/usr

DECLARE
  REGDS SYS.CHNF$_REG_INFO;
  regid NUMBER;
  empid VARCHAR2(40);
  qosflags NUMBER;
BEGIN
  qosflags := DBMS_CHANGE_NOTIFICATION.QOS_RELIABLE + DBMS_CHANGE_
NOTIFICATION.QOS_ROWIDS;
  REGDS := SYS.CHNF$_REG_INFO ('usr.orders_ntf_callback',
                               qosflags, 0,0,0);
  regid := DBMS_CHANGE_NOTIFICATION.NEW_REG_START (REGDS);
  SELECT empno INTO empid FROM usr.orders WHERE ROWNUM<2;
  DBMS_CHANGE_NOTIFICATION.REG_END;
END;
/

CONN /as sysdba

REVOKE CONNECT FROM usr;
```

By issuing the above anonymous PL/SQL block, you register the usr.orders table with the usr.orders_ntf_callback procedure. However, before you can execute this block, you have to temporarily grant CONNECT role to the usr schema and then connect as usr/usr.

In the above example, you use the qosflags variable to hold the options that are used during registration. In particular, you specify that the notification should include the ROWID information of the modified rows and notifications should persist in the database, surviving instance failure.

Then, you create a SYS.CHNF$_REG_INFO object, passing the qosflags variable to the constructor and specifying usr.orders_ntf_callback as the notification handler.

With the DBMS_CHANGE_NOTIFICATION.NEW_REG_START function, you begin a registration block. Next, you issue a query against the usr.orders table, so that it returns a single row. Finally, you end the registration by calling DBMS_CHANGE_NOTIFICATION.REG_END.

After the anonymous PL/SQL block defined in the listing is successfully executed, you can revoke the CONNECT role from the usr schema.

Quick Test

From now on, the usr.orders_ntf_callback procedure will be invoked whenever the usr.orders table changes. As a quick test, you might run the following INSERT statement from SQL*Plus:

```
CONN /as sysdba

INSERT INTO usr.orders VALUES(1045, 'maya', SYSDATE, 450.75);

COMMIT;
```

and then issue the following query:

```
SELECT * FROM usr.ntfresults;
```

As a result, you should see the following output:

```
NTF_DATE   TBL_NAME      EMP_ID     RSLT_MSG
---------  -----------   ---------  -------------
27-AUG-06  USR.ORDERS    maya       Not Found
```

This proves that the notification handler has been invoked. Not found in the rslt_msg field indicates that the script invoked by the postNtf procedure was not found. This is expected behavior in this case because you haven't yet created a dropCachedEmpOrders.php script specified in the HTTP request issued from within the postNtf procedure.

Implementing Notification-Based Caching with PEAR::Cache_Lite

Now that you have the notification system working, the next step is to create the dropCachedEmpOrders.php script that will be invoked in response to a change to the usr.orders table, removing the out-of-date data from the local cache on the web server.

The `dropCachedEmpOrders.php` script shown below should be invoked whenever a change is made to the `usr.orders` table. Depending on the hashed value of the employee ID passed to the script as the parameter, the script will remove the corresponding set of orders from the cache.

```php
<?php
//File: dropCachedEmpOrders.php
require_once 'Cache/Lite/Function.php';
require_once "DB.php";
$options = array(
    'cacheDir' => '/tmp/'
);
$dsn = 'oci8://app_conn:appconn@localhost:1521/orcl';
$dsn = DB::parseDSN($dsn);
$cache = new Cache_Lite_Function($options);
if (isset($_GET['par'])) {
    $cache->drop('getEmpOrders', $dsn, $_GET['par']);
}
?>
```

Although you are not going to connect to the database here, you include the DB.php file containing PEAR::DB. This is because you will use the DB::parseDSN method to parse the DSN, which is then passed to the drop method of PEAR::Cache_Lite_Function as a parameter. Since you have to pass the same DSN to the drop method as you pass to the call method, you define the same DSN here as you used in the testAuthor.php script discussed in the *Protecting Resources Based on Information about the Authenticated User* section in Chapter 6.

Another parameter you have to pass to the drop method is the hashed value of the employee ID, which in turn is passed to the dropCachedEmpOrders.php script from the postNtf PL/SQL procedure as a URL query-string variable. You check to see if this variable is set before calling the drop method. If so, you call the drop method, thus removing the specified set of orders from the cache.

After you have created the dropCachedEmpOrders.php script, it's time to see how you can put it into action. For this, you should turn back to the appPageOrdersCache.php script discussed in the *Caching Function Calls with the PEAR::Cache_Lite Package* section earlier in this chapter and modify it so that it passes the hashed value of an employee ID to the getEmpOrders function, rather than passing the employee ID itself.

The `appPageOrdersCacheNotify.php` script shown below caches `getEmpOrders` function calls in a secure manner. The script is a revision of the `appPageOrdersCache.php` script discussed earlier in this chapter. In this revision, to improve security, you pass the hashed value of an employee ID to the `getEmpOrders` function.

```php
<?php
//File: appPageOrdersCacheNotify.php
require_once "testAuthor.php";
require_once "getEmpOrders.php";
require_once 'Cache/Lite/Function.php';
$options = array(
  'cacheDir' => '/tmp/',
  'lifeTime' => 300
);
$ordersPage='"'."appPageEmpOrders.php".'"';
$rslt =$dbh->query("SELECT * FROM
  TABLE(sec_adm.cxt_ord_pkg.getRecentOrder)");
if (PEAR::isError($rslt)) {
    print $rslt->getMessage();
}
$cxt =$rslt->fetchRow(DB_FETCHMODE_ASSOC);
print '<font face="Arial">';
print "The most recent order was placed by ".$cxt['EMPNAME'].
                                " on ".$cxt['ORDDATE'];
$cache = new Cache_Lite_Function($options);
$hash_usr = sha1($username);
if ($rslt = $cache->call('getEmpOrders', $dbh->dsn, $hash_usr)){
 print "<h3>List of orders placed by ".
            $a->getAuthData('FULL_NAME')."</h3>";
 print '<table border="1" cellpadding="5">';
 print '<tr>';
 print '<th>Order No</th><th>Employee</th><th>
                          Order Date</th><th>Order Total</th>';
 print '</tr>';
 foreach ($rslt as $row) {
  print '<tr>';
  print '<td>'.$row['ORDNO'].
'</td><td>'.$row['EMPNAME'].'</td><td>'.$row['ORDDATE'].'
</td><td align="right">'.number_format($row['TOTAL'], 2).'</td>';
  print '</tr>';
 };
 print '</table>';
 } else {
 print "Some problem occurred while getting orders!\n";
```

```
     $cache->drop('getEmpOrders', $dbh->dsn, $hash_usr);
  }
  print '<br/>';
  print "Click <a href=".$ordersPage.">here</a> to see all
                       orders placed by all employees";
  print '</font>';
?>
```

In the script opposite, to get the hashed value of an employee ID, you use the `sha1` PHP function. This line of code is highlighted in the listing.

Then, you pass the hash to the `call` method of `Cache_Lite_Function` as a parameter when making a call to the `getEmpOrders` cached function. You also have to pass the hash to the `drop` method, which is invoked if the `call` method invoked here returns false.

You are now ready to test your caching system based on notifications issued by the database. To start with, run the `appPageOrdersCacheNotify.php` script shown opposite, and connect as `maya/mayapwd`. This should create a corresponding cache file in the `/tmp` directory on the web server. This cached data will be used in all subsequent executions of the `appPageOrdersCacheNotify.php` script made within the next 300 seconds. However, the cache file will be removed immediately, should you insert a new order or update an existing one on behalf of employee whose ID is `maya`.

Summary

Caching frequently accessed data can significantly reduce the use of system resources. By increasing the probability of cache hits, you reduce the amount of processing required to process a result set accessed by your application, thus improving application performance.

Although Oracle caches recently (in practice, this often means frequently) used metadata and data in memory by default, there are still a lot of details to master in order to take full advantage of these caching mechanisms. In this chapter, you learned how Oracle's caching mechanisms work when it comes to processing SQL and PL/SQL statements issued against the database, and why using bind variables can greatly increase the probability of shared pool cache hits. Also, you saw how global contexts can be used to boost performance by caching frequently used information in the memory of the database instance.

Another important topic discussed in this chapter is caching database data frequently accessed by the application on the web server. You learned that while using the PEAR::Cache_Lite package can help you build such a caching system on the web server side with a minimum of effort, with Oracle's database change notification feature you get the ability to keep the data cached on the web server up to date.

8

XML-Enabled Applications

Both PHP and Oracle provide comprehensive support for XML and XML-related technologies. Practically, this means you can perform any XML processing either with PHP or inside an Oracle database. While PHP allows you to construct and transform XML by using either PHP's XML extensions or PEAR XML packages, Oracle provides the Oracle XML DB, which has a wide set of XML features that can be used to efficiently store, retrieve, update, as well as transform XML data and generate it from relational data.

This chapter explains how to effectively use XML techniques and technologies available in PHP and Oracle when building XML-enabled PHP/Oracle applications. Specifically, you will see how to:

- Construct XML with the PHP DOM extension
- Navigate XML with XPath
- Transform XML with PHP XSL functions
- Generate XML from relational data with Oracle SQL/XML functions
- Store, retrieve, update, and transform XML with Oracle XML DB
- Validate XML documents against XML schemas
- Access XML stored in Oracle XML DB with standard internet protocols
- Query, construct, and transform XML with Oracle XQuery

Processing XML in PHP/Oracle Applications

As mentioned, there are two alternatives when it comes to performing XML processing in your PHP/Oracle application. You can perform any required XML processing using either PHP's XML extensions (or PEAR XML packages) or Oracle's XML features.

In the following sections, you will learn how to construct XML from relational data using the XML capabilities of both PHP and Oracle.

Processing XML Data with PHP

PHP provides three general extensions allowing you to work with XML. These extensions are listed in the following table:

PHP extension	Description
XML extension	The XML extension implements the SAX (Simple API for XML) approach to parsing and accessing XML content. The SAX parsing mechanism is memory efficient since it doesn't require the entire XML document to be stored in memory. This makes the SAX approach useful for certain type of operations on XML, for example, searching.
DOM extension	The DOM extension provides APIs for working with XML using DOM (Document Object Model). Unlike a SAX parser, a DOM parser builds an in-memory representation of an XML document, which in most cases makes performing modifying and updating operations more efficient.
SimpleXML extension	As its name implies, the SimpleXML extension provides the easiest way to work with XML. The SimpleXML approach allows you to access an XML document through its data structure representation and so can be especially useful when you simply need to read XML.

In practice, you should choose the extension that best suits the needs of your applications. For example, the XML extension implementing the SAX model can be very efficient when it comes to parsing large XML documents from which you only want to extract useful information. In contrast, the DOM extension comes in handy when you need to generate XML documents or modify existing ones. With the SimpleXML extension, XML documents are turned into data structures that can be then iterated like regular PHP arrays and objects, thus providing the most natural way for PHP developers to access data.

Since the Document Object Model (DOM) is best used for solving complex tasks, the following sections demonstrate how to use DOM extension APIs to generate, query, and manipulate XML documents in PHP.

Admittedly, the Document Object Model is widely used in web development. Web browsers, for example, use the DOM to represent web pages they display to the users. In Chapter 10 *AJAX-Based Applications*, you will learn techniques to access and manipulate the DOM tree of a web page sent to the browser by your application, thus allowing you to produce more interactive and responsive PHP/Oracle solutions.

Creating XML with the DOM PHP Extension

In fact, the PHP DOM extension is a set of classes that can be used to generate, access, and manipulate XML data. The DOM.php script defined in the following listing shows how to generate an XML document based on the result set retrieved from the database.

```php
<?php
//File: DOM.php
if(!$rsConnection = oci_connect('hr', 'hr', '//localhost/orcl')) {
    $err = oci_error();
    trigger_error('Could not establish a connection: ' .
                    $err['message'], E_USER_ERROR);
};
$dept_id = 90;
$query = "SELECT employee_id, last_name, salary FROM employees
                WHERE department_id = :deptid";
$stmt = oci_parse($rsConnection,$query);
oci_bind_by_name($stmt, ':deptid', $dept_id);
if (!oci_execute($stmt)) {
 $err = oci_error($stmt);
 trigger_error('Query failed: ' . $err['message'], E_USER_ERROR);
}
$dom = new DOMDocument('1.0', 'UTF-8');
$root = $dom->createElement('EMPLOYEES', '');
$root = $dom->appendChild($root);
while ($row = oci_fetch_assoc($stmt)) {
    $emp = $dom->createElement('EMPLOYEE', '');
    $emp = $root->appendChild($emp);
    $emp->setAttribute('id', $row['EMPLOYEE_ID']);
    $ename = $dom->createElement('ENAME', $row['LAST_NAME']);
    $ename = $emp->appendChild($ename);
    $salary = $dom->createElement('SALARY', $row['SALARY']);
    $salary = $emp->appendChild($salary);
}
echo $dom->saveXML();
$dom->save("employees.xml");
?>
```

To figure out what happens when you run the DOM.php script, let's take a closer look at this code.

You start by connecting to the database as hr/hr. Then, you define a query, which, when issued, retrieves some information about the employees working in the department whose ID is 90.

After the query is executed, you create a new DOM document that will be used to wrap the retrieved result set in XML format. You start generating a new DOM document by creating the root element and then appending it to the DOM tree.

In the next step you create the nodes of the DOM document based on the data retrieved from the database. For this, you fetch the data from the result set in a loop, creating the document structure.

In this example, you simply display the generated XML document using the saveXML method of the DOMDocument object and then save it to disk with the save method to the same folder where the script source file resides. However, in a real-world situation, you probably would continue processing this XML document, producing a result XML document that could then, for example, be sent to a web service or published as an RSS feed.

When you run the DOM.php script discussed here, you probably will see the following string in your browser:

```
King24000Kochhar17000De Haan17000
```

However, if you look at the source, you should see the following XML document:

```
<?xml version="1.0" encoding="UTF-8"?>
<EMPLOYEES>
 <EMPLOYEE id="100">
  <ENAME>King</ENAME>
  <SALARY>24000</SALARY>
 </EMPLOYEE>
 <EMPLOYEE id="101">
  <ENAME>Kochhar</ENAME>
  <SALARY>17000</SALARY>
 </EMPLOYEE>
 <EMPLOYEE id="102">
  <ENAME>De Haan</ENAME>
  <SALARY>17000</SALARY>
 </EMPLOYEE>
</EMPLOYEES>
```

After running the DOM.php script, the employees.xml file containing the document shown in the listing should appear in the folder where the script source file resides.

Querying a DOM Document with XPath

One way to access the DOM tree in a DOMDocument object is through an associated DOMXPath object. Identifying a specific node or nodes within the DOM tree of a DOMDocument object with this approach involves use of appropriate XPath expressions passed to the DOMXPath object as parameters.

 While the example in this section shows how XPath can be used in PHP, Oracle also has some SQL functions operating on XML, such as existsNode, extractValue, and updateXML, which take XPath-expression arguments.

The following script illustrates how to access XML content held in a DOMDocument object through the DOMXPath object associated with that DOMDocument.

```php
<?php
//File: XPath.php
$dom = new DomDocument();
$dom->load('employees.xml');
$xpath = new DOMXPath($dom);
$query = '//EMPLOYEE/SALARY[. > "15000"]';
$emps = $xpath->query($query);
print '<font face="Arial">';
print '<h3>Executive officers whose salaries > $15,000</h3>';
print '<table border="1" cellpadding="5">';
print '<th>Employee ID</th><th>Last Name</th><th>Salary</th>';
foreach ($emps as $emp) {
    print '<tr><td>'.$emp->parentNode->getAttribute('id').'</td>';
    print '<td>'.$emp->previousSibling->nodeValue.'</td>';
    print '<td>'.$emp->nodeValue.'</td></tr>';
}
print '</table>';
print '</font>';
?>
```

Unlike the preceding example where you generated an XML document from scratch, here you load it from a file, using the load method of the DOMDocument object. After the document is loaded, you create a new DOMXPath object, and associate it with the newly created DOMDocument object.

The XPath expression used in the above script is to be applied to the employees XML document loaded to DOMDocument object. You use this expression to identify all the SALARY nodes whose values exceed 15000, passing it to the DOMXPath's query method as the parameter.

 For more information on XPath, you can refer to the *W3C XML Path Language (XPath) Version 1.0 recommendation* at http://www.w3.org/TR/xpath.

To iterate over the result set returned by the query issued within the script, you use the foreach construct. Since each row of the result set represents a SALARY node defined within its parent EMPLOYEE node, you access that parent node using the parentNode method of the DOMNode object representing the SALARY node being processed. However, to access the corresponding ENAME node you use the previousSibling method of the DOMNode object.

If you run the XPath.php script discussed here, your browser should display an HTML table representing the list of employees whose salaries exceed 15,000.

Transforming and Processing XML with XSLT

In the preceding example, you transform XML into HTML directly in your script, wrapping the data extracted from the XML document into appropriate HTML tags. Alternatively, you might perform an XSL (Extensible Stylesheet Language) transformation to get the same general results.

However, before you can use the XSL extension you have to enable it in your PHP installation.

In UNIX, you have to recompile PHP with the following flag:

```
--with-xsl
```

In Windows, you have to uncomment the following line in the php.ini configuration file and then restart the Apache/PHP server:

```
extension=php_xsl.dll
```

Once you have enabled the XSL extension, you can use XSL functions to transform XML into HTML or another XML or a variety of other formats. The following figure depicts the general steps performed by a PHP/Oracle application that generates an HTML page with PHP, based on the result set retrieved from the database.

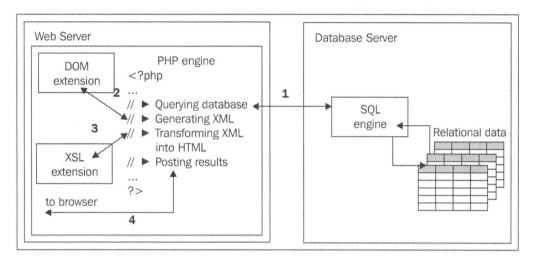

Here is the explanation of the steps in the above figure:

- The script queries the database to retrieve the data that will be used to construct an XML document.
- The script generates the XML document using the PHP DOM extension, based on the data retrieved in Step 1.
- The script transforms the XML document generated in step 2 into HTML format with the PHP XSL extension.
- The script posts the HTML page generated in step 3 to the user's browser.

As you can see, most of the XML processing work in the above scenario is performed by the PHP engine on the web server rather than on the database server. So, this may be efficient in cases where the database server becomes a performance bottleneck in your system.

Using this scenario, you might transform the employees XML document shown in the *Creating XML with the DOM PHP Extension* section into HTML so that the result page looks like the following figure:

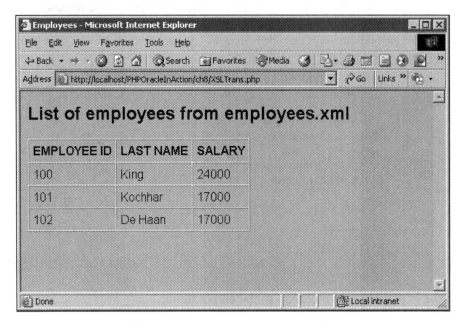

If you want to get the page shown in the above figure by applying an XSL transformation to the employees XML document, you first have to create an XSLT stylesheet describing the way the data is to be transformed.

The following `employees.xsl` stylesheet might be used to transform the employees XML document into HTML to get the page shown in the above figure.

```
<?xml version="1.0" encoding="utf-8" ?>
<xsl:stylesheet version="1.0" xmlns:xsl="http://www.w3.org/1999/XSL/
Transform">
    <xsl:template match="/">
     <html>
      <head>
        <title>Employees</title>
      </head>
       <body>
        <font face="Arial">
        <h2>List of employees from employees.xml</h2>
        <table border="1" cellspacing="0" cellpadding="5">
        <tr>
```

```
          <th><b>EMPLOYEE ID</b></th>
          <th><b>LAST NAME</b></th>
          <th><b>SALARY</b></th>
      </tr>
        <xsl:for-each select="EMPLOYEES">
        <xsl:for-each select="EMPLOYEE">
           <tr>
             <td><xsl:value-of select="@id"/></td>
             <td><xsl:value-of select="ENAME"/></td>
             <td><xsl:value-of select="SALARY"/></td>
           </tr>
          </xsl:for-each>
         </xsl:for-each>
        </table>
      </font>
    </body>
  </html>
 </xsl:template>
</xsl:stylesheet>
```

As you can see, the XSLT stylesheet shown in the listing is an XML document that contains elements and attributes defined in the XSLT namespace: `http://www.w3.org/1999/XSL/Transform`. Whereas the intent of these elements and attributes is to provide instructions to an XSLT processor, the HTML tags also presented in the stylesheet will be directly added to the resultant XML document.

While the `employees.xsl` stylesheet shown in the listing is designed to simply transform an employees XML document into HTML, you might create a more complicated stylesheet that would process XML data included in that XML document.

 It is interesting to note that XSLT is not limited to transforming XML data—it also can be used to process XML. Sometimes, performing the XML processing with XSLT may be much easier than using DOM operations to do the same job. For example, with XSLT, to calculate the total of all the orders included in the document, you don't need to write the code that will iterate over all the elements representing that orders, as you would with the DOM approach. Instead, you might use the `xsl:value-of select` element with the `sum` function in your stylesheet to get the job done.

Turning back to the `employees.xsl` stylesheet, suppose you want to add another column to the resultant HTML table, say, BONUS whose values are calculated based on the values from the SALARY column. In that case, the fragment of the stylesheet responsible for generating the HTML table might be modified as follows:

```
<table border="1" cellspacing="0" cellpadding="5">
<tr>
    <th><b>EMPLOYEE ID</b></th>
    <th><b>LAST NAME</b></th>
    <th><b>SALARY</b></th>
    <th><b>BONUS</b></th>
</tr>
  <xsl:for-each select="EMPLOYEES">
  <xsl:for-each select="EMPLOYEE">
      <tr>
        <td><xsl:value-of select="@id"/></td>
        <td><xsl:value-of select="ENAME"/></td>
        <td><xsl:value-of select="SALARY"/></td>
        <td><xsl:value-of select="SALARY*0.1"/></td>
      </tr>
    </xsl:for-each>
   </xsl:for-each>
   </table>
```

You might also want to calculate the average salary for the employees included in the employees XML document. To achieve this, you might further modify the `employees.xsl` stylesheet by adding the following XSLT construction immediately after the code shown above:

```
<p><b>Average salary is: </b><xsl:value-of
        select="format-number(sum(//SALARY) div
        count(//EMPLOYEE), '#######0.00')"/></p>
```

In this example, you sum the salaries of all employees included in the document with the `sum` function, and then divide the calculated sum by the number of employees obtained with the `count` function, thus getting the average salary formatted with the `format-number` function.

 For more examples of XSLT stylesheets, you can refer to the *W3C XSL Transformations (XSLT) Version 1.0 recommendation* available at `http://www.w3.org/TR/xslt`.

Now that you have a grasp on how to create XSLT stylesheets to be used for transforming and processing XML data, it's time to see an XSL transformation in action.

The following listing contains a simple PHP script that performs an XSL transformation, applying the employees.xsl XSLT stylesheet defined earlier in this section to the employees XML document shown in the *Creating XML with the DOM PHP Extension* section. It is assumed that the employees.xsl, employees.xml, and the XSLTrans.php files reside in the same directory.

```php
<?php
//File: XSLTrans.php
$domxsl = new DOMDocument();
$domxsl->load('employees.xsl');
$proc = new XSLTProcessor;
$xsl = $proc->importStylesheet($domxsl);
$domxml = new DOMDocument();
$domxml->load('employees.xml');
$rslt = $proc->transformToXml($domxml);
print $rslt;
?>
```

After you have created a new DOM document, you load the XSL stylesheet discussed earlier in this section into that document. Next, you create a new XSLTProcessor object that is then used to perform an XSL transformation. However, before you can do this, you need to import the stylesheet into the newly created XSLT processor, and you also need to create a new DOM document and then load the XML document to be transformed.

For simplicity, in this example you do not query the database, nor do you generate a new XML document from scratch with the DOM functions. Instead, you load the existing document employees.xml, which was generated and saved to disk during the execution of the DOM.php script discussed in the *Creating XML with the DOM PHP Extension* section earlier in this chapter.

The XSL transformation performed in the above script transforms the employees XML document into an HTML page that you then send to the user's browser.

When you run the XSLTrans.php script defined in the above listing, the result should be something like the previous figure.

Performing XML Processing inside the Database

When building XML-enabled applications on top of Oracle, there are many advantages to performing the XML processing inside the database when compared to performing it on the client. The key advantages to perform XML processing inside the database are as follows:

- Benefiting from the XML-specific memory optimizations provided by Oracle XML DB

- Eliminating overhead associated with parsing XML documents

- Reducing overhead associated with I/O disk operations and network traffic between the Web server and database server

Moving XML processing to the database may be especially useful if you are dealing with large XML documents stored in the database. In that case, your application won't need to transfer a large amount of data between the database and web server when processing XML inside the database—only the final product is sent across the wire.

Using Oracle SQL/XML Generation Functions

The simplest way to benefit from moving XML processing to the database is to use Oracle SQL/XML functions, which allow you to build SQL queries generating XML from relational data.

Turning back to the preceding sample, you might, for example, rewrite the query issued against the database so that it retrieves the generated employees XML document that is ready to be transformed into HTML with the PHP XSL extension functions.

Diagrammatically, this might look like the following figure:

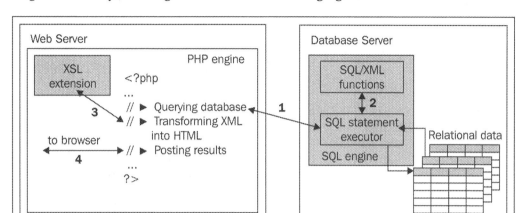

The explanation of the steps in the figure is the following:

- Step 1: The script issues the query containing SQL/XML functions so that it retrieves an XML document generated by the database server.

- Step 2: The database server generates the XML document, based on the query issued by the script in step 1.

- Step 3: The script transforms the XML document retrieved from the database into HTML format with the help of the PHP XSL extension functions.

- Step 4: The script posts the HTML page generated in step 3 to the user's browser.

In this scenario, you move some XML processing from the web server to the database server. In particular, the XML document is now generated on the database server with the help of the SQL/XML generation functions specified in the query, rather than generating that document on the web server with the PHP DOM extension functions as it was in the scenario depicted in the figure shown in the *Transforming and Processing XML with XSLT* section earlier in this chapter.

The following listing contains the SQLXMLQuery.php script that implements the above scenario. So, the script issues the query that makes Oracle generate the employees XML document, thus retrieving the employees XML document that is ready to be transformed with XSLT. The following script provides an example of using Oracle SQL/XML functions to generate XML from relational data. Using these functions lets you move the processing required to generate the employees XML document from the web server to the database server.

```php
<?php
  //File: SQLXMLQuery.php
  if(!$rsConnection = oci_connect('hr', 'hr', '//localhost/orcl')) {
      $err = oci_error();
      trigger_error('Could not establish a connection:
                                  '.$err['message'], E_USER_ERROR);
  };
  $dept_id = 90;
  $query = 'SELECT XMLELEMENT("EMPLOYEES",
              XMLAgg(
               XMLELEMENT("EMPLOYEE",
                XMLATTRIBUTES(employee_id AS "id"),
                XMLFOREST(last_name as "ENAME", salary as "SALARY"))))
              AS result
              FROM employees WHERE department_id=:deptid';
  $stmt = oci_parse($rsConnection,$query);
  oci_bind_by_name($stmt, ':deptid', $dept_id);
  if (!oci_execute($stmt)) {
   $err = oci_error($stmt);
   trigger_error('Query failed: '.$err['message'], E_USER_ERROR);
  }
  $xmlDoc = oci_fetch_assoc($stmt);
  $domxml = new DOMDocument();
  $domxml->loadXML($xmlDoc['RESULT']);
  $domxsl = new DOMDocument();
  $domxsl->load('employees.xsl');
  $proc = new XSLTProcessor;
  $xsl = $proc->importStylesheet($domxsl);
  $rslt = $proc->transformToXml($domxml);
  print $rslt;
?>
```

As you can see, the SQLXMLQuery.php script, unlike the DOM.php script discussed earlier in this chapter, does not use the PHP DOM functions to generate the employees XML document from scratch, based on the result set retrieved from the database. Instead, it issues a query that instructs the database server to generate that XML document. After executing the query, you fetch the result of the query and then load it to the newly created DOM document.

Next, you load the employees.xsl XSL stylesheet discussed in the *Transforming and Processing XML with XSLT* section earlier, assuming that this file resides in the same directory where you saved the SQLXMLQuery.php script discussed here.

Then, you create an XSLT processor, in which you import the employees.xsl stylesheet loaded into a DOM document. After performing the XSL transformation, you print the resultant HTML page.

When you run the `SQLXMLQuery.php` script, it should output a page that looks like the one shown in the figure in the *Transforming and Processing XML with XSLT* section.

Moving All the XML Processing into the Database

In the preceding example, the database server performs only a part of the XML processing while the rest is still performed by the PHP engine. Specifically, the database server generates an `employees` XML document based on the records from the `hr.employees` table, and the PHP script then transforms that document with XSLT into HTML format with the PHP XSL extension functions.

As an efficient alternative to PHP's XSLT processor, you might use Oracle's XSLT processor, thus benefiting from performing XSL transformations inside the database.

The following figure depicts the scenario where both generating XML and then transforming it into HTML take place inside the database.

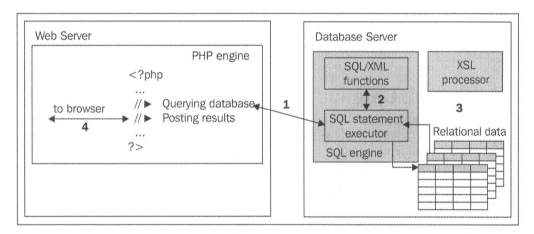

There are several advantages to performing XSLT transformations, as well as many other XML processing operations, inside the database. These advantages are outlined at the beginning of the *Performing XML Processing inside the Database* section earlier in this chapter.

The explanation of the steps in the figure is as follows:

- Step 1: The script issues the query containing SQL/XML functions so that it retrieves an HTML document generated by the database server.

- Step 2: The database server generates the XML document, based on the instructions in the query issued by the script in step 1.

- Step 3: The database server transforms the XML document into HTML with the XSL stylesheet specified in the query issued in step 1.

- Step 4: The script posts the HTML page retrieved from the database to the user's browser.

However, before you implement this scenario, you have to decide where to store the XSL stylesheet to be used for the XSL transformation. Obviously, retrieving the stylesheet from the web server before performing the transformation on the database server would be a bad idea in this case, since it would increase network overhead. In contrast, storing the stylesheet in the database would be the best solution for this situation.

When choosing the storage option for XSL stylesheets, you should bear in mind that an XSL stylesheet is in fact an XML document. So, it would be a good idea to choose one of the XML storage options available in Oracle database.

Storing XML Data in the Database

When using the database as a persistent storage for XML, you have several storage options. While all these options are discussed in the *Database Storage Options for XML Data in Oracle Database* section later in this chapter, this section provides a simple example of how you might store XML documents in an XMLType column in a database table as Character Large Object (CLOB) values. Once created, such a table can be used for storing different XML documents, including XSL stylesheets.

However, before creating this table you might want to create a new database schema. To create that schema and grant it all the required privileges, you might execute the SQL statements shown below:

```
CONN /as sysdba

CREATE USER xmlusr IDENTIFIED BY xmlusr;

GRANT connect, resource TO xmlusr;
```

Once the xmlusr schema is created and all the privileges required to work with it are granted, you can create the XSLTstylesheets table under this schema and populate it with the data. You might achieve this by issuing the SQL statements shown next:

```
CONN xmlusr/xmlusr

CREATE TABLE XSLTstylesheets (
    id NUMBER,
    stylesheet XMLType
);

INSERT INTO XSLTstylesheets VALUES (
 1,
 XMLType(
'<?xml version="1.0" encoding="utf-8" ?>
<xsl:stylesheet version="1.0" xmlns:xsl="http://www.w3.org/1999/XSL/
Transform">
    <xsl:template match="/">
     <html>
      <head>
        <title>Employees</title>
      </head>
       <body>
        <font face="Arial">
        <h2>List of employees from employees.xml</h2>
        <table border="1" cellspacing="0" cellpadding="5">
        <tr>
           <th><b>EMPLOYEE ID</b></th>
           <th><b>LAST NAME</b></th>
           <th><b>SALARY</b></th>
        </tr>
          <xsl:for-each select="EMPLOYEES">
          <xsl:for-each select="EMPLOYEE">
             <tr>
               <td><xsl:value-of select="@id"/></td>
               <td><xsl:value-of select="ENAME"/></td>
               <td><xsl:value-of select="SALARY"/></td>
             </tr>
           </xsl:for-each>
          </xsl:for-each>
         </table>
        </font>
       </body>
     </html>
    </xsl:template>
  </xsl:stylesheet>')
 );
COMMIT;
```

As you can see, inserting a new row into a table that contains an XMLType column is similar to inserting a new row into any other table—you use an INSERT statement and then issue the COMMIT to make the changes permanent. The only thing to notice here is that you have to explicitly convert the string representing an XML document to an XMLType value before inserting it to an XMLType column.

In this example, you insert only one row into the newly created XSLTstylesheets table. The stylesheet column of XMLType in this row includes the employees XSL stylesheet discussed in the *Transforming and Processing XML with XSLT* section earlier in this chapter. Once you have stored this stylesheet in the XSLTstylesheets table, you can access it with a SELECT statement when connected as xmlusr/xmlusr.

However, before you can move on to a script that will implement the scenario depicted in the figure shown in the *Moving All the XML Processing into the Database* section earlier in this chapter, you need to grant the SELECT privilege on the hr.employees table to the xmlusr database schema. This can be done by issuing the following statements from SQL*Plus:

```
CONN /as sysdba

GRANT SELECT ON hr.employees TO xmlusr;
```

By granting the SELECT privilege on the hr.employees table to xmlusr you permit the applications that will connect to the database through this schema to access data stored in the table.

Performing XSLT Transformations inside the Database

Now that you have the employees XSL stylesheet stored in the database and the xmlusr schema is permitted to access the hr.employees table, you can create a script that will instruct the database to build an HTML page based on the data stored in hr.employees.

The following listing contains the source code for such a script.

```php
<?php
  //File: DBServerXSLTrans.php
  if(!$rsConnection = oci_connect('xmlusr', 'xmlusr',
                              '//localhost/orcl')) {
      $err = oci_error();
      trigger_error('Could not establish a connection:
                      '.$err['message'], E_USER_ERROR);
  };
  $dept_id = 90;
  $query = 'SELECT XMLtransform(x.xmlcol,
```

```
   (SELECT stylesheet FROM XSLTstylesheets WHERE
     id = 1)).getStringVal()
   AS result FROM
   (SELECT XMLELEMENT("EMPLOYEES",
             XMLAgg(
               XMLELEMENT("EMPLOYEE",
                XMLATTRIBUTES(employee_id AS "id"),
                XMLFOREST(last_name AS "ENAME", salary AS "SALARY")
                )
                )
             ) AS xmlcol
   FROM  hr.employees WHERE department_id=:deptid) x';
   $stmt = oci_parse($rsConnection,$query);
   oci_bind_by_name($stmt, ':deptid', $dept_id);
   if (!oci_execute($stmt)) {
    $err = oci_error($stmt);
    trigger_error('Query failed: '.$err['message'], E_USER_ERROR);
   }
   $xmlDoc = oci_fetch_assoc($stmt);
   $dom = new DOMDocument();
   $dom->loadXML($xmlDoc['RESULT']);
   echo $dom->saveXML();
 ?>
```

As you can see, the select list of the SELECT statement used in the
DBServerXSLTrans.php script includes the XMLtransform SQL/XML function.
This function is used here to apply the employees XSL stylesheet retrieved from
the XSLTstylesheets table by the subquery to the employees XML document
generated by the subquery defined in the FROM clause of the query. The result of this
transformation should be an HTML page, which you load into a new DOMDocument
object and then display it in the browser. When displayed, the generated HTML page
should look like the figure shown in the *Transforming and Processing XML with XSLT*
section shown earlier in this chapter.

Building PHP Applications on Oracle XML DB

The preceding example shows how you might move the XML processing performed
by your PHP/Oracle application from PHP to Oracle, thus taking advantage of the
optimizations provided by the Oracle database server. In particular, you saw how to
generate an XML document from scratch and apply an XSL transformation inside the
database, rather than performing these operations with PHP.

In fact, Oracle XML Database provides much more functionality than what the sample demonstrates.

 Oracle XML DB refers to the set of Oracle Database XML technologies integrated with the relational database server, providing high-performance XML storage, retrieval, and processing.

The most significant features of Oracle XML DB, which make Oracle database ideal for XML-enabled database-driven applications, are listed below:

- Ability to store, retrieve, update, and transform XML data through the SQL and PL/SQL interfaces.
- Ability to perform XML operations on SQL data without physically migrating it into XML format.
- Oracle XML DB repository lets you manipulate XML content stored in the database with the standard Internet protocols, such as FTP, HTTP, and WebDAV.
- Support for the Worldwide Web Consortium (W3C) XML Schema Recommendation: `http://www.w3.org/TR/xmlschema-0/`, allowing you to validate XML documents against appropriate XML schemas registered in the database.
- XML-specific optimizations, reducing the cost of performing XML processing inside the database.

The subsections that follow show how you can make use of these features when building XML-enabled PHP/Oracle applications.

Using Oracle Database for Storing, Modifying, and Retrieving XML Data

With Oracle XML DB, you have various XML storage and XML processing options allowing you to achieve the required level of performance and scalability. One of the most interesting things about Oracle XML DB is that it allows you to perform SQL operations on XML data as well as XML operations on relational data, thus bridging the gap between the SQL and XML worlds.

Database Storage Options for XML Data in Oracle Database

When storing XML in Oracle database, you can choose between several storage options. The general XML storage options available in Oracle database are outlined in the following table:

XML storage option	Description
XMLType CLOB	Storing an XML document as a CLOB is a good idea if this document will be normally retrieved as a whole and updated by rewriting the entire document, rather than by performing piece-wise updates.
Native XMLType (Structured storage)	With structured storage, an XML document must conform to a certain XML schema and is stored in the database as a set of SQL objects, which provides excellent DML performance in most situations.
XMLType views	Using XMLType views lets you operate on XML data created on top of relational data, thus allowing you to construct XML representations of that data.

The following figure will help you understand better the ideas behind the storage methods outlined in the table.

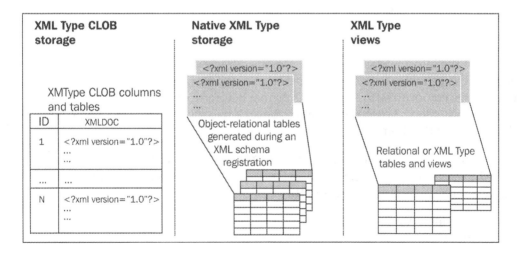

As you can see from the previous figure, when using CLOB storage for XMLType data, an XML document is stored in an XMLType column or table as a complete text document. Hence, updating an XML document stored as an XMLType CLOB is a very expensive operation that involves DOM parsing the document, performing the update operation on the DOM representation of the document, serializing the updated document back into text, and finally replacing it. Storing XML in CLOBs can be efficient when, for example, you're dealing with large XML documents, which are not updated frequently, and which you are going to retrieve as a whole.

In the preceding sample, you use XMLType CLOB storage for the employees XSL stylesheet, storing it in the `stylesheet` XMLType column of the `XSLTstylesheets` table, as discussed in the *Storing XML Data in the Database* section earlier. The XMLType CLOB storage is the best choice in that example because the only operation you are supposed to perform on the employees XSL stylesheet frequently is retrieving it as a whole when it comes to transforming an employees XML document into HTML.

In contrast, native XMLType storage, also known as structured or shredded storage, can be very efficient when you perform update operations on XML data frequently. This type of storage is created automatically by Oracle when registering an XML schema against the database.

 XML schemas are discussed in the *Using XML Schemas* subsection later in this section.

Based on the information in an XML schema, Oracle creates a set of SQL object types and XMLType tables to be used for managing and storing the contents of XML documents conforming to that XML schema. Before storing, a document is broken up, and its contents are stored as an instance of the appropriate object type generated during the XML schema registration process.

This approach makes it possible for Oracle XML DB to rewrite SQL statements issued to access or manipulate XML schema-based XML data to purely relational SQL statements, thus allowing for efficient processing of XML data.

XMLType views can be useful when you need to wrap existing relational data in XML format without physically migrating it into XML. In fact, you can define an XMLType view not only on relational tables and views but also on XMLType ones. For examples on using XMLType views, see the *Using XMLType Views* section later in this chapter.

As you can see, all the XML storage options presented in the table are based on XMLType. The following section discusses this native Oracle datatype in detail.

Using XMLType for Handling XML Data in the Database

Being an object type, XMLType can not only be used to store XML data in the database but also to operate on that data via its built-in methods. Regardless of the storage model you choose, XMLType provides a set of XML-specific methods to operate on XMLType instances.

The most commonly used methods of XMLType are listed in the following table:

XMLType method	Description
existsNode	Checks whether the XML document in a given XMLType instance contains a node that matches the XPath expression passed as the parameter. If the specified node is found, it returns 1; otherwise, it returns 0.
extract	Extracts a node or nodes from the XML document in an XMLType instance, based on the XPath expression passed as the parameter. Returns the result nodes as an XMLType instance.
createSchemaBasedXML	Explicitly associates an XML document in an XMLType instance with a registered XML schema specified in the parameter. You might want to perform this operation when inserting an XML document into an XML schema-based XMLType column or table.
schemaValidate	Validates an XML document in an XMLType instance against an XML schema specified in the parameter. On success, the status of the document is changed to VALIDATED; otherwise, an error is raised.
transform	Transforms an XML document in an XMLType instance with the XSL stylesheet specified in the parameter. Returns the resultant document as an XMLType instance.

You saw an example of using an XMLType method in the preceding sample application. In particular, in the DBServerXSLTrans.php script discussed in the *Performing XSLT Transformations inside the Database* section you use the getStringVal method of XMLType to retrieve the generated XHTML data as a VARCHAR value, so that it can then be loaded in a DOMDocument instance. If you recall, the query used in the DBServerXSLTrans.php script looks as follows:

```
$query = 'SELECT XMLtransform(x.xmlcol,
(SELECT stylesheet FROM XSLTstylesheets WHERE
    id = 1)).getStringVal()
AS result FROM
(SELECT XMLELEMENT("EMPLOYEES",
        XMLAgg(
```

```
                 XMLELEMENT("EMPLOYEE",
                  XMLATTRIBUTES(employee_id AS "id"),
                  XMLFOREST(last_name AS "ENAME", salary AS "SALARY")
                  )
                 )
               ) AS xmlcol
       FROM  hr.employees WHERE department_id=:deptid) x';
```

To see another XMLType method in action, namely `transform`, you might rewrite the above SQL statement as follows:

```
   $query = 'SELECT x.xmlcol.transform((SELECT stylesheet FROM
               XSLTstylesheets WHERE id = 1)).getStringVal()
   AS result FROM
   (SELECT XMLELEMENT("EMPLOYEES",
               XMLAgg(
                 XMLELEMENT("EMPLOYEE",
                  XMLATTRIBUTES(employee_id AS "id"),
                  XMLFOREST(last_name AS "ENAME", salary AS "SALARY")
                  )
                 )
               ) AS xmlcol
       FROM  hr.employees WHERE department_id=:deptid) x';
```

In the above query, you use the `transform` XMLType method as an alternative to the `XMLtransform` SQL function used in the original query. Since both `transform` and `XMLtransform` have the same functionality, the above queries will produce the same general result.

> `XMLtransform` is not the only example of an SQL function providing the same functionality as the appropriate XMLType method. In fact, Oracle XML DB provides analogous SQL functions for many XMLType methods. For example, XMLType methods `extract` and `existsNode` can be used instead of the SQL functions having the same names.

As you can see, the above queries operate on relational data, and transform it into XML format with SQL/XML generation functions. Before looking at the approaches you can take to retrieve XML data stored in the database natively, however, it would be a good idea to look at how you can create an XMLType storage in Oracle XML DB. The following section discusses how you can do this with the help of the XML Schema feature.

Using XML Schemas

The simplest way to create an XMLType storage structure in Oracle XML DB is by registering an appropriate XML schema against the database. As a part of the registration process, Oracle automatically creates the storage for a particular set of XML documents, based on the information provided by the schema.

 An XML schema can be thought of as the metadata describing a certain class of XML documents. So, an XML document conforming to a particular XML schema can be considered as an instance of this XML schema.

You might want to use an XML schema for:

- Building the storage for XML documents conforming the schema
- Setting up business rules on XML content of conforming documents
- Validating XML documents conforming to the schema

However, before you can use an XML schema, you have to create and then register it against the database. Both these tasks can be accomplished in one step with the registerschema procedure from the DBMS_XMLSCHEMA PL/SQL package. For example, to register an XML schema to which the following employee XML document conforms:

```
<EMPLOYEE id="100">
  <ENAME>King</ENAME>
  <SALARY>24000</SALARY>
</EMPLOYEE>
```

You might issue the following statements:

```
CONN /as sysdba

GRANT ALTER SESSION TO xmlusr;

CONN xmlusr/xmlusr

BEGIN
 DBMS_XMLSCHEMA.registerschema(
  'employee.xsd',
  '<xs:schema
           xmlns:xs="http://www.w3.org/2001/XMLSchema"
           xmlns:xdb="http://xmlns.oracle.com/xdb">
    <xs:element name="EMPLOYEE" type="EMPLOYEE_TYP"
           xdb:defaultTable="EMPLOYEES"
           xdb:columnProps=
```

```
                     "CONSTRAINT emp_pkey PRIMARY KEY (XMLDATA.empno)"/>
         <xs:complexType name="EMPLOYEE_TYP" xdb:SQLType="EMPLOYEE_T">
          <xs:sequence>
           <xs:element name="ENAME" type="xs:string" xdb:SQLName="ENAME"
                       xdb:SQLType="VARCHAR2"/>
           <xs:element name="SALARY" type="xs:double" xdb:SQLName="SALARY"
                       xdb:SQLType="NUMBER"/>
          </xs:sequence>
          <xs:attribute name="id" type="xs:positiveInteger"
                        xdb:SQLName="EMPNO"
                        xdb:SQLType="NUMBER"/>
         </xs:complexType>
        </xs:schema>',
        TRUE,
        TRUE,
        FALSE,
        TRUE
       );
      END;
      /
```

As you can see, the DBMS_XMLSCHEMA.registerschema procedure takes two arguments. The first one is the string representing the name under which you want to register the schema against the database, and the other one is the document containing the schema itself.

In this example, the root element of the XML schema includes two namespace declarations, namely the XML schema namespace declaration and Oracle XML DB namespace declaration. To denote these namespaces, you use prefixes: xs and xdb respectively.

By including the XML schema namespace declaration, you obtain the ability to use the elements and attributes defined in this namespace, as well as the data types defined by the XML Schema language. For example, in the above example you specify the positiveInteger XML Schema language data type for the id attribute of the EMPLOYEE element.

The Oracle XML DB namespace lets you use annotations in the schema. For example, you use the xdb:defaultTable annotation to tell Oracle to use the specified table name when generating an XMLType table that will be used for storing XML documents conforming to the schema, rather than using a system-generated name for that table. In this particular example, you specify EMPLOYEES as the name for this table.

Another interesting annotation used in this XML schema is the xdb:columnProps. In this example, you use this annotation to define a primary key on the EMPLOYEE element's id attribute mapped to the EMPNO attribute of the EMPLOYEE_T SQL object type.

By including the xdb:SQLName annotation you make sure that the name of the generated SQL object type will be EMPLOYEE_T.

Finally, note the use of the flags passed to the DBMS_XMLSCHEMA.registerschema procedure:

```
TRUE,
TRUE,
FALSE,
TRUE
```

The above flags indicate the following (in the same order as they appear in the listing):

- The schema is generated as local (visible only to the database user who created it)
- Appropriate SQL object types are generated
- Java beans are *not* generated
- Default tables are generated

After registering the schema, you might want to look at the database object generated during the registration. The following listing contains the SQL statements that you might issue from SQL*Plus to make sure that Oracle generated the objects annotated in the schema. For convenience, the listing also contains the output produced.

```
DESC employee_t

  employee_t is NOT FINAL
  Name                                    Null?    Type
  ---------------------------------------- -------- ------------------
  --
  SYS_XDBPD$                                        XDB.XDB$RAW_LIST_T
  EMPNO                                             NUMBER(38)
  ENAME                                             VARCHAR2(4000
CHAR)
  SALARY                                            NUMBER
DESC employees

  Name                                    Null?    Type
  ---------------------------------------- -------- ------------------
```

```
TABLE of
    SYS.XMLTYPE(
      XMLSchema "employee.xsd"
      Element "EMPLOYEE")
    STORAGE Object-relational TYPE "EMPLOYEE_T"
```

As you can see, Oracle generated the `employee_t` object type and `employees` XMLType table based on this object type, as a part of the XML schema registration process. Note that the names of the generated objects have been defined in the schema. If you recall, you set the value of the `xdb:SQLName` attribute of global element EMPLOYEE to EMPLOYEE_T, and the `xdb:defaultTable` attribute to EMPLOYEES.

 It's interesting to note that the names of database objects generated during the XML schema registration process are case sensitive. However, since SQL is case insensitive, you can refer to these objects in SQL disregarding the case of their names. The names of XML elements and attributes specified in an XML schema are also case sensitive. However, unlike SQL, XML is case-sensitive, which means you must refer to XML elements and attributes in XML code using the case with which they were defined in the XML schema.

Now that you have defined the XMLType storage for employee XML documents, you might want to load some data into the `employees` XML schema-based XMLType table generated during the schema registration. The simplest way to do this is to use the INSERT SQL statement, as follows:

```
CONN xmlusr/xmlusr

INSERT INTO employees VALUES(
 XMLType(
  '<EMPLOYEE id="100">
    <ENAME>King</ENAME>
    <SALARY>24000</SALARY>
   </EMPLOYEE>'
  ).createSchemaBasedXML('employee.xsd')
 );

COMMIT;
```

In the above example, you use the `createSchemaBasedXML` method of XMLType to explicitly identify the `employee` XML schema when inserting a new row into the `employees` table.

Now, if you try to issue the INSERT statement shown in the listing again, you will receive the following error message:

```
ERROR at line 1:
ORA-00001: unique constraint (XMLUSR.EMP_PKEY) violated
```

As you can see, an attempt to insert the same row into the employees table fails due to a EMP_PKEY primary key constraint violation. If you recall, you define the EMP_PKEY primary key on the id attribute of the EMPLOYEE element in the XML schema registered as discussed in this section earlier. This constraint makes it impossible to insert two employee XML documents with the same ID into the employees table.

 Another way to load data into the employees table is via one of the internet protocols supported by Oracle XML DB. This mechanism is discussed in the *Taking Advantage of Standard Internet Protocols* section later in this chapter.

Finally, it's worth noting that you can always delete a registered XML schema along with all the database objects generated during its registration. For example, to delete the employee XML schema registered as discussed earlier in this section, you might issue the following PL/SQL block:

```
CONN xmlusr/xmlusr

BEGIN
  DBMS_XMLSCHEMA.deleteSchema(
  SCHEMAURL => 'employee.xsd',
  DELETE_OPTION => dbms_xmlschema.DELETE_CASCADE_FORCE);
END;
/
```

 Since the employees table is used in the subsequent examples, make sure to register the employee XML schema again as discussed earlier in this section. Also make sure to insert a row into the table as shown earlier in this section.

Besides deleting the employee XML schema, the above code deletes the employee_t object type and employees XMLType table generated during the schema registration process.

For more information on using XML schemas in Oracle XML DB, you can refer to Oracle documentation: chapters: *XML Schema Storage and Query: Basic* and *XML Schema Storage and Query: Advanced* in the *Oracle XML DB Developer's Guide*. Also, for information on XML Schema language, you can refer to the *W3C XML Schema Recommendation* at `http://www.w3.org/TR/xmlschema-0/`.

Retrieving XML Data

To retrieve XML data from an XMLType table, you can use a SELECT SQL statement, just as you would if you had to query a relational table. For example, to select the employee with the id set to 100 from the employees XMLType table discussed in the preceding section, you might issue the following query from SQL*Plus when connected as xmlusr/xmlusr:

```
SELECT * FROM employees x WHERE existsNode(value(x),
                            '/EMPLOYEE/@id="100"') = 1;
```

This query should produce the following output:

```
SYS_NC_ROWINFO$
-----------------------
<EMPLOYEE id="100">
  <ENAME>King</ENAME>
  <SALARY>24000</SALARY>
</EMPLOYEE>
```

The QueryXML.php script defined below shows how the above query might be issued from PHP.

```php
<?php
//File: QueryXML.php
if(!$rsConnection = oci_connect('xmlusr', 'xmlusr',
                            '//localhost/orcl')) {
    $err = oci_error();
    trigger_error('Could not establish a connection:
                '.$err['message'], E_USER_ERROR);
};
$xpath_exp = '/EMPLOYEE/@id="100"';
$query = 'SELECT value(x).GetStringVal() as RESULT
        FROM employees x
        WHERE existsNode(value(x), :xpath) = 1';
$stmt = oci_parse($rsConnection,$query);
oci_bind_by_name($stmt, ":xpath", $xpath_exp);
if (!oci_execute($stmt)) {
```

```
    $err = oci_error($stmt);
    trigger_error('Query failed: '.$err['message'], E_USER_ERROR);
    }
    $xmlDoc = oci_fetch_assoc($stmt);
    $dom = new DOMDocument();
    $dom->loadXML($xmlDoc['RESULT']);
    print $dom->saveXML();
?>
```

In the above script, you set the $xpath_exp variable to the XPath expression that points to the EMPLOYEE node whose id attribute is set to 100. This variable is then bound to the :xpath placeholder.

Note the use of the value(x) pseudocolumn in the select list of the query. In this example, value(x) is used to access the XMLType object representing an employee XML document retrieved by the query. You use the GetStringVal XMLType method to convert the retrieved XML document into a string, so that it can be loaded into a DOMDocument.

When you run the QueryXML.php script shown in the listing, it should produce the following output:

```
<?xml version="1.0" ?>
<EMPLOYEE id="100">
 <ENAME>King</ENAME>
 <SALARY>24000</SALARY>
</EMPLOYEE>
```

If your browser omits XML tags, though, you will see the following:

```
King    2400
```

While the existsNode SQL function used in the preceding example checks for the existence of elements based on the XPath expression, the extractValue SQL function lets you extract the value of a node or attribute conforming to the specified XPath expression. So, the extractValue SQL function lets you access XML data, receiving results similar to those received when querying relational data.

The following figure illustrates this point diagrammatically.

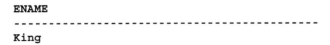

The following query is a simple example of extractValue in action:

```
SELECT extractValue(OBJECT_VALUE, '/EMPLOYEE/ENAME')
  ENAME FROM employees WHERE existsNode(OBJECT_VALUE,
  '/EMPLOYEE/@id="100"') = 1;
```

As you can see, the query extracts the value of the ENAME node under the EMPLOYEE node whose id attribute is set to 100. Note the use of the OBJECT_VALUE pseudocolumn in the query. This pseudocolumn is an Oracle Database 10g alternative to value(x). In this query, you use OBJECT_VALUE to access an employee XMLType object retrieved from the employees table.

When issued from SQL*Plus, the above query should return the following result:

```
ENAME
-------------------------------------------
King
```

You might rewrite the query to use the extract and existsNode XMLType methods as follows:

```
SELECT x.OBJECT_VALUE.extract('/EMPLOYEE/ENAME/text()').getStringVal()
  ENAME FROM employees x
  WHERE x.OBJECT_VALUE.existsNode('/EMPLOYEE/@id="100"')=1;
```

To test this query with PHP, you might write the `extractXML.php` script shown below:

```php
<?php
 //File: extractXML.php
 if(!$rsConnection = oci_connect('xmlusr', 'xmlusr',
                                 '//localhost/orcl')) {
     $err = oci_error();
     trigger_error('Could not establish a connection:
                   '.$err['message'], E_USER_ERROR);
 };
 $id = 100;
 $exist_exp = '/EMPLOYEE/@id='.$id;
 $extr_exp = '/EMPLOYEE/ENAME/text()';
 $query = 'SELECT x.OBJECT_VALUE.extract(:extr).getStringVal() ENAME
           FROM employees x
           WHERE x.OBJECT_VALUE.existsNode(:exist)=1';
 $stmt = oci_parse($rsConnection,$query);
 oci_bind_by_name($stmt, ":extr", $extr_exp);
 oci_bind_by_name($stmt, ":exist", $exist_exp);
 if (!oci_execute($stmt)) {
  $err = oci_error($stmt);
  trigger_error('Query failed: '.$err['message'], E_USER_ERROR);
 }
 $xmlDoc = oci_fetch_assoc($stmt);
 print '<h2>The name of employee whose id='.$id.' is:</h2>';
 print $xmlDoc['ENAME'];
?>
```

The query used in the script represents a simple example of using the `extractValue` SQL function. Usually, `extractValue` is used in complex SQL statements in which the data extracted from XML is then used in INSERT or UPDATE operations performed on relational tables.

Accessing Relational Data Through XMLType Views

Using relational tables to store shredded XML documents allows you to take advantage of both the Oracle XML technologies and Oracle database relational technologies when developing XML-enabled applications.

For example, you can easily implement fine-grained access when working with XML content built upon relational data. In Chapter 9 *Web Services*, you will see an example of how to secure XML data, based on the row-level security implemented on the relational data upon which that XML data is built.

In the preceding sections, you saw several examples of how to construct XML from SQL data with the help of SQL/XML generation functions. In the following sections, you will learn how to simplify the development of XML-enabled PHP/Oracle applications with XMLType views built upon relational tables.

Using XMLType Views

XMLType views provide a convenient way to construct XML representations of relational data without physically migrating that data into XML. Once written, an XMLType view may be used in various queries, making them simpler and so increasing their readability.

Turning back to the SELECT statement used in the SQLXMLQuery.php script discussed in the *Using Oracle SQL/XML Generation Functions* section earlier in this chapter, you might create an XMLType view based on that statement as shown below.

```
CONN /as sysdba
GRANT CREATE ANY VIEW TO xmlusr;
CONN xmlusr/xmlusr;
CREATE VIEW EmpsXML AS
  SELECT XMLELEMENT("EMPLOYEES",
            XMLAgg(
             XMLELEMENT("EMPLOYEE",
              XMLATTRIBUTES(employee_id AS "id"),
              XMLFOREST(last_name AS "ENAME", salary AS "SALARY")
             )
            )
           ) AS xmlcol,
        department_id AS dept_id
  FROM hr.employees GROUP BY department_id;
```

In this example, you start by granting the CREATE VIEW privilege to the xmlusr database schema and then, when connected as xmlusr/xmlusr, create the EmpsXML view based on the query that uses SQL/XML functions to generate XML from the data stored in the hr.employees relational table.

The good thing about the `EmpsXML` view is that it hides the details of generating an `employees` XML document, thus letting you write simpler and more readable queries. With it, the query used in the `SQLXMLQuery.php` script might be rewritten as follows:

```
$query = 'SELECT xmlcol as RESULT FROM EmpsXML WHERE
                                    dept_id=:deptid';
```

Before running the updated `SQLXMLQuery.php` script, make sure to specify the `xmlusr/xmlusr` schema in the `oci_connect` function at the beginning of the script as follows:

```
$rsConnection = oci_connect('xmlusr', 'xmlusr', '//localhost/orcl'))
```

Also, you might rewrite the query string used in the `DBServerXSLTrans.php` script discussed in the *Performing XSLT Transformations inside the Database* section earlier in this chapter as follows:

```
$query = 'SELECT XMLtransform(x.xmlcol,
(SELECT stylesheet FROM XSLTstylesheets
 WHERE id = 1)).getStringVal()
AS result FROM
(SELECT * FROM EmpsXML WHERE dept_id=:deptid) x';
```

As you can see, the above query is three times smaller than the one originally used in the `DBServerXSLTrans.php` script.

Creating XML Schema-Based XMLType Views

While the *Using XML Schemas* section earlier in this chapter focuses on how the XML Schema feature of Oracle XML DB can be used to create an XML schema-based storage structure, this section discusses how XML schema functionality might be used when working with existing relational data, without having to change the physical structure of that data.

 Creating an XML schema-based XMLType view is the most common way to take advantage of XML schema functionality when dealing with data stored relationally.

However, before you create an XML schema-based XMLType view, you must have the appropriate XML schema created and registered against the database. By executing the statement shown overleaf, you create and register the `emp.xsd` XML schema on which you will then create an XMLType view.

```
CONN xmlusr/xmlusr
BEGIN
 DBMS_XMLSCHEMA.registerschema(
  'emp.xsd',
  '<xs:schema
               xmlns:xs="http://www.w3.org/2001/XMLSchema"
               xmlns:xdb="http://xmlns.oracle.com/xdb">
   <xs:element name="EMPLOYEE" type="EMP_TYP"/>
   <xs:complexType name="EMP_TYP" xdb:SQLType="EMP_T"
                   xdb:maintainDOM="false">
    <xs:sequence>
     <xs:element name="ENAME" type ="enameType" xdb:SQLName="ENAME"
                 xdb:SQLType="VARCHAR2"/>
     <xs:element name="SALARY" type ="salaryType" xdb:SQLName="SALARY"
                 xdb:SQLType="NUMBER"/>
    </xs:sequence>
    <xs:attribute name="id" type="xs:positiveInteger"
                  xdb:SQLName="EMPNO"
                  xdb:SQLType="NUMBER"/>
   </xs:complexType>
   <xs:simpleType name="salaryType">
    <xs:restriction base="xs:double">
      <xs:maxExclusive value="100000"/>
    </xs:restriction>
   </xs:simpleType>
   <xs:simpleType name="enameType">
     <xs:restriction base="xs:string">
       <xs:minLength value="2"/>
       <xs:maxLength value="30"/>
     </xs:restriction>
   </xs:simpleType>
  </xs:schema>',
  TRUE,
  TRUE,
  FALSE,
  FALSE
 );
END;
/
```

As you can see from the listing, the EMPLOYEE element, which is the root element of the employee XML document described by this schema, is mapped to the EMP_T SQL object type. This object type will be automatically generated during schema registration as long as you set the DBMS_XMLSCHEMA.registerschema's fourth parameter, which is actually called GENTYPES, to TRUE.

At the same time, you set the sixth (GENTABLES) parameter to FALSE, thus instructing Oracle not to create any tables during schema registration. This makes sense in this case because you are going to map between this XML schema and an existing relational table later, with the help of an XMLType view.

After the PL/SQL block shown in the listing has been successfully executed, you might issue the DESC SQL command in order to make sure that the EMP_T object type was generated:

```
DESC EMP_T
```

This should return the following result:

```
EMP_T is NOT FINAL
  Name                                        Null?    Type
  ------------------------------------------- -------- -----------------
  --
   EMPNO                                                NUMBER(38)
   ENAME                                                VARCHAR2(4000
  CHAR)
   SALARY                                               NUMBER
```

Since DOM fidelity is not required when it comes to wrapping relational data in XML, you set the attribute maintainDOM to FALSE. As a result, the EMP_T type, unlike the EMPLOYEE_T type created as discussed in the *Using XML Schemas* section earlier, doesn't contain the SYS_XDBPD$ attribute.

The XML schema defined in the listing contains an example of how to add a constraint to an element described in the schema, restricting its content to values matching a set of conditions. In particular, you restrict the value of node SALARY in all employee XML documents conforming to the schema to be less than 100 000. To achieve this, you use a maxExclusive element under the restriction element defined in turn under the simpleType element for the SALARY element.

The following listing shows how to set up an XML schema-based XMLType view based on the hr.employees relational table. The view created here conforms to the employee XML schema created as discussed at the beginning of this section.

```
CONN xmlusr/xmlusr
CREATE TABLE emps
AS SELECT employee_id, last_name, salary FROM hr.employees;
ALTER TABLE emps
ADD constraint EMP_PRIMARYKEY
PRIMARY KEY (employee_id);
CREATE OR REPLACE VIEW empSch_v OF XMLType
  XMLSCHEMA "emp.xsd" ELEMENT "EMPLOYEE"
```

```
   WITH OBJECT ID (extract(OBJECT_VALUE, '/EMPLOYEE/@id/text()').
getNumberVal()) AS
 SELECT EMP_T(e.employee_id, e.last_name, e.salary)
 FROM emps e;
```

In the above listing, you start by creating relational table emps based on the hr.employees table. For simplicity, you include only three columns in the newly created table, while loading all the rows from hr.employees.

By specifying employee.xsd in the XMLSCHEMA clause and EMPLOYEE in the ELEMENT clause of the CREATE VIEW statement, you constrain a resultant row object in the view to be an instance of the element EMPLOYEE defined in the emp.xsd XML schema.

Since row objects in the empSch_v XMLType object view are synthesized from relational data, you must explicitly choose a set of unique identifiers to be used as object identifiers. In this example, in the WITH clause you specify the id attribute of the EMPLOYEE element as the object identifier because it is unique within the view row objects.

In the select list of the view, you explicitly convert the data retrieved from the relational table emps to the EMP_T SQL object type specified for the EMPLOYEE element in the emp.xsd XML schema.

Performing DML Operations on XML Schema-Based XMLType Views

Analyzing the underlying query of the empSch_v view discussed in the preceding section, you may note that each attribute of the EMP_T object used in the select list maps to a certain column of a single table, namely emps. What this means in practice is that the empSch_v view can be inherently updated, so you can perform DML operations against it without having to write INSTEAD-OF triggers.

The following figure gives a conceptual depiction of what occurs upon insertion of an XML document into an inherently updatable XML schema-based XMLType view.

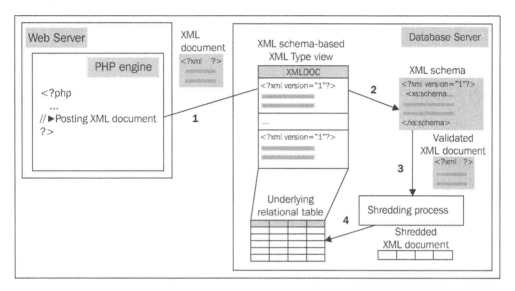

Here is the explanation of the steps outlined in the previous figure:

- Step 1: PHP script posts a schema-based XML document to be inserted into an XML schema-based XMLType view.
- Step 2: Oracle checks whether the XML document being inserted into the view conforms to the XML schema on which the view is defined.
- Step 3: If the document conforms to the schema, it is shredded into relational data conforming to the underlying relational table.
- Step 4: The shredded XML document is inserted into the underlying relational table, as a new row.

Turning back to the empSch_v view, you might issue the following INSERT statement against it from SQL*Plus in order to make sure that the view actually allows you to perform INSERT operations on it:

```
INSERT INTO empSch_v VALUES(XMLType(
   '<EMPLOYEE
   xmlns:xsi="http://www.w3.org/2001/XMLSchema-instance"
   xsi:noNamespaceSchemaLocation="emp.xsd"
   id="300">
```

```
      <ENAME>Silver</ENAME>
      <SALARY>12000</SALARY>
   </EMPLOYEE>')
   );


   COMMIT;
```

 Issuing a statement from SQL*Plus is always a good idea when you need to perform a quick test. All INSERT operations discussed in this section might be issued from within PHP code as well.

Note the use of the xsi:noNamespaceSchemaLocation attribute of the root document element EMPLOYEE in the above statement. This attribute is used to indicate the schema location. Alternatively, you might use the createSchemaBasedXML method of XMLType, as you did in the *Using XML Schemas* section when inserting a row into the employees table. However, in this example you would specify emp.xsd as the parameter of createSchemaBasedXML.

The data inserted through the empSch_v view can then be accessed not only through that view as XML, but also through its underlying table emps as relational data. For example, to retrieve the employee XML document inserted into the empSch_v view by the preceding query, you might use the following query:

```
SELECT * FROM empSch_v WHERE existsNode(OBJECT_VALUE,
                            '/EMPLOYEE/@id="300"')=1;
```

On the other hand, to see a relational representation of the inserted document, you might issue the following query against the emps underlying table:

```
SELECT * FROM emps WHERE employee_id=300;
```

This should produce the following output:

```
EMPLOYEE_ID LAST_NAME                      SALARY
----------- ------------------------ ----------
        300 Silver                         12000
```

Now, what happens if you try to insert an employee XML document into empSch_v, which doesn't conform the emp.xsd XML schema? Say, for example, the value of the SALARY element in the inserted document exceeds the maximum allowable value specified for this element in the schema. For example, you might issue the following statement and see what happens:

```
INSERT INTO empSch_v VALUES(XMLType(
   '<EMPLOYEE
```

```
    xmlns:xsi="http://www.w3.org/2001/XMLSchema-instance"
    xsi:noNamespaceSchemaLocation="emp.xsd"
    id="301">
    <ENAME>Jamison</ENAME>
    <SALARY>100000</SALARY>
  </EMPLOYEE>')
 );
```

You might be surprised to see that the above statement works without any problem. This is despite the fact that the value of the SALARY element is restricted to be less than 100000, as you might recall from the listing in the *Creating XML Schema-Based XMLType Views* section, describing emp.xsd XML schema registration.

The fact is that Oracle performs only a partial validation when it comes to inserting an XML document into an XML schema-based XMLType table or column or view. In particular, it checks to see whether the structure of the XML document being inserted conforms to the appropriate XML schema and does not check the contents of the document.

So, to ensure that the employee XML documents inserted into the empSch_v view are fully compliant with the emp.xsd XML schema, you need to explicitly invoke an XML schema validation when performing INSERT operations. The simplest way to do this is to use a PL/SQL function that might be created as follows:

```
CONN xmlusr/xmlusr
CREATE OR REPLACE FUNCTION val_xml (xmldoc XMLType)
RETURN XMLType
IS
   tmpxml XMLType;
BEGIN
   tmpxml := xmldoc;
   XMLTYPE.schemavalidate(tmpxml);
   RETURN xmldoc;
END;
/
```

Issuing a statement from SQL*Plus is always a good idea when you need to perform a quick test. All INSERT operations discussed in this section might be issued from within PHP code as well.

After you have created the `val_xml` function, you might use it in `INSERT` operations issued against XML schema-based tables and views as follows:

```
INSERT INTO empSch_v VALUES(VAL_XML(XMLType(
    '<EMPLOYEE
    xmlns:xsi="http://www.w3.org/2001/XMLSchema-instance"
    xsi:noNamespaceSchemaLocation="emp.xsd"
    id="302">
    <ENAME>Johnson</ENAME>
    <SALARY>100000</SALARY>
  </EMPLOYEE>')
    )
);
```

Now, a full XML schema validation takes place. Since the value of the `SALARY` element in the above `employee` XML document is greater than the maximum allowable value defined in the schema, you should receive the following error message:

```
ERROR at line 1:
ORA-31154: invalid XML document
ORA-19202: Error occurred in XML processing
LSX-00292: value "100000" is greater than maximum "100000" (exclusive)
ORA-06512: at "SYS.XMLTYPE", line 345
ORA-06512: at "XMLUSR.VAL_XML", line 7
```

However, it is important to note that while a full XML schema validation allows you to validate both the structure and contents of an instance document, it comes at the cost of processing time and memory usage, thus adding overhead to your application and decreasing performance.

Using Oracle XML DB Repository

Another variation on accessing and manipulating XML content stored in Oracle database is provided by Oracle XML DB repository, which is an essential component of Oracle XML DB.

 Oracle XML DB repository, also known as XML repository, is a hierarchically organized repository seamlessly integrated with Oracle Database, containing resources that can be manipulated using a file/folder/URL metaphor.

The most significant thing about XML repository is that it makes it possible to access and manipulate XML data in a number of different ways, including SQL, PL/SQL, and standard internet protocols, such as HTTP, FTP, and WebDAV. Graphically, it looks as shown in the following figure.

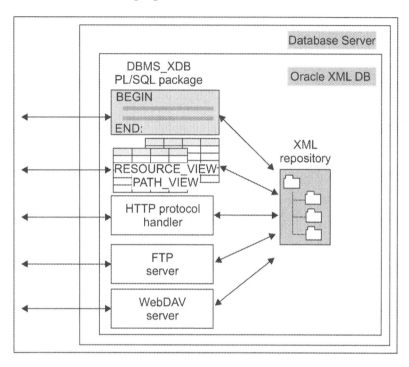

You may find it convenient to think of Oracle XML DB repository as a file system whose metadata and data are stored in the database. Like a conventional file system, Oracle XML DB repository contains resources: files and folders. However, in the case of XML repository, each resource also can be accessed through SQL.

 Although XML repository is optimized for working with XML data, you can use it to store non-XML data as well. For example, you might store a collection of pictures there.

Manipulating Repository Resources with PL/SQL

Oracle XML DB provides PL/SQL package DBMS_XDB to access Oracle XML DB repository programmatically from within PL/SQL code.

For example, to create a repository folder and then a resource in that folder, you might use the DBMS_XDB.createFolder and DBMS_XDB.createResource function respectively, as follows:

```
CONN xmlusr/xmlusr;
DECLARE
  rslt BOOLEAN;
  xmldoc VARCHAR2(250) :=
  '<EMPLOYEE
    xmlns:xsi="http://www.w3.org/2001/XMLSchema-instance"
    xsi:noNamespaceSchemaLocation="employee.xsd"
    id="303">
    <ENAME>Locke</ENAME>
    <SALARY>7000</SALARY>
  </EMPLOYEE>';
BEGIN
 IF (NOT DBMS_XDB.existsResource('/public/xmlusr')) THEN
  rslt:=DBMS_XDB.createFolder('/public/xmlusr');
 END IF;
 IF (NOT DBMS_XDB.existsResource('/public/xmlusr/emps')) THEN
  rslt:=DBMS_XDB.createFolder('/public/xmlusr/emps');
 END IF;
 rslt := DBMS_XDB.createResource('/public/xmlusr/emps/emp303.xml',
xmldoc);
 COMMIT;
END;
/
```

As you can see, when creating a resource, regardless of whether it is a file or folder, you must specify an absolute path to that resource. This is required because, as in a conventional file system, each resource in the XML repository is identified by a path and name.

Accessing Repository Resources with SQL

In fact, Oracle XML DB repository resources are stored in a set of database tables and indexes, which can be accessed via SQL. You are not supposed to access those tables directly. Instead, Oracle XML DB provides two public views RESOURCE_VIEW and PATH_VIEW through which you can access repository resources.

For example, you might issue the following query against the RESOURCE_VIEW view to access the employee XML document stored in the XML repository as /public/xmlusr/emps/emp303.xml, assuming that you have executed the PL/SQL block shown in the preceding section.

```
SELECT extract(r.RES, '/Resource/Contents/*').getStringVal()
  RESULT FROM RESOURCE_VIEW r
  WHERE equals_path(res, '/public/xmlusr/emps/emp303.xml') = 1;
```

This should produce the following result:

```
<EMPLOYEE
    xmlns:xsi="http://www.w3.org/2001/XMLSchema-instance"
    xsi:noNamespaceSchemaLocation="employee.xsd"
    id="303">
  <ENAME>Locke</ENAME>
  <SALARY>7000</SALARY>
</EMPLOYEE>
```

However, in this particular example you don't have to query RESOURCE_VIEW to retrieve the above XML document through SQL. Instead, you might issue the following query against the employees XMLType table:

```
SELECT extract(OBJECT_VALUE,'/').getStringVal()
  RESULT FROM employees
  WHERE existsNode(OBJECT_VALUE, '/EMPLOYEE/@id="303"') = 1;
```

You might be asking yourself: How could that have happened—a document uploaded into the XML repository appeared in an XMLType table? As you might recall from the listing describing the employee.xsd XML schema registration in the *Using XML Schemas* section, the employees XMLType table is specified as a default table in the employee.xsd XML schema and so it must have been generated during the schema registration process. Since the employee XML document inserted into the XML repository by the PL/SQL code as discussed in the preceding section is based on the employee.xsd XML schema, this document has been automatically inserted into the employees XMLType table.

Taking Advantage of Standard Internet Protocols

As mentioned, Oracle XML DB provides native support for standard internet protocols, such as HTTP(S), WebDAV, and FTP. Continuing with the preceding sample, you might, for example, upload another employee XML document into the XML repository with one of the above protocols, say, FTP.

Starting with Oracle Database 10*g* Release 2, FTP is disabled by default, for security reasons. This is achieved by setting the FTP port to 0. To enable FTP, you must manually set the FTP port number to an appropriate value, such as 2100, which is the default value in Oracle Database releases before 10*g* Release 2. Changing the FTP port to an appropriate value can be easily done with the help of Oracle Enterprise Manager, a graphical tool supplied with Oracle Database. For more information on Oracle Enterprise Manager, refer to Oracle documentation: chapter *Getting Started with Oracle Enterprise Manager* in the *Oracle Database 2 Day DBA* manual.

The uploadXML.php script shown below provides a simple example of how you might upload an XML document into the XML repository through FTP protocol.

```php
<?php
//File: uploadXML.php
$host='localhost';
$port=2100;
$timeout=30;
$db_user='xmlusr';
$db_pswd='xmlusr';
$root_dir='/public/xmlusr/emps';
$empid=304;
$file='emp'.$empid.'.xml';
$cnt=
'<?xml version="1.0"?>
  <EMPLOYEE
     xmlns:xsi="http://www.w3.org/2001/XMLSchema-instance"
     xsi:noNamespaceSchemaLocation="employee.xsd"
     id="'.$empid.'">
    <ENAME>Polonski</ENAME>
    <SALARY>8200</SALARY>
  </EMPLOYEE>';
$temp = tmpfile();
fwrite($temp, $cnt);
fseek($temp, 0);
$ftpcon = ftp_connect($host, $port, $timeout);
$login = ftp_login($ftpcon, $db_user, $db_pswd);
ftp_chdir($ftpcon, $root_dir);
ftp_fput($ftpcon, $file, $temp, FTP_ASCII);
ftp_close($ftpcon);
?>
```

In the above script, you start by setting up the parameters required to connect to the FTP server running on the database server.

By including the value of the employee's `id` attribute in the name of the XML file to be uploaded into the XML repository, you ensure the uniqueness of file names within the repository folder that contains `employee` XML documents in single files.

Then, you create a temp file and write XML content in it. Then, you connect to the Oracle FTP server and upload the file into the XML repository.

After the `uploadXML.php` script is executed, to make sure that the `employee` XML document has been successfully uploaded into the XML repository, you might issue the following query from SQL*Plus:

```
CONN xmlusr/xmlusr
SELECT extract(OBJECT_VALUE,'/').getStringVal()
  RESULT FROM employees
  WHERE existsNode(OBJECT_VALUE, '/EMPLOYEE/@id="304"') = 1;
```

If everything is OK, this query should output the `employee` XML document uploaded by the `uploadXML.php` script:

```
<?xml version="1.0"?>
  <EMPLOYEE
      xmlns:xsi="http://www.w3.org/2001/XMLSchema-instance"
      xsi:noNamespaceSchemaLocation="employee.xsd"
      id="304">
    <ENAME>Polonski</ENAME>
    <SALARY>8200</SALARY>
  </EMPLOYEE>
```

So, after the `uploadXML.php` script is executed, the XML document inserted by the script becomes permanent immediately.

Handling Transactions

As you can see from the preceding example, changes made through internet protocols to repository resources become permanent once a single operation on a resource has been completed.

In contrast, all SQL and PL/SQL operations that you perform on the XML data stored in Oracle XML DB are transactional, irrespective of whether you're using XMLType storage or the XML repository. This allows you to combine SQL and PL/SQL statements operating on XML data within a logical unit of work and explicitly commit the transaction or roll it back if necessary.

Suppose you want to create a folder in the XML repository and then upload an XML document in it. The following code fragment shows how this can be done in PL/SQL:

```
rslt:=DBMS_XDB.createFolder('/public/xmlusr/emps/303');
rslt:=DBMS_XDB.createResource('/public/xmlusr/emps/303/emp303.xml',
xmldoc);
COMMIT;
```

The above PL/SQL code is transactional. If an error occurs during the execution of the `createFolder` function, then the results of execution of `createFolder` are discarded automatically.

On the other hand, when performing the same operations through FTP protocol, failure to create the resource doesn't affect the results of preceding operation. So, the following fragment of PHP code is not transactional:

```
$login = ftp_login($ftpcon, $db_user, $db_pswd);
ftp_chdir($ftpcon, '/public/xmlusr/emps');
ftp_mkdir($ftpcon, '303');
ftp_chdir($ftpcon, '/public/xmlusr/emps/303');
ftp_fput($ftpcon, 'emp303.xml', $xmldoc, FTP_ASCII);
ftp_close($ftpcon);
```

Chapter 4 *Transactions*, presented earlier in this book, explains in detail how to use transactions in PHP/Oracle applications.

Querying Data with Oracle XQuery

Starting with Oracle Database 10g Release 2, you can take advantage of a full-featured native XQuery engine integrated with the database. With Oracle XQuery, you can accomplish various tasks involved in developing PHP/Oracle XML applications, operating on any kind of data that can be expressed in XML.

The following figure shows the data sources with which Oracle XQuery can work.

Relational data

Database Server

XML data

```
<?xml version="1.0"?>
```

```
<?xml version="1.0"?>
...
...
```

Xquery engine

External
sources

As you can see from the figure, XQuery can be used to query any data stored in the database and out of it.

Please note that XQuery is not available in the Express Edition of
Oracle Database. For more information on Oracle XQuery, you can
refer to Oracle documentation: chapter *Using XQuery with Oracle XML DB*
in the *Oracle XML DB Developer's Guide*. You can also refer to the
XQuery 1.0: An XML Query Language W3C Recommendation at
http://www.w3.org/TR/xquery/.

Using XQuery to Construct XML from Relational Data

In the preceding sections, you saw several examples of how to construct XML representations of relational data using the SQL/XML generation function, as well as using object types when creating XMLType views on relational tables. In this section, you will learn how to build XML on relational data with XQuery.

Turning back to the *Using Oracle SQL/XML Generation Functions* section, you might modify the listing containing the SQLXMLQuery.php script that uses PHP DOM extension functions to produce an XML representation of relational data to use XQuery instead of those functions, as shown overleaf:

```php
<?php
  //File: XQuery.php
  if(!$rsConnection = oci_connect('hr', 'hr', '//localhost/orcl')) {
      $err = oci_error();
      trigger_error('Could not establish a connection: ' .
                    $err['message'], E_USER_ERROR);
  };
  $dept_id=90;
  $query =
   'SELECT XMLQuery('.
   "'".'for $j in 1
    return (
    <EMPLOYEES> {
      for $i in ora:view("hr", "employees")/ROW
      where $i/DEPARTMENT_ID = $deptid
      return (<EMPLOYEE id="{xs:integer($i/EMPLOYEE_ID)}">
                 <ENAME>{xs:string($i/LAST_NAME)}</ENAME>
                 <SALARY>{xs:integer($i/SALARY)}</SALARY>
             </EMPLOYEE>)} </EMPLOYEES>)'."'".
      'PASSING XMLElement("deptid", :deptid) AS "deptid"
       RETURNING CONTENT).getStringVal() RESULT FROM DUAL';
  $stmt = oci_parse($rsConnection,$query);
  oci_bind_by_name($stmt, ':deptid', $dept_id);
  if (!oci_execute($stmt)) {
   $err = oci_error($stmt);
   trigger_error('Query failed: ' . $err['message'], E_USER_ERROR);
  }
  $xmlDoc = oci_fetch_assoc($stmt);
  $domxml = new DOMDocument();
  $domxml->loadXML($xmlDoc['RESULT']);
  print $domxml->saveXML();
?>
```

The Oracle SQL function XMLQuery can be used to construct or query XML data, based on an XQuery expression passed as the parameter. In this example, you use the XMLQuery function to generate an XML representation of some data stored in the relational table hr.employees.

You start the FLWOR expression used in this example with the for clause performing only one iteration.

 FLWOR stands for for, let, where, order by, return—the clauses used when composing an XQuery expression.

Next, in the nested FLWOR expression that starts with the for clause, you iterate over the hr.employees rows selected based on the condition specified in the where clause. With the help of the ora:view XQuery function, you query relational table hr.employees, as it were an XMLType table, creating XML documents on the fly.

In the return clause of the FLWOR expression, you construct the EMPLOYEE nodes of the resultant EMPLOYEES document.

You bind dynamic variable deptid to an XQuery expression using the PASSING clause. This variable is used in the where clause of the nested FLWOR expression, restricting the retrieved employee records to those that belong to the specified department.

When executed, the XQuery.php script shown in the listing opposite should produce the same XML document as the one shown in the *Creating XML with the DOM PHP Extension* section at the beginning of this chapter. If you want to print the resultant XML document in HTML format, you might perform an XSL transformation before outputting it. To achieve this, you might replace the last line of code in the script:

```
print $domxml->saveXML();
```

with the following lines:

```
$domxsl = new DOMDocument();
$domxsl->load('employees.xsl');
$proc = new XSLTProcessor;
$xsl = $proc->importStylesheet($domxsl);
$rslt = $proc->transformToXml($domxml);
print $rslt;
```

Assuming that you have created the employees.xsl stylesheet as discussed in the *Transforming and Processing XML with XSLT* section earlier in this chapter, with the above replacement, the XQuery.php script shown in the listing should produce the HTML table as shown in the *Transforming and Processing XML with XSLT* section earlier.

Breaking up XML into Relational Data

While the preceding example shows how to construct an XML representation over relational data, the example in this section illustrates how you can shred XML data back into relational data. This reverse operation can be useful if your application works with relational data rather than XML, but the data which you work with, is stored in XML format.

Turning back to the `employees` XMLType table generated during the registration of the `employee.xsd` XML schema discussed in the *Using XML Schemas* section, you might use the SQL function `XMLTable` to shred the `employee` XML documents into individual columns of a virtual table, as shown below:

```
CONN xmlusr/xmlusr
SELECT emps.empno,emps.ename, emps.salary FROM employees,
   XMLTable(
   'for $i in /EMPLOYEE
    return $i'
    PASSING OBJECT_VALUE
    COLUMNS empno NUMBER        PATH '/EMPLOYEE/@id',
            ename VARCHAR2(30)  PATH '/EMPLOYEE/ENAME',
            salary NUMBER       PATH '/EMPLOYEE/SALARY') emps;
```

Assuming that you have followed the instructions in the preceding sections, the output generated by the query shown in the listing might look like this:

```
EMPNO ENAME                                      SALARY
----- ------------------------------------- ----------
  100 King                                    24000
  101 Horka                                   25000
  303 Locke                                    7000
  304 Polonski                                 8200
```

In a real-world situation, in order to hide data complexity, you might find it useful to build a view on the query shown in the listing, so that the people designing SQL queries against that view have no idea they are dealing with data actually stored in XML format.

Summary

When building XML-enabled PHP/Oracle applications, the database can not only be used as an efficient means for storing XML data, but also to operate on any kind of data that can be expressed in XML.

In this chapter you learned how to use XML techniques and technologies available in PHP and Oracle when building XML-enabled PHP/Oracle applications. In particular, you saw how to use PHP's XML extensions and how to take advantage of Oracle XML DB, a set of Oracle XML technologies making Oracle Database an ideal choice for data-driven XML applications.

By now you should have a good understanding of how you can use XML techniques and technologies available in PHP and Oracle to build robust XML-enabled PHP applications on Oracle Database. Armed with this knowledge, you will be able to understand better XML Web Services discussed in the next chapter.

9

Web Services

Web Services is a powerful technology that enables different systems to communicate with each other over the Internet in a uniform way, without having to worry about implementation details. The most popular protocol for accessing web services today is **SOAP**—a lightweight, XML-based, messaging protocol designed for exchanging structured and typed information between distributed applications over standard transport protocols, such as HTTP.

When developing a SOAP web service to expose the functionality of a PHP/Oracle application, you have a number of choices. For example, you could employ the PEAR::SOAP package or the PHP SOAP extension to implement a SOAP web service in PHP while implementing its business logic partly in PHP and partly within the database. As far as Oracle is concerned, you might, of course, implement the key business logic of a SOAP web service within the database, while still having the SOAP server implemented in PHP and, therefore, running on the web/PHP server. Finally, you might implement a SOAP web service, including its business logic, entirely within the database.

In this chapter you learn how to build a SOAP web service exposing the functionality of a PHP/Oracle application, using the PHP SOAP extension and Oracle XML technologies.

Exposing a PHP/Oracle Application as a Web Service Using PHP SOAP Extension

PHP's SOAP extension is an implementation of the SOAP protocol for PHP. Written in C, it provides a performance advantage over the PEAR::SOAP implementation, which is written in PHP.

In the following sections, you will learn how to expose a PHP/Oracle application as a web service with the help of PHP's SOAP extension.

Communicating Using SOAP

As mentioned, SOAP is a messaging protocol. What this means is that SOAP clients and SOAP servers interact by sending SOAP messages to each other.

 A SOAP message is a SOAP-formatted XML document used to transport information between SOAP-based interfaces. For more information on SOAP, you can refer to the W3C SOAP Recommendation documents. Links to the latest versions of these documents can be found at http://www.w3.org/TR/soap/.

The following figure illustrates the general structure of a SOAP message.

```
<?xml version='1.0' ?>
<Envelope ...>
  <Header>
    . . .
  </Header>
  <Body>
    . . .
  </Body>
</Envelope>
```

As you can see in the figure, an XML document representing a SOAP message includes two key elements, namely `Header` and `Body`, under the `Envelope` root element.

While the body of a SOAP message contains the actual message payload, the SOAP header is optional and is used to pass meta-information related to the processing of the message itself. For example, the header might be used to supply security measures to protect the data passed in the message body.

The most commonly used messaging pattern in SOAP is the RPC (Remote Procedure Call) pattern, in which the client calls a remote function available on the server and then gets the results back, sending requests and responses as SOAP messages.

The following figure gives a conceptual depiction of how an RPC scenario works with SOAP.

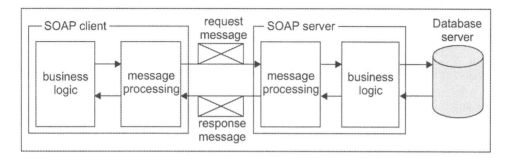

As you can see in the figure, the SOAP client initiates a communication with the corresponding SOAP server by sending a SOAP request message, by which the client invokes the required business logic component (in other words, it calls a remote function) available on the server.

The server in turn processes the request message and then invokes the called function. After performing the called function, the server generates a SOAP response message and then sends it back to the client. The response message normally contains the results produced by the invoked function or information about the fault thrown by that function.

What you Need to Build a SOAP Web Service

When developing a web service, you normally use several technologies such as XML, SOAP, XML Schema, and WSDL in a complementary way. This section outlines which software components you need to build your own SOAP web service with PHP's SOAP extension, and how these components interact with each other.

The key components required to build a SOAP web service with PHP's SOAP extension are listed in the following table:

Component	Description
PHP's SOAP extension	Written in C, the SOAP extension provides an efficient alternative to the PEAR::SOAP package, which is written in PHP. The SOAP extension supports WSDL, which simplifies the process of writing SOAP servers and SOAP clients.
PHP class	Normally you use a PHP class to encapsulate the web service logic. For this purpose, you might use an existing class, adding SoapFault class functionality to be able to use the PHP exception mechanism to throw a SOAP fault.
WSDL document	WSDL stands for Web Service Definition Language. When developing a SOAP web service with the PHP SOAP extension, you have to develop an accompanying WSDL file as well. In this document, you describe the SOAP messages to be used when interacting with the SOAP service.

While the above table gives a short functional description of each component needed to build a SOAP web service with PHP SOAP extension, the following figure gives you a high-level view of how these components interact with each other.

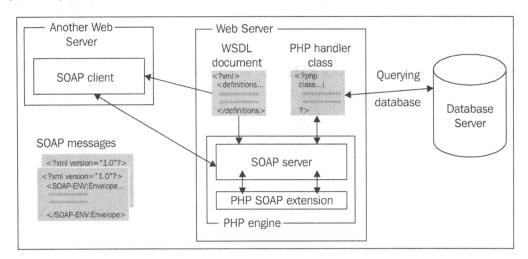

For simplicity, the diagram shown in the figure illustrates only one SOAP client interacting with the SOAP server. In reality, of course, there may be more than one client requesting a SOAP server simultaneously. Although the SOAP server presented in the figure is build upon the PHP SOAP extension, a SOAP client interacting with this server may be built with other software and even running on another operating system platform.

Looking at the figure, notice the use of the WSDL document, which describes the public interface to the server and is used by the client to determine what functions are available on the server. The same WSDL document is used when creating a SOAP server object. In this example, the WSDL describes the public methods of the PHP handler, which is a custom class implementing the web service logic.

Building a SOAP Web Service on Top of a PHP/Oracle Application

Now that you know which key components are required to build a SOAP web service, it's time to look at an example that should give you an idea of how to expose a PHP/Oracle application as a SOAP web service.

Suppose you want to expose the functionality of a po custom PHP class as a web service. Let's say this class contains a placeOrder method that takes an XML document representing a purchase order as its parameter and then sends it to the database for validating it against a registered XML schema and storing it in XML format.

Diagrammatically, this might look like the following figure.

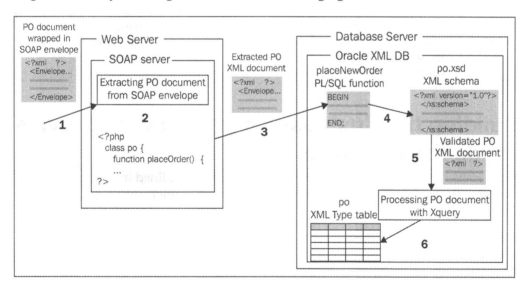

Here is the explanation of the steps in the previous figure:

- Step 1: The SOAP server running on the web/PHP server receives a PO XML document wrapped by the client in a SOAP envelope, and then extracts it.
- Step 2: The `po` class's `placeOrder` method exposed by the SOAP web service takes the PO XML document extracted in step 1 as its parameter.
- Step 3: The `placeOrder` method then invokes the `placeNewOrder` PL/SQL function, sending the extracted PO document as the parameter.
- Step 4: The first thing that the `placeNewOrder` function does is to initiate the process of validation of the XML PO document against the `po.xsd` XML schema.
- Step 5: The validated PO document is then processed with XQuery. During this phase, the automatically generated PO's ID and some other information are added to the document.
- Step 6: Finally, the PO XML document is inserted into the `po` XMLType table.

In the next sections, you will see each of the above steps in detail, as the sample application is built.

Although a SOAP client initiates a communication with the corresponding SOAP server, you start building the sample discussed here with the latter. It makes sense to do so, because the main focus here is the server rather than the client. In this example, you need a very simple client to be used only to test the server, once you've built the latter.

Building the Business Logic of a Web Service Inside the Database

When implementing a SOAP web service that works as outlined in the above scenario, you can start by creating the database objects implementing the web service's business logic.

In the following sections, you create the `placeNewOrder` PL/SQL function that will be invoked by the web service whenever a new PO arrives, and the PO XML schema that will be used to validate arrived PO documents.

Creating an XML Schema to Validate Incoming Documents

You can start by creating and registering the PO XML schema within the database. This schema will be used to validate all incoming PO XML documents. Moreover, while registering the schema, Oracle will automatically create the po XMLType table to be used for storing that documents.

> Alternatively, you might embed a PO XML schema in the WSDL document describing the web service, thus moving XML Schema validation from the database server to the SOAP server, which in this example, is implemented with the PHP SOAP extension and is therefore running on the web/PHP server. Or you might use two XML schemas simultaneously, performing validation at both the database server and web/PHP server. However, in either case you should understand that XML Schema validation consumes a great deal of processor time and physical memory. So, in most cases, it is more efficient to perform XML Schema validation within the database rather than at the web/PHP server, since it allows you to take advantage of the XML-specific memory optimizations provided by Oracle XML DB.

The following listing shows the code you need to execute from SQL*Plus in order to create and register a po.xsd XML schema against the database. It is assumed that you have the xmlusr/xmlusr database account created as discussed in the *Storing XML Data in the Database* section in Chapter 8 *XML-Enabled Applications*.

```
CONN xmlusr/xmlusr;

BEGIN
 DBMS_XMLSCHEMA.registerschema(
  'po.xsd',
  '<?xml version="1.0" encoding="UTF-8"?>
<xs:schema
        xmlns:xs="http://www.w3.org/2001/XMLSchema"
        xmlns:xdb="http://xmlns.oracle.com/xdb"
        xdb:storeVarrayAsTable="true" >
   <xs:element name="purchaseOrder" type="purchaseOrder_typ"
              xdb:defaultTable="PO"
              xdb:columnProps=
              "CONSTRAINT po_pkey PRIMARY KEY (XMLDATA.pono)"/>
   <xs:complexType name="purchaseOrder_typ" >
    <xs:sequence>
     <xs:element name="orderDate" type="xs:date" minOccurs="0"/>
```

```
        <xs:element name="shipDate" type="xs:date" minOccurs="0"/>
        <xs:element name="shipTo" type="Address"/>
        <xs:element name="billTo" type="Address"/>
        <xs:element name="items" type="Items"/>
      </xs:sequence>
      <xs:attribute name="id" xdb:SQLName="PONO" >
        <xs:simpleType>
         <xs:restriction base="xs:string">
          <xs:pattern value="[A-Z]{2}-\d{6}"/>
         </xs:restriction>
        </xs:simpleType>
      </xs:attribute>
    </xs:complexType>
    <xs:complexType name="Address" >
     <xs:sequence>
      <xs:element name="name" type="xs:string" />
      <xs:element name="street" type="xs:string" />
      <xs:element name="city" type="xs:string" />
      <xs:element name="state" type="xs:string" />
      <xs:element name="zip">
       <xs:simpleType>
        <xs:restriction base="xs:string">
         <xs:pattern value="\d{5}"/>
        </xs:restriction>
       </xs:simpleType>
      </xs:element>
     </xs:sequence>
     <xs:attribute name="country" type="xs:NMTOKENS" fixed="US"/>
    </xs:complexType>
    <xs:complexType name="Items" >
     <xs:sequence>
      <xs:element name="item" minOccurs="0" maxOccurs="unbounded" >
       <xs:complexType>
        <xs:sequence>
         <xs:element name="partId" >
         <xs:simpleType>
          <xs:restriction base="xs:string">
           <xs:pattern value="\d{3}"/>
          </xs:restriction>
         </xs:simpleType>
        </xs:element>
        <xs:element name="quantity" >
         <xs:simpleType>
          <xs:restriction base="xs:positiveInteger">
```

```
            <xs:maxExclusive value="100"/>
          </xs:restriction>
        </xs:simpleType>
      </xs:element>
      <xs:element name="price" type="xs:decimal"/>
    </xs:sequence>
  </xs:complexType>
</xs:element>
</xs:sequence>
</xs:complexType>
</xs:schema>',
TRUE,
TRUE,
FALSE,
TRUE
);
END;
/
```

With the help of the xdb:defaultTable annotation, you specified that XML documents compliant with the schema will be stored in the po XMLType table. Another annotation in the purchaseOrder element, namely xdb:columnProps, instructs Oracle to define a primary key on the pono attribute in the po XMLType table. This guarantees the uniqueness of PO IDs within the documents stored in the po XMLType table. In this case, you are able to refer to the pono attribute when setting up the xdb:columnProps annotation because you explicitly specify the name for that attribute with the help of the xdb:SQLName annotation. Also, you specify a matching pattern that restricts the value of the pono attribute to a nine-character string that begins with two capital letters followed by the dash character followed by six digits.

Note that the orderDate and shipDate elements defined in the above schema have attribute minOccurs set to 0. This means that these elements need not be present in XML documents compliant with this XML schema. This allows you to validate incoming PO XML documents, which actually should not contain these elements. On the other hand, it doesn't prevent you from including them in resultant PO XML documents to be stored in the po XMLType table based on this XML schema.

When defining the restriction for the quantity element, you specify that the maximum allowed value for that element is 100. This means that an incoming PO document cannot contain items whose quantity exceeds 100.

As mentioned, during the registration of the PO XML schema as shown in the previous listing, Oracle implicitly creates the po XMLType table based on that XML schema. To make sure it has done so, you can issue the following query from SQL*Plus, when connected as xmlusr/xmlusr:

```
DESC po
```

The above should produce the following output:

```
TABLE of SYS.XMLTYPE(XMLSchema "po.xsd" Element "purchaseOrder")
   STORAGE Object-relational TYPE "purchaseOrder_typ"
```

 Using XML schemas is discussed in more detail in the section *Using XML Schemas* in Chapter 8 *XML-Enabled Applications*.

Generating Unique IDs for Incoming Documents

Before you start developing PL/SQL code that will process incoming POs and then insert resultant documents into the po table, you have to figure out which mechanism will be used to generate unique IDs for incoming POs. Since the web service discussed here is designed to receive PO documents from more than one client, it is fairly obvious that generating IDs must be performed on the server side rather than on the client.

As discussed in the preceding section, the last 6 characters in a PO ID are digits. To guarantee uniqueness across generated PO IDs, the combination of those digits must be unique for each generated ID. To achieve this, you might want to use a sequence number generator that will generate unique sequential numbers. You might issue the following statement from SQL*Plus to create such a sequence number generator inside the database:

```
CONN xmlusr/xmlusr;

CREATE SEQUENCE orders_seq
START WITH 1
INCREMENT BY 1
MAXVALUE 999999
NOCYCLE;
```

With the help of the orders_seq sequence created above, you will be able to obtain a sequential number to be used as part of the generated ID for an incoming PO document. To do this, you can access the orders_seq's NEXTVAL pseudocolumn in an SQL statement, as you will see in the next section.

Since an Oracle sequence is irrevocably incremented upon accessing its NEXTVAL pseudocolumn, it is obvious that you have to generate the ID for an incoming PO only if it has been successfully validated against the PO XML schema created and registered as shown in the listing in the preceding section.

In the above CREATE SEQUENCE statement, you used several clauses, which are described in the following table.

Clause	Description
START WITH	Specifies the first sequential number to be generated upon accessing the NEXTVAL pseudocolumn of the sequence. In this example, you explicitly set this number to 1.
INCREMENT BY	Specifies the interval between generated sequence numbers. In this example, you explicitly set this interval to 1.
MAXVALUE	Specifies the maximum allowed value for the sequence. You set it to 999999 because the PO ID's pattern defined in the PO XML schema requires that you use a six-digit number for the number portion of a PO ID.
NOCYCLE	Specifies that the sequence will not start a new cycle upon reaching the maximum allowed value specified in the MAXVALUE clause. In this case, this guarantees uniqueness across PO IDs.

Besides the clauses described in the table, there are a few other clauses that can be used with the CREATE SEQUENCE statement. For detailed information, see Oracle documentation: section *CREATE SEQUENCE* in chapter *SQL Statements* in the *Oracle Database SQL Reference* manual.

Creating PL/SQL Subprograms Implementing the Business Logic of the Web Service

Now that you have a sequence in hand, you are ready to develop PL/SQL code that will be used to process incoming POs and then insert resultant documents into the table.

For the purpose of this sample, you will create two PL/SQL functions, namely placeNewOrder and transOrder. The placeNewOrder function will be invoked from PHP code, taking an incoming PO document as the parameter. After validating the incoming document, placeNewOrder invokes the transOrder function that will transform that document to the resultant document. Then, placeNewOrder will save the resultant document in the po XMLType table.

You start by creating the `transOrder` PL/SQL function that will take an incoming PO XML document as its parameter and then transform it to the resultant document. To create the function from SQL*Plus, you can run the CREATE FUNCTION statement shown below:

```
CONN xmlusr/xmlusr;

CREATE OR REPLACE FUNCTION transOrder (xmldoc XMLType)
RETURN XMLType
IS
 rsltdoc XMLType;
 ordid VARCHAR2(9);
 ordno VARCHAR2(6);
 orderDate DATE;
 shipDate DATE;
BEGIN
 ordid:='US-000000';
 SELECT orders_seq.nextval INTO ordno FROM DUAL;
 ordid:=SUBSTR(ordid, 1, 9-LENGTH(ordno))||ordno;
 orderDate:=SYSDATE;
 shipDate:=SYSDATE+1;
 SELECT XMLQuery(
   'for $p in $xmldoc/purchaseOrder
    return (<purchaseOrder
            xmlns:xsi="http://www.w3.org/2001/XMLSchema-instance"
            xsi:noNamespaceSchemaLocation="po.xsd"
            id="{$ordid}">
          {$orderDate,
           $shipDate,
           $p/shipTo,
           $p/billTo,
           $p/items}
        </purchaseOrder>)'
   PASSING  xmldoc as "xmldoc",
          XMLElement("ordid", ordid) AS "ordid",
          XMLElement("orderDate", orderDate) AS "orderDate",
          XMLElement("shipDate", shipDate) AS "shipDate"
   RETURNING CONTENT) INTO rsltdoc FROM DUAL;
 RETURN rsltdoc;
END;
/
```

As you can see, the `transOrder` PL/SQL function takes only a parameter that is of type XMLType. Through this parameter, the function will receive an incoming PO to be transformed into a resultant PO document.

The executable part of the `transOrder` function starts with the code that generates an ID for the PO document passed to the function as the parameter. The first PO ID generated by this code should be: `US-000001`.

However, adding a generated ID to an incoming document is not the only thing to take care of in this example. You also need to add the `orderDate` and `shipDate` elements to the XML document representing an incoming PO, specifying appropriate values for those elements. You set variable `orderDate` to the current date and `shipDate` to the date of the next day. These variables then are passed to the XQuery expression, which in turn is passed to the XMLQuery function as the argument.

In the `return` clause of the XQuery expression, you construct the resultant PO document, which is then returned to the caller.

> Using Oracle XQuery to query, construct, and transform XML is discussed in more detail in the section *Querying Data with Oracle XQuery* in Chapter 8 *XML-Enabled Applications*.

Now that you have the `transOrder` function created, you can move on to the `placeNewOrder` function. The following listing shows the SQL statement to be executed from SQL*Plus to create this function.

```
CONN xmlusr/xmlusr;
CREATE OR REPLACE FUNCTION placeNewOrder (xmldoc IN XMLType,
                                          msg OUT VARCHAR2)
RETURN NUMBER
IS
   tmpxml XMLType;
   errcode NUMBER;
   errmesg VARCHAR2(256);
BEGIN
   tmpxml := xmldoc;
   XMLTYPE.schemaValidate(tmpxml);
   tmpxml:=transOrder(tmpxml);
   INSERT INTO po VALUES(tmpxml);
   COMMIT;
   msg:='Ok!';
   RETURN 1;
   EXCEPTION
    WHEN OTHERS THEN
      errcode := SQLCODE;
      errmesg := SUBSTR(SQLERRM, 1, 256);
      msg:= errcode || ': ' || errmesg;
      RETURN 0;
END;
/
```

As you can see, the `placeNewOrder` PL/SQL function takes two parameters. The first one, called `xmldoc`, is an input parameter of XMLType through which an incoming PO document is passed to the function. The other one, called `msg`, is an output parameter through which `placeNewOrder` tells the caller whether the incoming PO has been successfully processed and inserted into the `po` XMLType table.

With the help of the XMLType `schemaValidate` method, you validate the incoming PO against the PO XML schema created as shown in the listing in the *Creating an XML Schema to Validate Incoming Documents* section earlier. If the incoming PO has been successfully validated, you transform it into the resultant document with the `transOrder` PL/SQL function created as shown in the listing at the beginning of this section, and then insert it into the `po` XMLType table created by Oracle during registering the PO XML schema.

If either the validation or insertion fails then control is transferred to the code in the WHEN OTHERS THEN section in the exception-handling part of the `placeNewOrder` PL/SQL function. This code sets the `msg` output parameter to an appropriate error message string and returns 0 to the caller.

Although you created the `placeNewOrder` PL/SQL function to be called from PHP code encapsulating the functionality of the PO web service discussed here, you can test this function from SQL*Plus to make sure that everything works as expected so far.

The following listing shows SQL and PL/SQL code that you might execute to test the `placeNewOrder` PL/SQL function created as shown in the preceding listing.

```
CONN xmlusr/xmlusr;
VARIABLE rslt_msg VARCHAR2(300);

DECLARE
 rslt NUMBER;
BEGIN rslt:=placeNewOrder(XMLType('
<purchaseOrder xmlns:xsi="http://www.w3.org/2001/XMLSchema-instance"
               xsi:noNamespaceSchemaLocation="po.xsd" >
    <shipTo country="US">
     <name>Maya Silver</name>
     <street>5th West Street</street>
     <city>Shell Valley</city>
     <state>CA</state>
     <zip>90950</zip>
    </shipTo>
    <billTo country="US">
     <name>Jonathan Jamison</name>
     <street>277 Nevada Road</street>
```

```
        <city>North Town</city>
        <state>CA</state>
        <zip>90952</zip>
      </billTo>
      <items>
        <item>
         <partId>948</partId>
         <quantity>3</quantity>
         <price>15.75</price>
        </item>
        <item>
         <partId>943</partId>
         <quantity>1</quantity>
         <price>34.95</price>
        </item>
      </items>
</purchaseOrder>'),  :rslt_msg); END;
/
PRINT rslt_msg;
```

In the above listing, you start by declaring the rslt_msg bind variable that is used
in the next anonymous PL/SQL block to hold an output message produced by the
placeNewOrder function invoked in that PL/SQL block.

In the PL/SQL block, you call placeNewOrder, passing the PO XML document
as the first parameter. By setting the xsi:noNamespaceSchemaLocation attribute
of the purchaseOrder root element in the PO document to po.xsd, you explicitly
specify that this document is compliant with the po.xsd XML schema, created and
registered as discussed in the *Creating an XML Schema to Validate Incoming Documents*
section earlier.

The rslt_msg bind variable declared in the above listing is passed as the second
parameter to placeNewOrder when it is invoked within the PL/SQL block. Then,
you access the rslt_msg variable from SQL*Plus with the PRINT command,
displaying the resultant message that tells you whether the PO document has been
successfully validated and stored in the database. If everything is OK, you should see
the following output:

```
RSLT_MSG
--------
Ok!
```

Building a PHP Handler Class

As stated earlier, the `placeNewOrder` PL/SQL function discussed in the preceding section will be invoked from PHP code encapsulating the web service functionality. This PHP code passes an incoming PO document to the `placeNewOrder` function as the parameter. `placeNewOrder` in turn processes that PO and then inserts the resultant document into the `po` XMLType table, returning 1 on success or 0 on failure.

The following listing shows the `po` PHP class whose `placeOrder` method will be exposed by the web service. This method encapsulates the web service functionality, receiving an incoming PO from a web service client and then passing it to the `placeNewOrder` PL/SQL function for further processing.

```php
<?php
//File po.php
class po {
  function placeOrder($po) {
    if(!$conn = oci_connect('xmlusr', 'xmlusr', '//localhost/orcl')){
       throw new SoapFault("Server","Failed to connect to database");
     };
    $sql = "BEGIN :rslt:=placeNewOrder(XMLType(:po).
        createSchemaBasedXML('po.xsd'), :msg); END;";
    $query = oci_parse($conn, $sql);
    oci_bind_by_name($query, ':rslt', $rslt);
    oci_bind_by_name($query, ':po', $po);
    oci_bind_by_name($query, ':msg', $msg, 300);
    if (!oci_execute($query)) {
      throw new SoapFault("Server","Failed to execute query");
    };
    if ($rslt==0) {
      throw new SoapFault("Server","Failed to validate
        or insert PO".$msg);
     };
     return $msg;
    }
  }
 ?>
```

In the above PHP code, you establish a connection to the database with the `oci_connect` function. Upon failure to do so, you throw a SOAP exception, thus informing the SOAP client about the error occurred.

Like `SoapServer` and `SoapClient`, which are required to build a SOAP server and SOAP client respectively, `SoapFault` is a predefined class of the PHP SOAP extension, which is not enabled by default, however. You can enable it with the configure option `--enable-soap`, or, if you are a Windows user, append `extension=php_soap.dll` to the list of extensions in the `php.ini` configuration file.

Note that the SQl string used in the `placeOrder` function contains three placeholders for bind variables that are bound to those placeholders by using `oci_bind_by_name`. As you might recall from the preceding section, the `placeNewOrder` PL/SQL function takes two parameters—the first one is input, and the second is output.

However, the fact is that the `oci_bind_by_name` function doesn't let you specify whether the bind variable is used for input or output—this is determined during execution of the script. So, you bind each of the three bind variables to the corresponding placeholder in the same general way, regardless of whether you are dealing with the bind variable representing the input or output parameter of the `placeNewOrder` function, or the `rslt` bind variable used to hold the return value of the function.

However, it is important to note that there is a difference between the way binding of input variables works and the way binding of output variables does. The fact is that binding takes place before output variables are assigned their values generated during execution of the SQL or PL/SQL statement.

So, your application has no idea about the length of the value that will be assigned to an output bind variable, and allocates a small, actually 1-character, buffer for the output value. If an output value is supposed to be greater than 1 character, you have to explicitly set the maximum allowable length for this bind, specifying it as the fourth parameter in the `oci_bind_by_name` function. In this sample application, for example, you explicitly set the maximum length for the `$msg` bind variable to 300. On the other hand, you don't specify the maximum length for the `rslt` bind variable used to hold the return value of the `placeNewOrder` function. This is because the `placeNewOrder` function returns either 0 or 1, a 1-digit value.

In contrast, input bind variables are set to their values before binding takes place, which makes it possible for the application to automatically allocate the necessary storage space for the bind. That is why in this sample you don't specify the maximum length for the bind when binding the `$po` variable to the `:po` placeholder representing the `xmldoc` input parameter of the `placeNewOrder` function.

To gain a basic understanding of how to use bind variables in PHP scripts interacting with Oracle via the OCI extension, you can refer to the *Using Bind Variables* section in Chapter 2 *PHP and Oracle Connection*.

Using WSDL

The last piece of software you have to build before you can move on to create the PHP code implementing the SOAP web server is a WSDL document describing the web service to the clients that will use that service.

Web Service Definition Language (WSDL) is a standard way for SOAP web services to describe themselves to their clients, providing all the required information in an XML document. This document describes support by the service operations, expected parameters, and what the service returns.

Schematically, a WSDL document, which is actually an XML document, look like the following:

```
<?xml version="1.0" ?>
<definitions ...>
 <types>
 ...
 </types>
 <message>
 ...
 </message>
 <portType>
 ...
 </portType>
 <binding>
 ...
 </binding>
 <service>
 ...
 </service>
</definitions>
```

Looking through this schematic representation, you may notice that the top-level element of a WSDL document is named definitions that and contains a sequence of other elements. For simplicity, the above representation shows only the top-level child elements under the definitions root element. The key elements used in WSDL documents are outlined in the following table:

Element	Description
definitions	This is the root element of a WSDL document. Apart from the elements describing the web service, this root element contains several attributes declaring a number of namespaces.
types	This element is optional. It contains data type definitions normally described with XML Schema Definition Language (XSD) type system. These data type definitions can be used then to describe the payload data transmitted with the messages through which the service interacts with its clients.
message	A WSDL document may include several message elements, each of which contains one or more part elements describing the data that will be transmitted with the message.
portType	This element contains one or more individual operations, each of which is defined using an operation element.
operation	Each operation element represents a certain action performed by the web service, and includes an input message and output message elements referring to an appropriate message element defined earlier in the document, thus specifying the input and output messages for the operation.
binding	This element defines a concrete protocol and message format for operations defined in the portType construct declared earlier in the document. The binding element contains one or more operation constructs, each of which corresponds to the particular operation element defined in the portType construct.
service	This element contains one or more ports, or endpoints, each of which is defined with a port element.
port	This element is used to associate a specific network address with a binding defined with a binding element earlier in the document. Essentially, it defines a communication endpoint operating on the messages associated with the operations defined earlier in the document.

As you can see, a WSDL description document has a standard structure implemented in XML, containing everything a client of a SOAP web service needs to know to be able to call that service.

 For more information on WSDL, you can refer to the Web Services Description Language (WSDL) W3C Note available at http://www.w3.org/TR/wsdl.

Having covered the fundamentals behind WSDL, let's now turn back to the sample application discussed in the preceding sections. The following listing shows the WSDL document describing the PO web service discussed in this chapter. It is assumed that you save this document as the `po.wsdl` file in the same directory where the `SOAPServer.php` script discussed in the next section will be located.

```xml
<?xml version="1.0" encoding="utf-8"?>
<definitions name ="poService"
             xmlns:http="http://schemas.xmlsoap.org/wsdl/http/"
             xmlns:soap="http://schemas.xmlsoap.org/wsdl/soap/"
             xmlns:xsd="http://www.w3.org/2001/XMLSchema"
             xmlns="http://schemas.xmlsoap.org/wsdl/"
             targetNamespace="http://localhost/PHPOracleInAction/ch9/
po.wsdl">
    <message name="getPlaceOrderInput">
        <part name="body" element="xsd:string"/>
    </message>
    <message name="getPlaceOrderOutput">
        <part name="body" element="xsd:string"/>
    </message>
    <portType name="poServicePortType">
        <operation name="placeOrder">
            <input message="tns:getPlaceOrderInput"/>
            <output message="tns:getPlaceOrderOutput"/>
        </operation>
    </portType>
    <binding name="poServiceBinding" type="tns:poServicePortType">
        <soap:binding style="document" transport="http://schemas.
xmlsoap.org/soap/http"/>
        <operation name="placeOrder">
            <soap:operation soapAction="http://localhost/
PHPOracleInAction/ch9/placeOrder"/>
            <input>
                <soap:body use="literal"/>
            </input>
            <output>
                <soap:body use="literal"/>
            </output>
        </operation>
    </binding>
    <service name="poService">
        <port name="poServicePort" binding="tns:poServiceBinding">
            <soap:address location="http://localhost/PHPOracleInAction/
ch9/SOAPserver.php"/>
        </port>
    </service>
</definitions>
```

You start by creating the definitions element along with a collection of the namespaces that will be used within the document.

In this example, you don't use the types construct to define data types for the data being communicated. Instead, you use native XML Schema types directly when describing the message parts in the part elements defined within the message constructs. In particular, you specify that the payload data in both the input and output messages will be of standard XSD type xsd:string.

In the above WSDL, the operation defined within the portType construct refers to the input message and output message defined earlier in the document. Later, within the binding construct, you define another operation element with the same name to specify the binding information for the operation.

In this example, the port element is used to associate the network address of the SOAP server representing the PO web service with the poServiceBinding binding defined with the binding element. To achieve this, you set the binding attribute of the port element to poServiceBinding and then define the soap:address element within the port element. With soap:address, you specify the URL of the PO web service, so that a client can invoke the web server.

Creating a SOAP Server with PHP's SOAP Extension

The next step in building the PO web service is to implement the SOAP server that will be invoked by the clients using the service. Creating this SOAP server with the PHP SOAP extension is simple. The following listing shows that you just need to write four lines of code to implement the server.

```php
<?php
 //File: SOAPServer.php
 require_once "po.php";
 $srv= new SoapServer("po.wsdl");
 $srv->setClass("po");
 $srv->handle();
?>
```

In the above script, you start by including the po.php file containing the po PHP handler class whose method placeOrder will be exposed as the PO web service.

Further, you create a new SoapServer object, specifying the po.wsdl document discussed in the preceding section. Also you set the po class located in the po.php file as the handler class.

Finally, you use the `handle` method to get the job done. Specifically, this method processes a SOAP request received from the client, calls the `placeOrder` method of the `po` class, and finally sends a response back to the client.

It is important to note that you must not run the `SOAPServer.php` script to make the PO web service available for the clients. When executed, each client, based on the information in the `po.wsdl` document, will run `SOAPServer.php` implicitly.

Building a SOAP Client to Test the SOAP Server

Now that you have your SOAP server built and ready for action, it's time to test it out. To do this, you might want to build a SOAP client that will connect to the SOAP server and call the `placeOrder` exposed method, thus consuming your PO web service.

Since a client of the PO web service is supposed to send a PO XML document to the server, you might want to create such a document on disk, so that it can be reused for testing purposes. For the purpose of this example, you might create the PO XML document shown below, saving it as the `po.xml` file on disk.

```
<purchaseOrder>
    <shipTo country="US">
      <name>John Davidson</name>
      <street>11 Maple Road</street>
      <city>Fairfax</city>
      <state>VA</state>
      <zip>22030</zip>
    </shipTo>
    <billTo country="US">
      <name>John Davidson</name>
      <street>11 Maple Road</street>
      <city>Fairfax</city>
      <state>VA</state>
      <zip>22030</zip>
    </billTo>
    <items>
       <item>
        <partId>942</partId>
        <quantity>2</quantity>
        <price>75</price>
       </item>
       <item>
```

```
        <partId>943</partId>
        <quantity>3</quantity>
        <price>34.95</price>
      </item>
    </items>
  </purchaseOrder>
```

As you can see, the `purchaseOrder` root element in the PO XML document shown in the listing doesn't contain the `noNamespaceSchemaLocation` attribute, thus excluding information on the XML schema with which the document is compliant. Although this makes it easier for the client to build such a PO document, it requires the server to provide this information before processing that document anyway. In this example, you use the XMLType `createSchemaBasedXML` method to explicitly identify the XML schema, namely `po.xsd`, when transforming the `po` parameter of the `placeNewOrder` PL/SQL function to XMLType.

Having the PO XML document shown in the above listing saved as `po.xml`, you can now move on to the client script. Assuming that you have the SOAP extension enabled, you can test the PO web service you have just built with the client script shown in the listing below.

> The client script shown below is implemented with the PHP SOAP extension. However, it is interesting to note that since the SOAP protocol is independent of any particular programming language and implementation specifics, you are not limited to using the PHP SOAP extension when implementing a SOAP client to interact with a SOAP web service built with that PHP extension. Instead, you might, for example, build a SOAP client with .NET or Java.

The client shown below wraps a purchase order document in a SOAP envelope and sends it to the server. The server in turn extracts the purchase order from the SOAP message and then processes the extracted document by the `placeOrder` method of the `po` custom PHP class discussed in the *Building a PHP Handler Class* section earlier.

```php
<?php
//File: SoapClient.php
$handle = fopen("po.xml", "r");
$po= fread($handle, filesize("po.xml"));
fclose($handle);
$client = new SoapClient("http://localhost/PHPOracleInAction/ch9/
po.wsdl");
try {
  print($client->placeOrder($po));
}
catch (SoapFault $e) {
```

```
    print $e->getMessage();
  }
?>
```

In the `SoapClient.php` script shown in the listing, you start by opening and then reading from the `po.xml` file shown at the beginning of this section. In this example, it is assumed that the `po.xml` file is located in the same directory where you saved the `SOAPClient.php` script shown in the listing.

Next, you create a new `SoapClient` object in the WSDL mode, specifying the same WSDL document specified when creating the `SoapServer` object in the `SOAPServer.php` script discussed in the preceding section. The `SoapClient` object is then used to call the `placeOrder` remote method exposed by the PO web service. You call `placeOrder` within the `try` block, trapping possible SOAP fault responses sent by the PHP handler in the `catch` block.

Now if you run the `SoapClient.php` script, it should invoke the `placeOrder` remote method exposed by the PO web service, providing the PO XML document stored in the `po.xml` file as the parameter. The PO web service in turn should validate this PO document against the `po.xsd` XML schema created as discussed in the *Creating an XML Schema to Validate Incoming Documents* section earlier in this chapter and then insert the document into the `po` XMLType table created during registration of the `po.xsd` XML schema. If everything is OK, the service returns an `Ok!` message to the client, which in turn will post that message to your browser.

To make sure that the PO XML document has been successfully inserted into the `po` XMLType table, you might connect to SQL*Plus as `xmlusr/xmlusr` and issue the following query:

```
SET LONG 1000

SELECT * FROM po;
```

This should produce the following output:

```
SYS_NC_ROWINFO$
-------------------------------------------------------------------
<purchaseOrder xmlns:xsi="http://www.w3.org/2001/XMLSchema-instance"
xsi:noNamespaceSchemaLocation="po.xsd" id="US-000001">
  <orderDate>2006-11-03</orderDate>
  <shipDate>2006-11-04</shipDate>
  <shipTo country="US">
    <name>John Davidson</name>
    <street>11 Maple Road</street>
    <city>Fairfax</city>
    <state>VA</state>
```

```
      <zip>22030</zip>
   </shipTo>
   <billTo country="US">
      <name>John Davidson</name>
      <street>11 Maple Road</street>
      <city>Fairfax</city>
      <state>VA</state>
      <zip>22030</zip>
   </billTo>
   <items>
      <item>
         <partId>942</partId>
         <quantity>2</quantity>
         <price>75</price>
      </item>
      <item>
         <partId>943</partId>
         <quantity>3</quantity>
         <price>34.95</price>
      </item>
   </items>
</purchaseOrder>
```

As you can see, the above PO is not quite the same as the original PO shown at the beginning of this section. In particular, the purchaseOrder root element in the above document contains the noNamespaceSchemaLocation and id attributes specifying the XML schema and generated PO ID respectively. Also the above document contains the shipDate and orderDate elements that were not present in the original PO.

Adding Security

One issue with the PO web service discussed in the preceding sections is that no authentication is required when consuming this service. What this means is that everyone may submit a PO document to the service, without having to provide any credentials. However, in a real-world situation you might want only legitimate users to be able to consume the service.

One simple way to achieve this could be to provide legitimate users with a token, which they will then supply with a request message when consuming the service. A significant disadvantage of this approach is that an unauthorized user may obtain the token and then consume the service on behalf of a legitimate user.

To work around this issue, you might use, in place of a fixed token, a hash generated from the value of a particular element or elements in the PO document being passed to the service. On the client, you might include that hash as a part in the SOAP message body containing the PO document in the other part. The server in turn is responsible for retrieving the hashed token from the message and checking whether this hash corresponds to the PO that arrived in the same message. Depending on the algorithm used to generate a hash, each new PO document may come with a potentially different hashed token, which makes it harder for a malicious user to illegally access the service.

As you can see, with the above approach, you don't even need to create and hold security accounts in the database, since the security measures are incorporated in a SOAP message itself, thus enabling message-level security.

 As an alternative to including credentials in the SOAP message body, you might include them in the SOAP message header. To achieve this with the SOAP extension, you might use the following predefined classes: `SoapHeader`, `SoapParam`, and `SoapVar`. A discussion of how to use SOAP message headers to send secure messages, as well as a discussion of how to implement WS-Security authentication is beyond the scope of this chapter.

In the following sections, you learn how to implement a secure version of the PO web service, based on the approach outlined above.

Implementing Authorization Logic Inside the Database

Once the server has received a message containing a PO document and corresponding hashed token, it has to make sure that the token actually conforms to the document, and, thus, the sender is allowed or authorized to consume the service. When implementing authorization logic, you have the usual two choices. You can either implement it with PHP or inside the database with PL/SQL. This example discusses the latter.

In this case, you might implement authorization logic inside the database in a single PL/SQL subprogram that will check whether a supplied token actually conforms to the document that arrived in the same message.

The following listing shows the code you need to execute from SQL*Plus to create the checkCred PL/SQL procedure that takes the PO document and hashed token extracted from the SOAP message that arrived, and verifies whether the token corresponds with the document. If there is a mismatch, the checkCred procedure throws an exception.

```
CONN /as sysdba

GRANT EXECUTE ON dbms_crypto TO xmlusr;

CONN xmlusr/xmlusr;

CREATE OR REPLACE PROCEDURE checkCred (xmldoc XMLType, pswd VARCHAR2)
IS
 billName VARCHAR2(30);
 hashName VARCHAR2(40);
BEGIN
 SELECT extractValue(xmldoc, '/purchaseOrder/billTo/name')
                     INTO billName FROM DUAL;
 hashName := DBMS_CRYPTO.HASH (
 UTL_I18N.STRING_TO_RAW (billName, 'AL32UTF8'),
 DBMS_CRYPTO.HASH_SH1);
 hashName:=NLS_LOWER(hashName);
 IF (hashName != pswd) THEN
   raise_application_error(-20101, 'Specified token is not valid');
 END IF;
END;
/
```

As you can see in the listing, the checkCred procedure takes two parameters. The first one is used to pass a PO document as an XMLType, and the second one is used to pass the token that goes along with that PO document.

In this example, you extract the value of element name specified under the billTo construct in the PO and than hash that value using the hash function from the DBMS_CRYPTO PL/SQL package. By specifying the DBMS_CRYPTO.HASH_SH1 constant as the third parameter of the hash function, you instruct the function to use the Secure Hash Algorithm (SHA) when generating the hash value.

The checkCred procedure shown in the listing is supposed to be invoked before any processing of the PO document takes place. If checkCred determines that the supplied token is not valid, it raises an exception that is supposed to be caught and handled in the caller.

Now you can modify the placeNewOrder PL/SQL function created as discussed in the *Creating PL/SQL Subprograms Implementing the Business Logic of the Web Service* section earlier, so that it takes a hashed token as a parameter and then invokes the checkCred function discussed above. For the purpose of this example, however, you might create new PL/SQL function placeNewOrderSecure to be used in place of placeNewOrder used in the preceding sample.

The following listing shows the SQL statement that you might execute from SQL*Plus to create the `placeNewOrderSecure` PL/SQL function. It is assumed that you have the `po.xsd` PO XML schema created as discussed in the *Creating an XML Schema to Validate Incoming Documents* section at the beginning of this chapter. Also you must have the `transOrder` PL/SQL function created as discussed in the *Creating PL/SQL Subprograms Implementing the Business Logic of the Web Service* section.

The PL/SQL function `placeNewOrderSecure` created as shown below will verify whether the client is allowed to consume the service before performing any processing of the incoming PO document.

```
CONN xmlusr/xmlusr;

CREATE OR REPLACE FUNCTION placeNewOrderSecure (xmldoc
        IN XMLType, pswd IN VARCHAR2, msg OUT VARCHAR2)
RETURN NUMBER
IS
  tmpxml XMLType;
  errcode NUMBER;
  errmesg VARCHAR2(256);
BEGIN
  tmpxml := xmldoc;
  checkCred(tmpxml, pswd);
  XMLTYPE.schemaValidate(tmpxml);
  tmpxml:=transOrder(tmpxml);
  INSERT INTO po VALUES(tmpxml);
  COMMIT;
  msg:='Ok!';
  RETURN 1;
  EXCEPTION
    WHEN OTHERS THEN
      errcode := SQLCODE;
      errmesg := SUBSTR(SQLERRM, 1, 256);
      msg:= errcode || ': ' || errmesg;
      RETURN 0;
END;
/
```

As you can see, the `placeNewOrderSecure` PL/SQL function takes two input parameters where the second one is used to pass the hashed token that goes along with the PO document passed as the first parameter.

You invoke the checkCred function that verifies whether the token passed in the second parameter corresponds with the PO document passed in the first parameter, and generates an exception if the token doesn't conform to the document. In that case, control transfers to the code in the WHEN OTHERS THEN section in which the msg output parameter of the placeNeworderSecure PL/SQL function is set to the error message issued.

Creating a PHP Handler Class

The placeNewOrderSecure PL/SQL function created in the preceding section is supposed to be invoked from within a method of the PHP handler class encapsulating the service functionality.

The following listing shows the po_sec PHP class whose placeOrderSecure method will be exposed by the secure version of the PO web service. The po_sec PHP class is a revision of the po class discussed in the *Building a PHP Handler Class* section earlier. The placeOrderSecure method of the po_sec class takes an incoming PO and a corresponding hashed token as parameters and then passes them to the placeNewOrderSecure PL/SQL function for further processing.

```php
<?php
//File po_sec.php
class po_sec {
   function placeOrderSecure($po, $pswd) {
     if(!$conn = oci_connect('xmlusr', 'xmlusr', '//localhost/orcl')){
         throw new SoapFault("Server","Failed to connect to
                             database");
     };
     $sql = "BEGIN :rslt:=placeNewOrderSecure(XMLType(:po).
createSchemaBasedXML
                            ('po.xsd'), :pswd, :msg); END;";
     $query = oci_parse($conn, $sql);
     oci_bind_by_name($query, ':rslt', $rslt);
     oci_bind_by_name($query, ':po', $po);
     oci_bind_by_name($query, ':pswd', $pswd);
     oci_bind_by_name($query, ':msg', $msg, 300);
     if (!oci_execute($query)) {
         throw new SoapFault("Server","Failed to execute query".$msg);
     };
     if ($rslt==0) {
         throw new SoapFault("Server","Failed to validate or
                             insert PO. ".$msg);
     };
     return $msg;
   }
 }
?>
```

As you can see, the `placeOrderSecure` method takes two parameters. The first passes an incoming PO document, while the other passes the hashed token corresponding to that PO. What the `placeOrderSecure` method does is invoke the `placeNewOrderSecure` PL/SQL function discussed in the preceding section, transmitting the above parameters to that function.

If the `checkCred` PL/SQL procedure, which in turn is invoked from within the `placeNewOrderSecure` PL/SQL function, determines that the supplied token doesn't conform to the supplied PO document, it makes `placeNewOrderSecure` stop execution, returning an appropriate error message. This message is then wrapped in the SOAP fault message and thrown back to the client.

Creating a WSDL Document

Before moving on to creating the SOAP server for the secure version of PO web service discussed here, you need to create the WSDL document describing this service.

This document is shown below:

```
<?xml version="1.0" encoding="utf-8"?>
<definitions name ="poService"
             xmlns:http="http://schemas.xmlsoap.org/wsdl/http/"
             xmlns:soap="http://schemas.xmlsoap.org/wsdl/soap/"
             xmlns:xsd="http://www.w3.org/2001/XMLSchema"
             xmlns="http://schemas.xmlsoap.org/wsdl/"
             targetNamespace="http://localhost/PHPOracleInAction/ch9/
po_sec.wsdl">
    <message name="getPlaceOrderInput">
        <part name="po" element="xsd:string"/>
        <part name="pswd" element="xsd:string"/>
    </message>
    <message name="getPlaceOrderOutput">
        <part name="body" element="xsd:string"/>
    </message>
    <portType name="poServicePortType">
        <operation name="placeOrderSecure">
            <input message="tns:getPlaceOrderInput"/>
            <output message="tns:getPlaceOrderOutput"/>
        </operation>
    </portType>
    <binding name="poServiceBinding" type="tns:poServicePortType">
        <soap:binding style="rpc"
```

```
                    transport="http://schemas.xmlsoap.org/soap/http"/>
          <operation name="placeOrderSecure">
            <soap:operation soapAction="http://localhost/
  PHPOracleInAction/ch9/placeOrderSecure"/
    >
                <input>
                    <soap:body use="literal"/>
                </input>
                <output>
                    <soap:body use="literal"/>
                </output>
            </operation>
      </binding>
      <service name="poService">
          <port name="poServicePort" binding="tns:poServiceBinding">
              <soap:address location="http://localhost/PHPOracleInAction/
  ch9/SOAPServerSecure.php
    "/>
          </port>
      </service>
  </definitions>
```

As you can see, the input message defined in this document consists of two parts:
po and pswd, indicating that the body of a message passed from a client to the server
will include a PO document and token.

Since the input message defined in the document consists of more than one part, you
set the style attribute of the soap:binding element to rpc, thus specifying that each
contained operation is RPC-oriented.

It is assumed that you save the WSDL document shown in the listing as the po_sec.
wsdl file in the same directory in which you will save the SOAPServerSecure.php
script shown below:

```php
<?php
//File: SOAPServerSecure.php
require_once "po_sec.php";
$srv= new SoapServer("po_sec.wsdl");
$srv->setClass("po_sec");
$srv->handle();
?>
```

As you can see, the SOAPServerSecure.php script shown in the listing differs from
SOAPServer.php discussed in the *Creating a SOAP Server with PHP's SOAP Extension*
section earlier only in that it contains references to other files.

Creating a Client Script

Now, to test the newly created secure PO web service, you need to build the client that will connect to the server and call the `placeOrderSecure` method, thus consuming the service.

The client below might be used to test the secure version of the PO web service discussed in this chapter.

```php
<?php
//File: SoapClientSecure.php
$handle = fopen("po.xml", "r");
$po= fread($handle, filesize("po.xml"));
fclose($handle);
$xmlpo = simplexml_load_string($po);
$billName = $xmlpo->shipTo->name;
$pswd=sha1($billName);
$client = new SoapClient("http://localhost/PHPOracleInAction/ch9/
                                                po_sec.wsdl");
try {
  print($client->placeOrderSecure($po, $pswd));
}
catch (SoapFault $e) {
  print $e->getMessage();
}
?>
```

In this example, you use the `SimpleXML` extension, enabled by default in PHP 5, to work with the PO XML document. After the `po.xml` document is loaded from disk, you load it into a `SimpleXML` object using the `simplexml_load_string` function. Next, you access the `purchaseOrder/shipTo/name` element in the PO XML document and then hash the extracted value with the `sha1` PHP hashing function.

From the user's point of view, the secure PO web service discussed here behaves in the same way as the PO web service discussed earlier in this chapter. Assuming that you have the `po.xml` document as shown at the beginning of the *Building a SOAP Client to Test the SOAP Server* section earlier, you can execute the `SoapClientSecure.php` script to test the newly created service. If everything is OK, your browser should yield an `Ok!` message.

Summary

Web Services is a popular technology that makes it possible for developers to expose application's functionality over the Web, enabling computer systems implemented on any software platform to communicate with each other. As a developer, you should not necessarily build new code when it comes to implementing the business logic of a web service. Instead, you can easily add a web service to an existing application, thus reusing well-written pieces of existing code.

In this chapter, you learned how to build a simple web service, using the PHP SOAP extension and Oracle XML technologies. You also saw a simple way to secure a web service so that only legitimate users can consume it.

10

AJAX-Based Applications

As you learned in the preceding chapters, if you want to have an efficient PHP/
Oracle application, you have to think about how to effectively distribute the
application processing between the web/PHP server and the Oracle database server
and try to find some optimal balance point.

However, besides the web/PHP server and the Oracle database server, there may
be another player in the field of application processing, namely the browser. With
the help of browser-side technologies such as JavaScript and AJAX—an acronym
for Asynchronous JavaScript and XML—you might achieve better performance
by moving some application processing from the above-mentioned servers to the
browser. More importantly though, using these technologies allows you to update
the content viewed by the user in the browser without reloading the entire page, thus
producing more responsive solutions.

This chapter explains how AJAX and some other client-side (browser-side) JavaScript
technologies can be used along with the Oracle database technologies as well as PHP
features to improve the responsiveness of PHP/Oracle applications.

Building AJAX-Based PHP/Oracle Applications

Sometimes, the processing performed by your PHP/Oracle application may take
time, making the user wait until the database server produces the results and then
the web/PHP server sends them to the browser. To get through that problem, you
might incorporate rich, interactive UIs into your application, allowing the user to
keep working with the page displayed in the browser while the web/PHP and
database servers are still working in the background on preparing the results to
return. This is where the AJAX technologies may come in very handy.

AJAX is a new, yet effective approach to web development, employing a combination of technologies, such as JavaScript, XML and DOM, which, when used together, makes it possible for a browser to asynchronously interact with the web server, significantly improving the responsiveness of your application. You can think of AJAX as providing a way to dynamically modify a certain portion of the page displayed in the browser, without having to perform the whole page reload.

In the following sections, you learn how you might improve the responsiveness of a PHP/Oracle application with AJAX.

AJAX Interactions

As mentioned, using browser-side technologies such as JavaScript and AJAX allows you to move some application processing to the browser, thereby reducing the network traffic as well as the load on the web/PHP and database servers. However, the real power of AJAX lies in the fact that the JavaScript in an AJAX-based application can interact with the web server asynchronously, thus enabling users to continue working with the page displayed while waiting for a response to the request made to the web server.

Schematically, an AJAX-based PHP/Oracle application might look like the following figure.

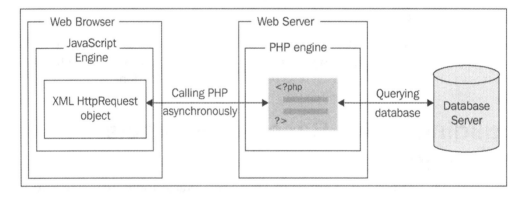

As you can see in the figure, JavaScript code executed on the web browser asynchronously calls PHP code, using the XMLHttpRequest built-in JavaScript object.

To be able to run an AJAX-based application, the user must use a JavaScript-enabled browser supporting the XMLHttpRequest object. You will see this JavaScript object in action in the section *Using the XMLHttpRequest JavaScript Object* later.

The PHP code called from the browser, in turn, interacts with the database server as needed, returning the results back to the browser. The most important thing to note about the interaction between the browser and web/PHP server is that it is performed in the background, without causing the whole page to be reloaded and redrawn.

 Going one step further in improving the responsiveness of your application, you might cache database result sets on the web server, using techniques discussed in Chapter 7 *Caching*. In that case, the PHP script invoked by the JavaScript code performed on the browser could actually retrieve database data from the local cache on the web server, rather than from the database.

Designing an AJAX/PHP/Oracle Monitoring Application

While using AJAX can significantly improve the responsiveness of your application, it's important to understand that AJAX as a technology is not a magic bullet that is appropriate for any situation. Using AJAX can be useful only in those applications where you perform dynamic page processing, updating part of a page rather than the whole page.

Consider a monitoring application that is supposed to display some rapidly changing information, automatically updating the page viewed by a user after a given period of time. Say, for example, you need to create an application that makes the database calculate the number of orders inserted into an orders table for today as well as their total amount, automatically redisplaying the results after a 30-second period of time.

The page generated by the above application might look like the following figure.

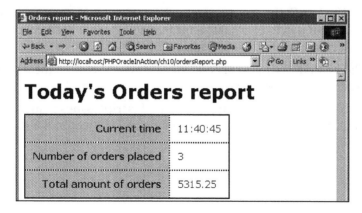

Using AJAX is quite appropriate in this application, since this makes it possible to avoid a full reload of the application page every 30 seconds, allowing the user to continue viewing the page while a successive request is sent and processed, and then a response is received.

Using a 30-second interval between successive requests to the database here implies that the requested data may change quickly. In this particular example, this means that new orders are inserted into the `orders` table very often. Of course, this doesn't mean that new orders arrive in equal time intervals and each new request necessarily returns a different result—you may have no new order for, say, 5 minutes, and then a bunch of them arrive in another 30 seconds. So, it would be a good idea to send a real request to the database only if a change on the requested data has occurred, and satisfy the request from the local cache of the web/PHP server otherwise. To achieve this, you might implement a caching system based on the Oracle Database Change Notification feature, as discussed in Chapter 7 *Caching*.

The following figure gives you a high-level view of how the above application works.

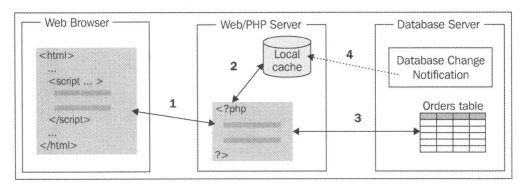

Here is the explanation of the steps in the figure:

- Step 1: The JavaScript running in the browser makes an asynchronous call to the web/PHP server every 30 seconds, invoking the PHP script that returns the most recent figures to be displayed.

- Step 2: The PHP script invoked in step 1 tries to retrieve the data from the local cache of the web server.

- Step 3: If the local cache is empty, the PHP script issues a query against the database, making it calculate the latest figures, based on the data stored in the `orders` table.

- Step 4: The Oracle change notification mechanism, which is working in the background, invokes the PHP script emptying the local cache of the web server, in response to changing data in the orders table.

In the following 0 sections, you will learn how to build an application that works as described in the above scenario.

Building Blocks of an AJAX-Based Solution

Now you are ready to move on and create the building blocks that will work together, making the AJAX-based PHP/Oracle application described in the preceding section. To start with, you might create the required data structures that will be used by the application.

Creating the Data Structures

As you might have guessed, the sample application discussed here will use information calculated based on the data stored in an orders database table. So, you might create a new database schema ajax/ajax, a new table orders in that schema, and then populate the newly created orders table with data.

The following listing contains the SQL script that you can run from SQL*Plus to accomplish the above tasks.

```
CONN /as sysdba

CREATE USER ajax IDENTIFIED BY ajax;

GRANT connect, resource TO ajax;

CONN ajax/ajax;

CREATE TABLE orders(
   ordno   NUMBER PRIMARY KEY,
   orddate DATE,
   total   NUMBER(10,2)
);

INSERT INTO orders VALUES
(1024, '14-nov-2006', 180.50);

INSERT INTO orders VALUES
(1025, '15-nov-2006', 3480.00);

INSERT INTO orders VALUES
(1026, '15-nov-2006', 1700.75);

COMMIT;
```

Building the PHP Script that will Process AJAX Requests

The next step in building the sample is to create the PHP script that will process the AJAX requests issued by the sample's main page. The following listing shows the code for such a script. The getOrdersTotal.php script shown below is designed to process AJAX GET requests that will be issued by the main page of the sample.

```php
<?php
//File:getOrdersTotal.php
$dat = '15-nov-2006';
if(!$dbConn = oci_connect('ajax', 'ajax', '//localhost/orcl')) {
        $err = oci_error();
        trigger_error('Could not establish a connection: ' .
                        $err['message'], E_USER_ERROR);
    };
$strSQL = "SELECT TO_CHAR(SYSDATE, 'HH:MI:SS') time, count(*) num,
                    SUM(total) total FROM orders WHERE orddate= :dat";
$stmt = oci_parse($dbConn,$strSQL);
oci_bind_by_name($stmt, ':dat', $dat);
if (!oci_execute($stmt)) {
        $err = oci_error($stmt);
        trigger_error('Query failed: ' . $err['message'],
                        E_USER_ERROR);
};
oci_fetch($stmt);
$rslt[0] = oci_result($stmt, 'TIME');
$rslt[1] = oci_result($stmt, 'NUM');
$rslt[2] = oci_result($stmt, 'TOTAL');
print $rslt[0]."/".
        $rslt[1]."/".
        $rslt[2];
?>
```

As you can see, the SQL statement issued from within the script retrieves the following information:

- The current time set for the operating system on which the database server is running

- The total number of orders inserted into the orders table for the day specified in $dat

- The total amount of the orders inserted into the orders table for the day specified in $dat

In this simple example, you use a certain date, namely 15-nov-2006, in the WHERE clause of the query, since you have a few orders with this date inserted into the orders table, as discussed in the preceding section. However, in a real-world situation you might use the date specified by the user and passed to the script, or, if you are interested in generating today's report, you might rewrite the WHERE clause as follows:

```
WHERE orddate= TRUNC(SYSDATE)
```

The condition in the above WHERE clause ensures that only rows inserted today are selected.

In this example, you use an array to hold the query results returned by the oci_result function. Then, the script concatenates these results in a single string, using "/" as the delimiter, and outputs it with print.

You might be wondering why you would want to return the results as a single string in this script. The reasons for this will become clear when you read the next section *Using the XMLHttpRequest JavaScript Object*, which explains how to build the JavaScript code that will make asynchronous calls to the getOrdersTotal.php script discussed here, processing the results returned as a single string.

Using the XMLHttpRequest JavaScript Object

XMLHttpRequest—a standard JavaScript class allowing browsers to make asynchronous requests to a web server—lies at the heart of AJAX. As mentioned, users of an AJAX-based application must use a JavaScript-enabled browser supporting the XMLHttpRequest object.

A good overview of the XMLHttpRequest class can be found at http://developer. apple.com/internet/webcontent/xmlhttpreq.html. You can also visit the AJAX page on the Mozilla Developer Center at http://developer.mozilla. org/en/docs/AJAX, on which you will find comprehensive examples on using XMLHttpRequest.

One problem with creating an instance of the XMLHttpRequest class is that it is implemented a bit differently in different browsers. In particular, creating an XMLHttpRequest class's instance may have a different syntax depending on the browser. So, you might find it useful to create a custom JavaScript function that will wrap the code for creating an instance of the XMLHttpRequest class.

The following listing shows such a JavaScript function. It is assumed that you save it in the `ajax.js` file in a folder that will be used to hold all other sample application files, including the PHP script files discussed in the following sections.

```javascript
//File: ajax.js
var req = null;
function initRequest() {
  if (!req) {
   try {
    req = new XMLHttpRequest();
   }
   catch (e) {
    try {
     req = new ActiveXObject('MSXML2.XMLHTTP');
    }
    catch (e) {
     try {
      req = new ActiveXObject('Microsoft.XMLHTTP');
     }
     catch (e) {
      req = null;
     }
    }
   }
  }
}
```

Let's take a closer look at how the above script works.

You start by declaring the `req` variable, initially setting it to null. This variable is then used to hold an instance of the `XMLHttpRequest` class supported now by most of the popular web browsers.

First, you try to create an instance of the `XMLHttpRequest` class. This should work for Mozilla and Safari browsers. However, it doesn't work for Internet Explorer where `XMLHttpRequest` is implemented as an ActiveX object. In that case, you create an instance of `XMLHttpRequest` with the following code: `new ActiveXObject('MSXML2.XMLHTTP')` or, in case of failure, with the following: `new ActiveXObject('Microsoft.XMLHTTP')`. If all of the above attempts to create an `XMLHttpRequest` object fail, you set the `req` variable to `null` again.

Although there are differences in creating an `XMLHttpRequest` instance between Internet Explorer and other major browsers, this object, once created, behaves in the same way, regardless of the browser it is created in.

Now that you can create an instance of the XMLHttpRequest object, you are ready for the next step: building the JavaScript code that will use that instance to make an asynchronous request to the web/PHP server.

This JavaScript code is shown below. You have to save it in a separate file called ordersTotal.js in the same directory as the ajax.js script shown in the preceding listing. The JavaScript code shown below makes an asynchronous call to the getOrdersTotal.php script discussed in the *Building the PHP Script that will Process AJAX Requests* section every 30 seconds.

```
//File: ordersTotal.js
function getOrdersTotal() {
    initRequest();
    req.open("GET", "getOrdersTotal.php?temp="+new Date().
                    getTime(), true);
    req.onreadystatechange = updateOrdersTotal;
    req.send(null);
  }
window.onload = getOrdersTotal;
function updateOrdersTotal() {
 if (req.readyState == 4) {
  var ordersInfo = req.responseText;
  var param = ordersInfo.split("/");
  var curTime = document.getElementById("currentTime");
  var ordNumber = document.getElementById("ordersNumber");
  var ordTotal = document.getElementById("ordersTotal");
  if (curTime.firstChild) {
     curTime.removeChild(curTime.firstChild);
  }
  curTime.appendChild(document.createTextNode(param[0]));
  if (ordNumber.firstChild) {
     ordNumber.removeChild(ordNumber.firstChild);
  }
  ordNumber.appendChild(document.createTextNode(param[1]));
  if (ordTotal.firstChild) {
     ordTotal.removeChild(ordTotal.firstChild);
  }
  ordTotal.appendChild(document.createTextNode(param[2]));
  var tmId = setTimeout(getOrdersTotal, 30000);
 }
}
```

To figure out how the above JavaScript works, let's take a closer look at its code, walking through it step by step.

In the first line of code in the getOrdersTotal JavaScript function shown in the listing, you call the initRequest function from the ajax.js script created as shown in the preceding listing. This function, when invoked, creates the req object, which is nothing but an instance of the XMLHttpRequest JavaScript class.

Once you've got an instance of XMLHttpRequest, you can call its open method to initialize a connection to the web/PHP server, passing three parameters to this method. You set the first parameter to GET, thus telling the browser to use the GET HTTP request method when interacting with the web/PHP server. You pass the name of the PHP script that will be requested as the second parameter. The path to the PHP script is not specified in this particular example, since this script is assumed to be located in the same folder as the page that will use the ordersTotal.js JavaScript discussed here.

Also notice the use of the dummy URL parameter temp within the second argument of the open method. You set this parameter to the current date and time, appending it to the request URL in order to get around Internet Explorer's caching. Using this simple technique guarantees uniqueness of request URLs made with XMLHttpRequest, preventing the browser from using its caching table when dealing with those URLs. From an end-user perspective, this ensures that the application always displays the most recent information rather than out-of-date data taken from the browser's caching table.

As an alternative to the above technique, you might use the setRequestHeader method of the XMLHttpRequest class, setting the If-Modified-Since header to some past date. In that case, the getOrdersTotal JavaScript function discussed here might look like the following:

```
function getOrdersTotal() {
  initRequest();
  req.open("GET", "getOrdersTotal.php", true);
  req.onreadystatechange = updateOrdersTotal;
  req.setRequestHeader("If-Modified-Since", "Thu,
                    25 Nov 2004 00:00:00 GMT");
  req.send(null);
}
```

Finally, by setting the last parameter of the open method to true, you explicitly specify that the request to the web/PHP server will be asynchronous.

After calling the open method of the req object, you have to specify a JavaScript function that will be invoked by the browser when it receives a response from the getOrdersTotal.php script. To achieve this, you have to set the onreadystatechange property of the req object to the name of that JavaScript function. In this particular example, you set onreadystatechange to updateOrdersTotal, which is defined later in this same script.

Now you can send the request to the web/PHP server by invoking the `send` method of the `req` object. Since you don't need to pass any data to the server along with a GET request, you set the `send` method's parameter to null.

Now that you have the `getOrdersTotal` JavaScript function defined, you can call it. By setting the `onload` event property of the `window` JavaScript object to `getOrdersTotal`, you tell the browser to invoke this JavaScript function upon completion of loading a page containing the `ordersTotal.js` script.

The next step is to define a `updateOrdersTotal` JavaScript function, which you specify to be called by the browser when it receives a response from the `getOrdersTotal.php` script. However, note that the browser will invoke `updateOrdersTotal`, every time the request's state changes. That is why, when implementing this function, you first have to make sure that the function has been invoked upon changing the request's state to the one that indicates that the response from the `getOrdersTotal.php` script has been loaded and, therefore, the request is completed. To achieve this, you check whether the `readyState` property of the `req` object representing an instance of `XMLHttpRequest` is set to 4, which indicates just the above state.

Through the `responseText` property of the `XMLHttpRequest` instance used here, you gain access to the result string returned by the `getOrdersTotal.php` script. Then, you use the `split` method of the `string` standard JavaScript object to cut up this result string into pieces, based on the / delimiter, storing the resulting pieces into an array.

 As you might recall from the *Building the PHP Script that will Process AJAX Requests* section, the `getOrdersTotal.php` script concatenates its results into a single string, using / as a delimiter. Here, you extract those results from the result string. Based on using the GET HTTP request method, this technique is appropriate when you deal with small portions of data to be sent between the web/PHP server and the browser. If you need to send a large amount of data, though, you should use a POST request, which is also appropriate when you need to send formatted or sensitive data. Using AJAX POST HTTP requests will be discussed later in this chapter.

Now that you have the results returned by the `getOrdersTotal.php` script, you can update the document loaded in the browser. The first step toward it is to assign each HTML element that you want to update to a JavaScript variable. Then, you update the values of those elements through the associated variables.

Finally, you use the standard JavaScript function `setTimeout` to invoke the `getOrdersTotal` function defined earlier in this same script at a 30 second interval.

Actually, setTimeout executes a JavaScript function specified as the first parameter only once. However, in this particular example, the getOrdersTotal function passed as the first argument to setTimeout, in turn, invokes the updateOrdersTotal function, which then calls setTimeout again, thus ensuring that getOrdersTotal will be invoked again in 30 seconds time.

Putting It All Together

Now you are ready to build the main application page that will use AJAX to asynchronously communicate with the web/PHP server. The following listing shows the source code for such a page. Save this code in the ordersReport.php file in the same folder in which you saved all the script files discussed in the preceding sections.

After the page generated by the code shown in the listing is loaded in a browser, the JavaScript invokes the getOrdersTotal.php script every 30 seconds to retrieve the most recent results from the database, updating the content on the page without performing a full reload.

```html
<html>
 <head>
  <title>Orders report</title>
  <style type="text/css">
   body {
      font-family:     Verdana, Geneva, Arial, Helvetica, sans-serif;
      font-size:       small;
   }
   table {
     border:            2px solid black;
     border-collapse: collapse;
   }
   td, th {
     border:            2px dotted grey;
     padding:          .8em;
   }
   td {
     text-align:       left;
   }
   th {
     text-align:       right;
     background-color: #cccccc;
   }
  </style>
```

```
  <script type="text/javascript" src="ajax.js"> </script>
  <script type="text/javascript" src="ordersTotal.js"> </script>
</head>
<body>
 <h1>Today's Orders report</h1>
  <table>
   <tr><th>Current time</th>
    <td><span id="currentTime"></span></td></tr>
   <tr><th>Number of orders placed</th>
    <td><span id="ordersNumber"></span></td></tr>
   <tr><th>Total amount of orders</th>
    <td><span id="ordersTotal"></span></td></tr>
  </table>
 </body>
</html>
```

The `style` section is used here to put CSS styles in the page, thus improving the look and feel of it.

 For detailed information about CSS, you can refer to the W3C's page on CSS at `http://www.w3.org/Style/CSS`.

Then, you include the JavaScript code discussed in the preceding section. To achieve this, you create two `<script>` tags, setting their `src` attributes to `ajax.js` and `ordersTotal.js` respectively.

Now if you run the script shown in the above listing, it should produce a page that looks like the one as shown in the figure in *Designing an AJAX/PHP/Oracle Monitoring Applications* section in the earlier in this chapter.

Next, you might want to make sure that the page generated is automatically updated in 30 seconds time, displaying the most recent information about the orders stored in the `orders` database table. So, you might insert a new order or orders into that table and then check to see what happens. For example, you might insert new orders into the `orders` table from SQL*Plus by issuing the statements shown below:

```
CONN ajax/ajax;

INSERT INTO orders VALUES
(1027, '15-nov-2006', 134.50);

INSERT INTO orders VALUES
(1028, '15-nov-2006', 1020.00);

COMMIT;
```

With that done, you can switch you focus back to the window in which the browser is displaying the page produced by the ordersReport.php script earlier. After a while, you should notice that the content on the page has been updated, though without full reloading.

Using Caching to Further Improve Responsiveness

Now that you have a working AJAX-based PHP/Oracle application, you might take the next, actually an optional, step towards improving application responsiveness and implement a caching system that will cache the information coming from the database on the web/PHP server. To be efficient, that caching system must update the cache immediately after changing the data in the orders table.

To implement such a caching system, you might use the PEAR::Cache_Lite package in conjunction with the Oracle database change notification feature, as discussed in Chapter 7 *Caching*.

As you might recall from Chapter 7, to make use of the database change notification feature, you have to perform the following two general tasks. First, you have to create a notification handler, a PL/SQL subprogram, which will be executed in response to a change notification. Then, you have to register any query on the orders table, so that the notification handler is invoked whenever a transaction changes the orders table and commits. For full detail on how the above tasks can be implemented, you can go back to Chapter 7 *Caching*, to the section *Using Database Change Notification*.

Implementing Master/Detail Solutions with AJAX

The sample application discussed in the preceding sections is a basic example, of course. Nevertheless, it shows you how to use the XMLHttpRequest JavaScript class to make asynchronous calls to PHP/Oracle scripts.

In the following sections, you will build a more complex sample application showing how to make a PHP/Oracle application more responsive and dynamic with the help of AJAX.

Planning a Master/Detail Solution that uses AJAX

In the preceding sample, you use AJAX to automatically update a page displaying some rapidly changing data stored in the database, actually updating a few numbers on the page. Of course, you might use AJAX to solve more complicated tasks. For example, you might implement an AJAX-based solution that makes the database generate blocks of well-formed HTML code and then dynamically insert those blocks in the browser's HTML tree, significantly updating the loaded page without actually performing a full reload. Fortunately, Oracle database provides tools that can be used to generate an HTML representation of SQL data; for example, XQuery discussed in Chapter 8 *XML-Enabled Applications*, section *Querying Data with Oracle XQuery*.

The following figure gives you a high-level view of how the above application might work.

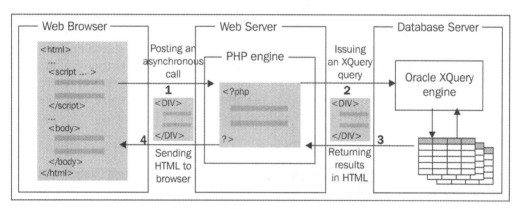

As you might guess, each arrow in the figure represents a certain step in the interactions within the application. Here is the explanation of the steps:

- Step 1: The JavaScript running in the browser posts an asynchronous call to the PHP script on the web/PHP server.

- Step 2: The PHP script invoked in step 1 issues an XQuery query against the database.

- Step 3: Based on the XQuery issued by the PHP script in step 2, the database constructs HTML code from SQL data and then returns it back to the PHP script.

- Step 4: The HTML code constructed in step 3 is returned to the JavaScript running in the browser, and then is inserted directly into the browser's HTML tree, thus dynamically updating the page displayed in the browser.

The above scenario might be used in an application that allows a user to view master/detail data, displaying details on demand. For example, the detail description of an item presented on the page will be downloaded from the database and then displayed on the page only if the user clicks a **Full Description** link related to that item.

In the following sections, you will learn how to build such an application.

Building the Sample Application

For simplicity, the sample application discussed here will have only one page, through which a user will be able to view master/detail information retrieved from the database. In particular, the sample's page, when loaded, will display a list of articles stored in an `articles` database table, much in the way a WWW search engine displays links to the articles that match the criteria specified, along with a short description for each item. However, unlike a page generated by a search engine, a page produced by the sample application will contain a **Full Description** link for each article displayed, allowing a user to asynchronously download additional information about an article of interest from the `articles` and `resources` database tables, and then add this information to the page without performing a full reload.

When loaded, the sample's page might look like the following figure.

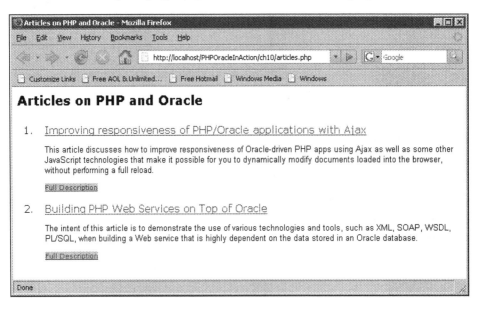

If a user clicks a **Full Description** link on the page shown in the figure, the browser in turn should output a corresponding **Full Description** section, inserting it after the **Full Description** link clicked. The updated page might look like the following figure.

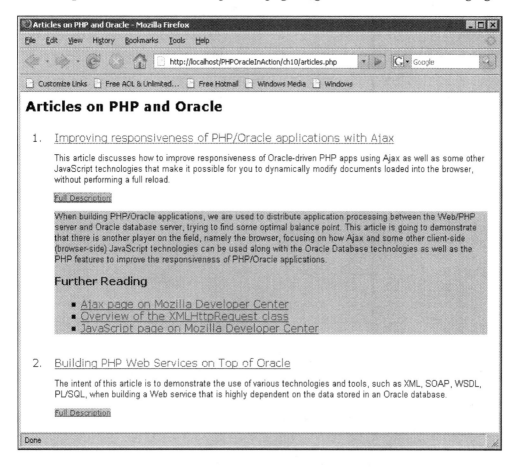

To roll up the **Full Description** section, the user should click the **Full Description** link again.

Now that you have seen what the sample application's page should look like and how it should behave, it's time to move on and build the application.

Creating the Data Structures

As mentioned, the sample application discussed here will use the data stored in `articles` and `resources` database tables. The `article` table is supposed to hold information about the articles that will be displayed on the sample's page. The information stored in the `resources` table will be used to fill up the `Further Reading` column when generating the full description section for an article.

The following listing contains the SQL statements that you might issue from SQL*Plus to create the `articles` table, and then populate it with data.

```
CONN ajax/ajax;

CREATE TABLE articles(
    artno        NUMBER PRIMARY KEY,
    url          VARCHAR2(100),
    title        VARCHAR2(100),
    author       VARCHAR2(50),
    pubdate      DATE,
    shortdesc    VARCHAR2(300),
    fulldesc     VARCHAR2(2000)
);

INSERT INTO articles VALUES(
1,
'http://localhost/articles/AJAXPHPOracle.html',
'Improving responsiveness of PHP/Oracle applications with AJAX',
'Yuli Vasiliev',
'25-nov-2006',
'This article discusses how to improve responsiveness of Oracle-driven
PHP apps using AJAX as well as some other JavaScript technologies that
make it possible for you to dynamically modify documents loaded into
the browser, without performing a full reload.',
'When building PHP/Oracle applications, we are used to distribute
application processing between the Web/PHP server and Oracle database
server, trying to find some optimal balance point. This article is
going to demonstrate that there is another player on the field, namely
the browser, focusing on how AJAX and some other client-side (browser-
side) JavaScript technologies can be used along with the Oracle
Database technologies as well as the PHP features to improve the
responsiveness of PHP/Oracle applications.'
);

INSERT INTO articles VALUES(
2,
'http://localhost/articles/PHPWebServicesOnOracle.html',
```

```
'Building PHP Web Services on Top of Oracle',
'Yuli Vasiliev',
'25-nov-2006',
'The intent of this article is to demonstrate the use of various
technologies and tools, such as XML, SOAP, WSDL, PL/SQL, when building
a Web service that is highly dependent on the data stored in an Oracle
database.',
'The PHP SOAP extension can serve as a good alternative to PEAR::SOAP.
As compared with PEAR::SOAP that is written in PHP, the SOAP extension
has more features and is written in C; thus, another advantage of
using the SOAP extension is speed. By implementing the business logic
of the Web service inside the database, you can reduce overhead for
cross-tier data communication. This can be particularly useful if your
Web service is highly dependent on the data stored in the database.'
);


COMMIT;
```

Now that you have the `articles` table created and populated with some records representing articles, you can create the `resources` table and populate it with links to additional resources each of which is to be related to a certain article stored in the `articles` table.

To create the `resources` table and then populate it with data, you might issue the SQL statements shown below:

```
CONN ajax/ajax;

CREATE TABLE resources(
  resno   NUMBER PRIMARY KEY,
  artno   NUMBER REFERENCES articles(artno),
  url     VARCHAR2(100),
  title   VARCHAR2(100)
);

INSERT INTO resources VALUES(
1,
1,
'http://developer.mozilla.org/en/docs/AJAX',
'AJAX page on Mozilla Developer Center'
);

INSERT INTO resources VALUES(
2,
1,
'http://developer.apple.com/internet/webcontent/xmlhttpreq.html',
```

```
'Overview of the XMLHttpRequest class'
);

INSERT INTO resources VALUES (
3,
1,
'http://developer.mozilla.org/en/docs/JavaScript',
'JavaScript page on Mozilla Developer Center'
);
INSERT INTO resources VALUES (
4,
2,
'http://www.w3.org/TR/soap/',
'W3C SOAP Recommendation documents'
);

COMMIT;
```

When creating the `resources` table, you define and enable a foreign key on the `artno` column that references the primary key defined on the `artno` column of the `articles` table, thus establishing a parent/child relationship between `articles` and `resources` tables.

Generating HTML with Oracle XQuery

As you learned in Chapter 8 *XML-Enabled Applications*, section *Querying Data with Oracle XQuery*, Oracle XQuery can be used to perform various tasks involved in developing XML-enabled database-driven applications, including constructing XML or HTML from SQL data.

The following listing contains the source code for the `getFullDesc.php` script that issues an XQuery query returning HTML code generated from the data stored in the `articles` and `resources` tables set up in the preceding section. This script will be asynchronously called whenever a user clicks a **Full Description** link on a page generated by the sample.

```php
<?php
 //File:getFullDesc.php
 if (isset($_POST['artid'])) {
   $artid=$_POST['artid'];
   if(!$dbConn = oci_connect('ajax', 'ajax', '//localhost/orcl')) {
     $err = oci_error();
     trigger_error('Could not establish a connection: ' .
                   $err['message'], E_USER_ERROR);
```

```
    };
    $sql='SELECT XMLQuery('.'"'.
            'for $i in ora:view("articles")/ROW
            where $i/ARTNO = $artno
            return (
              <div class="fulldesc">
              <p>{xs:string($i/FULLDESC)}</p>
              <h3>Further Reading</h3>
              <ul type="square"> {
              for $j in ora:view("resources")/ROW
              where $i/ARTNO = $j/ARTNO
              return (<li>
                    <a href="{xs:string($j/URL)}">{xs:string($j/
TITLE)}</a>
                    </li>)
                  } </ul></div>)'.'"'.
            'PASSING XMLElement("artno", :artno) AS "artno"
            RETURNING CONTENT) AS FULLDESC FROM DUAL';
    $stmt = oci_parse($dbConn,$sql);
    oci_bind_by_name($stmt, ':artno', $artid);
    if (!oci_execute($stmt)) {
        $err = oci_error($stmt);
        trigger_error('Query failed: ' .
                                $err['message'], E_USER_ERROR);
    };
    oci_fetch($stmt);
    $fullDesc = oci_result($stmt, 'FULLDESC');
    print $fullDesc;
  }
?>
```

In the first line of the script, you check to see if the artid POST variable has been passed in. If so, you set the $artid variable to the value of the artid POST variable and then proceed to connect to the database in order to retrieve the full description of the article whose artno is equal to the value in the $artid variable.

After a connection has been established, you define and then issue an XQuery against the database. You start the FLWOR expression in the XQuery with the for clause, which defines a loop iterating over the rows in the articles table. However, the condition specified in the where clause limits this loop to only one iteration. Specifically, it instructs Oracle to retrieve the information on the article of interest.

In the return clause of the FLWOR expression, you generate the HTML fragment that will be returned by the XQuery. The root element in this fragment is an HTML div tag with the class attribute set to fulldesc.

When it comes to including links to resources related to the article of interest, you define an inner `for` loop that will iterate over the `resources` table's rows that satisfy the condition in the `where` clause.

Using the `PASSING` clause of the `XMLQuery` function, you pass the `$artid` variable to the XQuery as a context item, which is used in the `where` clause to define the article of interest.

After you fetch and then retrieve the HTML code generated by the XQuery query, you send that HTML to the caller, in the way you usually do when it comes to printing out results generated by a script.

Sending Post Requests with AJAX

Now that you have the `getFullDesc.php` script that will be invoked whenever a user clicks a **Full Description** link on the sample's page, you need to create the JavaScript that, in fact, will invoke `getFullDesc.php`.

The following listing shows the source code for such a JavaScript script. Save this code in the `fullDesc.js` file in the same folder in which you saved the `getFullDesc.php` script discussed in the preceding section. The following JavaScript code makes an asynchronous call to the `getFullDesc.php` script, and then dynamically embeds the retrieved HTML code into the page displayed.

```
//File: fullDesc.js
function setFullDesc (artid) {
    var thisFullDesc = document.getElementById('fullDesc'+artid);
    var thisArticle = document.getElementById('article'+artid);
    if (!thisFullDesc){
      initRequest();
      req.open("POST", "getFullDesc.php?temp="+new Date().
                                        getTime(), true);
      req.onreadystatechange = function(){
       if (req.readyState == 4) {
         var fullDescHTML = req.responseText;
         var newFullDesc = document.createElement("div");
         newFullDesc.setAttribute("id", "fullDesc"+artid);
         newFullDesc.innerHTML=fullDescHTML;
         thisArticle.appendChild(newFullDesc);
        }
       };
      req.setRequestHeader("Content-Type",
                         "application/x-www-form-urlencoded");
      req.send("artid=" + artid);
     } else {
```

```
        thisArticle.removeChild(thisFullDesc);
    }
}
```

As you can see, the `setFullDesc` function defined in this JavaScript takes one parameter, namely `artid`. This parameter is then posted along with the `XMLHttpRequest` request to the `getFullDesc.php` script, as a POST parameter specifying the article of interest.

With the help of the `getElementById` method of the JavaScript `document` object representing the page displayed by the browser, you assign the HTML element representing the article of interest to a `thisArticle` JavaScript variable. Also, you assign the HTML element representing the `Full Description` section related to the article of interest to a `thisFullDesc` variable.

As you will learn a bit later, the HTML element whose ID is `"article"+artid`, and which is assigned to the `thisArticle` JavaScript variable here will be actually a `div` HTML element wrapping other HTML elements used to display information about the article of interest. And the element assigned to the `thisFullDesc` variable in this script will be actually another `div` HTML element generated dynamically.

When the user clicks a **Full Description** link on the sample's page, the JavaScript checks to see if the full description information on the article of interest has been displayed. To discover this, you simply check to see if the HTML element assigned to the `thisFullDesc` variable exists. If so, this means that the user likely wants to roll up the full description section. In that case, you remove this section. Otherwise, you create an instance of the `XMLHttpRequest` class and then make an asynchronous request to the web/PHP server, invoking the `getFullDesc.php` script discussed in the preceding section.

When initializing a connection to the web/PHP server, you set the first parameter of the `open` method to `POST`, thus telling the browser to use the POST HTTP request method when interacting with the web/PHP server.

After you get a response from the web/PHP server, you access the request object's `responseText` property to get the results returned by the `getFullDesc.php` script. As you might recall from the preceding section, the `getFullDesc.php` script returns a full description for the specified article in HTML format.

Now that you have the full description of the article of interest as HTML, all you need to do is dynamically embed this HTML into the document loaded in the browser, so that the full description section appears under the **Full Description** link clicked by the user. To achieve this, you first create a `div` HTML element that will be used as a container for the HTML received. Then, you set the `innerHTML` property of the newly created `div` element to that HTML code. Finally, you insert the `div` element into the page as the last child of the HTML element assigned to the `thisArticle` variable. By doing so, you, in fact, directly embed the HTML generated by the database into the loaded page, dynamically updating it.

Since you are sending a POST request to the web/PHP server, you set the `Content-Type` header for the request to `application/x-www-form-urlencoded`.

In this particular example, the `send` method takes one parameter to be posted with the request. Specifically, you post the ID of the article for which you want to get a full description.

Styling with CSS

Before moving on to create the PHP script that will generate the page to be accessed by a user, you might want to define CSS styles that will be used to improve the look and feel of that page. In the preceding example, you simply put CSS styles inside the `style` HTML tag of the sample application's page. In this example, you will put them in a separate file.

The following listing shows the CSS styles that might be used for the sample discussed here. Save this code in the `styles.css` file in the same folder in which you saved the script files discussed in the preceding sections.

```css
body {
    font-family:    Verdana, Geneva, Arial, Helvetica, sans-serif;
    font-size:      small;
}
h3, a {
    font-size:      1em;
}
p {
    font-family: Arial, Helvetica, sans-serif;
    font-size:      .8em;

}
.fulldesc {
    background:#ccc;
}

.desclink {
    font-size:      0.7em;
    background:#ccc;
}
```

Putting It All Together

Now you are ready to build the PHP script that will generate the sample application's page. The listing below shows the source code for such a script. Save this code in the `articles.php` file in the same folder in which you saved the script files discussed in the preceding sections.

```php
<?php
   //File:articles.php
    if(!$dbConn = oci_connect('ajax', 'ajax', '//localhost/orcl')) {
        $err = oci_error();
        trigger_error('Could not establish a connection: ' .
                        $err['message'], E_USER_ERROR);
    };
    $sql='SELECT artno, url, title, shortdesc FROM articles';
    $stmt = oci_parse($dbConn,$sql);
    if (!oci_execute($stmt)) {
        $err = oci_error($stmt);
        trigger_error('Query failed: ' .
                        $err['message'], E_USER_ERROR);
    };
?>
<html>
 <head>
  <title>Articles on PHP and Oracle</title>
  <link rel="stylesheet" type="text/css" href="styles.css" />
  <script type="text/javascript" src="ajax.js"> </script>
  <script type="text/javascript" src="fullDesc.js"> </script>
 </head>
<body>
 <h2>Articles on PHP and Oracle</h2>
 <table cellpadding = "8">
 <?php
  while ($emp = oci_fetch_array($stmt, OCI_ASSOC)) {
   print '<tr>';
   print '<td valign ="top">'.$emp['ARTNO'].'</td>';
   print '<td>'.
            '<div id="article'.$emp['ARTNO'].'">'.
             '<a href="'.$emp['URL'].'" >'.$emp['TITLE'].'</a>'.
             '<p>'.$emp['SHORTDESC'].'</p>'.
             '<a href="#" onclick="setFullDesc('.$emp['ARTNO'].')"
                 class = "desclink">Full Description</a>'.
            '</div>'.
            '</td>';
    print '</tr>';
```

```
    }
  ?>
  </table>
  </body>
</html>
```

The SELECT statement used in this script will return the information on all the articles stored in the `articles` table. After this statement is executed, you fetch and display its results in the `while` loop, styling and formatting the output as specified in the `styles.css` defined in the preceding section.

Now if you run the script shown in the listing, you should see a page something like the one shown in the figure at the beginning of the *Building the Sample Application* section earlier in this chapter. Then, if you click a **Full Description** link on this page, the browser should output a corresponding **Full Description** section, inserting it after the **Full Description** link clicked. The updated page might look like the figure at the end of the *Building the Sample Application* section. You can always remove a **Full Description** section by clicking the **Full Description** link above that section.

Summary

As you learned in this chapter, using AJAX is a great way to improve the responsiveness of PHP/Oracle applications, making them more dynamic and interactive, and faster to respond to user actions. In particular, you saw an example of an AJAX-based PHP/Oracle application whose page automatically updates itself at a certain time interval, displaying the most recent data retrieved from the database. The other sample application discussed in this chapter demonstrated how you might benefit from using AJAX in a PHP/Oracle application that provides access to master/detail information stored in the database, retrieving and displaying details on demand.

However, it's important to understand that the AJAX approach to web development is not a magic bullet that is appropriate for any situation. Before you start building an AJAX-based solution or begin ajaxifying an existing one, the first thing you have to consider is whether AJAX is appropriate for the application you're working on. Using AJAX can be useful in applications where you need to perform dynamic page processing, updating part of a page rather than the whole page, while still allowing the user to work with the page being updated.

A

Installing PHP and Oracle Software

To follow the examples provided throughout this book, you need to have a few pieces of software installed and working properly, so that you have the following servers up and running in your system:

- Oracle database server
- Web/PHP server

To achieve this, you have to install the following software components:

- Oracle Database Server software
- Oracle database
- SQL command-line tool to interact with the database
- Oracle Client libraries
- Web server with activated support for PHP

While Chapter 1 briefly discusses the above software components, this appendix provides a quick-and-dirty guide to obtaining, installing, and configuring them to work together.

Installing Oracle Database Software

As discussed in Chapter 1 *Getting Started with PHP and Oracle* in the *Obtaining Oracle Database Software* section, although most of the Oracle products are available on a commercial basis, you can download them from Oracle Technology Network at `http://www.oracle.com/technology/software/index.html` for free. Then, you can use the downloaded software for free while developing and prototyping your applications, and buy the license only for those Oracle products that will be used in your final product.

The Oracle Technology Network Developer License can be found at
`http://www.oracle.com/technology/software/htdocs/`
`devlic.html.`

As you learned in Chapter 1 in the section *Choosing Between Oracle Database Editions*, Oracle Database is available in several editions. An important thing to consider when choosing between Oracle Database editions is what edition best suits your needs and budget.

Once you have decided which edition of Oracle Database to use, it's time to download the appropriate installation archive file and then walk through the installation process. The following section describes the basic installation steps for Oracle Database 10g Enterprise/Standard editions on both Windows and Unix systems. It is followed by a section that describes the basic installation steps for Oracle Database 10g Express Edition.

 For detailed information on how to install Oracle Database software, see Oracle documentation: *Oracle Database Installation Guide* for your operating system platform. Oracle documentation is available from the documentation section of the OTN website at: `http://www.oracle.`
`com/technology/documentation/index.html.`

Installing Oracle Database Enterprise/ Standard Editions

Once you have downloaded the installation archive file, you can extract it on your hard disk and then start the installation.

Most installation steps are common to all operating system platforms and involve running the Oracle Universal Installer, a Java-based graphical user interface tool that is used to install and remove Oracle software.

Here are the basic installation steps for Oracle Database 10g Enterprise/Standard Editions. By following these steps, you will not only install Oracle Database Server software but also an Oracle database, Oracle Client libraries, and SQL*Plus — an SQL command-line tool to interact with the database.

- Log on to the computer as a user with the administrative privileges so that you can install Oracle Database software and run the database.
- Navigate to the directory where you downloaded the installation archive file, extract it, and then execute `setup.exe` to start Oracle Universal Installer on Windows. On Linux, run the following command: `$ ./runInstaller`

The following figure shows what the first screen of the Oracle Universal Installer looks like on Windows.

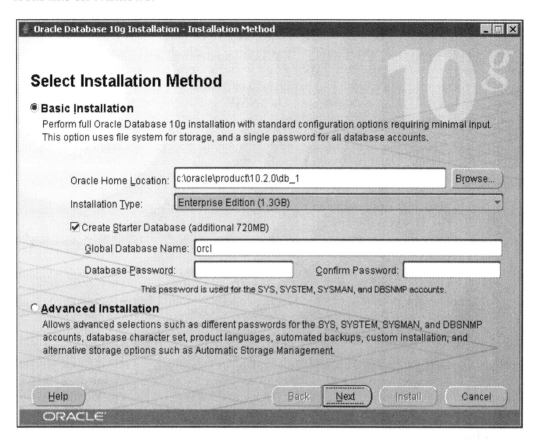

- On the first screen of the Oracle Universal Installer, select either **Basic Installation** to quickly install Oracle Database software or **Advanced Installation** to have advanced installation choices.

Selecting the **Advanced Installation** option allows you to customize your installation. For information about advanced installation choices, see *Oracle Database Installation Guide* for your platform.

From now on, it is assumed that you have chosen the **Basic Installation** option.

- On the same screen, specify the full path to the directory where you want to install the database.

- On the same screen, choose what database product you want to install: **Enterprise Edition**, **Standard Edition**, **Personal Edition**, or **Custom Installation**.

- On the same screen, check the **Create Starter Database** box to create a database during installation. This option is available on this screen when you select **Basic Installation**. Having checked the **Create Starter Database** box, you have to specify the **Global Database Name** and the password for the **SYS**, **SYSTEM**, **SYSMAN**, and **DBSNMP** administrator accounts.

 A global database name consists of the database name and database domain, and must be unique within the same network. So, you may find it convenient to use the network domain name as the database domain, but generally speaking you don't have to follow this rule. For simple cases, you need not specify a database domain at all—you may use only the database name.

- On the same screen, click **Next** to continue.

- (For Unix and Linux only) On the **Specify Inventory Directory and Credentials** screen, specify the full path to a directory for installation files and make sure to specify an operating system group that has "write" permission to this directory.

 This screen appears only during the first installation of Oracle software on this computer.

On the **Product-Specific Prerequisite Checks** screen, make sure that your system meets the minimum requirements for installing the chosen products. Once all the checks have been successfully completed, click **Next** to continue.

 You can proceed with the installation only if the status of each check performed in this stage is **Succeeded** or **Warning**.

- On the summary screen, review the installation information and click the **Install** button to start the installation. This opens the Install screen that shows installation progress.

- On the **Configuration Assistants screen**, review the status information for the configuration assistants that are started automatically and used to configure the software and create a database.

- (For Unix and Linux only) On the **Execute Configuration Scripts** screen, read the instructions and then run the scripts mentioned on this screen as the root user.

- On the **End** screen, note the information and exit the Installer.

That is it. Your database is up and ready for use now.

Installing Oracle Database Express Edition (XE)

If you want to use an Oracle database for free even in the final product, consider Oracle Database Express Edition—a lightweight Oracle database that is free to develop, deploy, and distribute. This section describes the basic installation steps for this Oracle Database edition.

One word of warning before you proceed with Oracle Database Express Edition. Note that some Oracle Database features are not available in this lightweight edition of Oracle Database. For example, the XQuery feature discussed in Chapter 8 in the *Querying Data with Oracle XQuery* section is not available in Oracle Database XE. Also, the Oracle Virtual Private Database (VPD) feature discussed in Chapter 6 in the *Row-Level Security Using VPD* section is available only in Enterprise Edition of Oracle Database.

Once you have completed the following installation steps, you will have an Oracle Database XE Server (including an Oracle database), Oracle Database XE Client, and SQL*Plus installed on your computer.

Installing Oracle Database XE on Windows

Here are the installation steps for Oracle Database 10g Express Edition on Windows:

- Log in to Windows as a user of the Administrators group.

- Make sure that the ORACLE_HOME environment variable is not set in your system. Otherwise delete it. This can be done from the System Properties dialog, which can be invoked from **Control Panel | System**.

- Double-click the Oracle Database XE installation executable downloaded from OTN to run Oracle Database XE Server installer.

The following figure shows what the screen of the Oracle Database XE Server installer looks like after you run it.

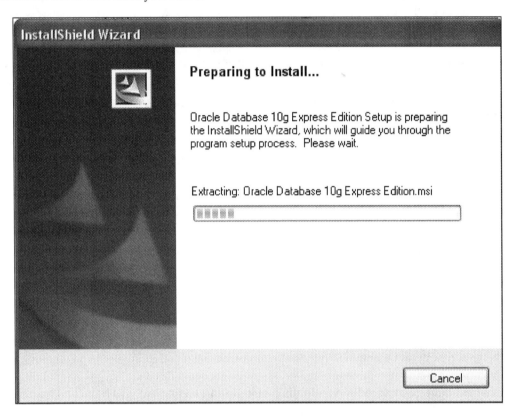

- In the Welcome window of the Wizard, click **Next**.

- In the **License Agreement** window, click **I accept** and then click **Next**.

- In the **Choose Destination Location** window, choose the directory for installation and click **Next**.

- If at least one of the following port numbers: 1521, 2030, 8080 is already in use in your system, you will be prompted to enter an available port number. Otherwise, the above numbers will be used automatically.

- In the **Specify Database Passwords** window, enter the passwords for the SYS and SYSTEM database accounts and click **Next**.

- In the Summary window, click **Install** to proceed to installation, or **Back** to turn back and modify the settings.

- After the installation is complete, click **Finish**.

That is it. Your database is up and ready for use now.

Installing Oracle Database XE on Linux

Here are the installation steps for Oracle Database 10g Express Edition on Linux:

- Log in to your computer as root.

- Change directory to the one in which you downloaded the Oracle Database XE oracle-xe-10.2.0.1-1.0.i386.rpm installation executable and install the RPM:
  ```
  $ rpm -ivh oracle-xe-10.2.0.1-1.0.i386.rpm
  ```

- When prompted, run the following command to configure the database:
  ```
  $ /etc/init.d/oracle-xe configure
  ```

- When entering configuration information, accept the default port numbers for the Oracle Database XE graphical user interface and Oracle database listener: 8080 and 1521 respectively. Also, enter and confirm the passwords for the SYS and SYSTEM default user accounts.

> If, when configuring the database, you select **Yes** to the question of whether you want the database to automatically start along with the computer, then the database is up and ready for use now. Otherwise you have to start it manually as follows:
> ```
> $ /etc/init.d/oracle-xe start
> ```

Installing Apache HTTP Server

Before you can install PHP, you must have a web server installed and working in your system. Although PHP has support for most of the web servers worth mentioning, Apache/PHP remains the most popular combination among developers.

The Apache HTTP server is distributed under the Apache License, a free software/open-source license whose current version can be found on the licenses page of the Apache website at: http://www.apache.org/licenses/.

You can download the Apache HTTP server from the download page of the Apache website at: http://httpd.apache.org/download.cgi.

As mentioned in Chapter 1 in the *Apache HTTP Server* section, Oracle recommends that you install a web server on another machine but on the same network as the database server. However, for simplicity you can have both the Oracle database server and web server on the same machine.

In fact, installing Apache is a very easy process: On Windows, if you have downloaded the version of Apache for Windows with the .msi extension (the recommended way), you just run the Apache .msi file and then follow the wizard. On Unix-like systems, once you have downloaded a source version of the Apache HTTP server, you perform standard operations that you normally deal with when it comes to installing new software from sources: extract, configure, compile, and install.

Once you have Apache installed and configured, you can start it. On Windows, Apache is normally run as a service. You can configure service startup by choosing Automatic, Manual, or Disabled. On Unix-like systems, Apache, the httpd program, is run as a demon. It is recommended that you use the apachectl control script to invoke the httpd executable:

```
# /usr/local/apache2/bin/apachectl start
```

To make sure that your web server is up and running on your machine, open your web browser to the URL http://localhost/.

The following figure shows what the default page of Apache web server looks like.

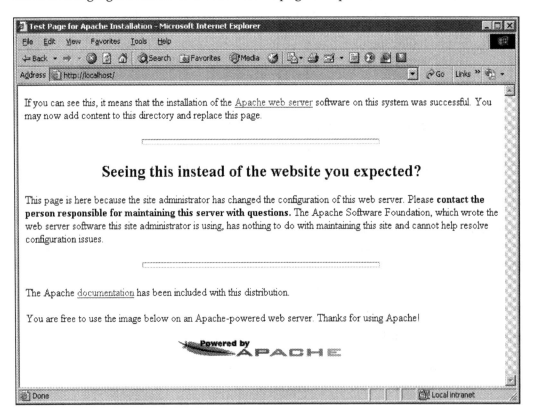

Now that you have your web server up and running, you can move on to the next step, obtaining and installing PHP.

Installing PHP

The current recommended releases of PHP are available for download from the downloads page of the php.net site at:

    http://www.php.net/downloads.php

From this page, you can download the latest stable release of PHP 5 and then follow the steps below to install PHP in your system. For further assistance along the way, you may consult the *Installation and Configuration* manual available on the php.net web site at: http://www.php.net/manual/install.php. Alternatively, you might read the install.txt file that is shipped with PHP.

Installing PHP on Windows

Here are the basic installation steps for PHP 5 on Windows:

- Extract the distribution file into the c:\php directory.
- Add the C:\php directory to the PATH to make php5ts.dll available to the web server modules.
- Rename php.ini-recommended to php.ini.
- In php.ini, set the doc_root to your htdocs directory of Apache. For example:

      doc_root = c:\Program Files\Apache Group\Apache2\htdocs

- In the Apache httpd.conf configuration file, to install PHP as an Apache module, insert the following two lines:

      LoadModule php5_module "c:/php/php5apache2.dll"
      AddType application/x-httpd-php .php

- In the Apache httpd.conf configuration file, configure the path to php.ini:

      PHPIniDir "C:/php"

- Restart Apache.

As an alternative to the above manual installation, you might use the Windows PHP installer that is also available from the downloads page of the php.net website.

[Although the Windows PHP installer is the fastest way to make PHP work, it doesn't allow you to set every option as you might want to. So, using the installer isn't the recommended method for installing PHP.]

Once you have PHP installed on your Windows system, you might want to set some extensions for added functionality. It is important to note that many extensions are built into the Windows version of PHP. To use these extensions, you just uncomment them in the php.ini configuration file—no additional DLLs are required. However, some of the extensions require extra DLLs to work. For example, the PHP OCI8 extension needs the Oracle Client libraries.

Installing PHP on Unix-Like Systems

Here are basic installation steps for PHP 5 on Unix-like systems:

- Extract the distribution file:

```
# gunzip php-5xx.tar.gz
# tar -xvf php-5xx.tar
```

- Change dir to the directory containing the PHP sources:

```
# cd php-5xx
```

- Configure your PHP installation:

```
# ./configure --with-apxs2=/usr/local/apache2/bin/apxs
```

[You cannot configure PHP to support the PHP OCI8 extension until you install the Oracle Client libraries required to run OCI applications (unless you have PHP and Oracle installed on the same computer). You'll need to recompile PHP for OCI8 support once you have these libraries installed. See the Oracle Instant Client section for details.]

- Compile and then install PHP:

```
# make
# make install
```

- Set up `php.ini`.

  ```
  # cp php.ini-dist /usr/local/lib/php.ini
  ```

- Edit the `httpd.conf` Apache configuration file to load the PHP module into Apache:

  ```
  LoadModule php5_module modules/libphp5.so
  ```

- In `httpd.conf`, add handlers for files with the `.php` and .phps extensions:

  ```
  AddType application/x-httpd-php .php
  AddType application/x-httpd-php-source .phps
  ```

- Restart Apache:

  ```
  # usr/local/apache2/bin/apachectl start
  ```

By now you should have a working Apache/PHP web server.

Testing PHP

Once you have finished the installation steps, you might want to test PHP. The easiest way to make sure that PHP works properly is by using the following simple PHP script:

```
<?php
  phpinfo();
?>
```

Save this script as `phptest.php` in the `htdocs` directory of Apache and then run it in your browser by opening the following URL:

```
http://yourservername/phptest.php
```

Provided your Apache/PHP web server is up and running, the `phptest.php` script should output a large amount of information about the current state of PHP. Graphically it might look like the following figure.

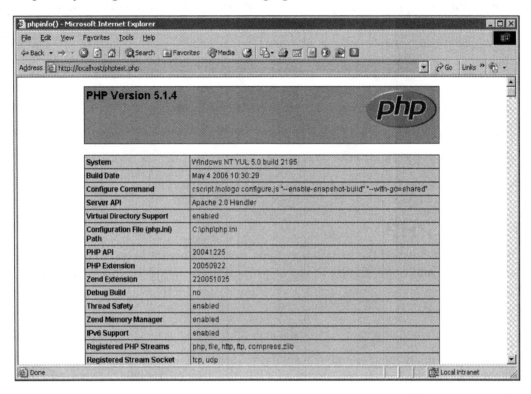

As expected, the `phpinfo` output doesn't contain an OCI8 section—we have installed PHP without OCI8 support. The next section discusses how to add the OCI8 support to an existing installation of PHP.

Bridging the Gap Between Oracle and PHP

By now you should have an Oracle database and Apache/PHP web server installed and working. However, before you can start developing PHP/Oracle applications, you have to enable the OCI8 extension in your PHP installation.

Oracle Instant Client

If you have both the database and web server installed on the same computer then you already have all the required Oracle components—no Instant Client is required, and so you can skip to the next section *Enabling the OCI8 Extension in an Existing PHP Installation*.

However, if you have the database and web server installed on different computers, you will need to install another piece of software, which will bridge the gap between Oracle and PHP. Specifically, you have to install the Oracle client libraries needed by the PHP OCI8 extension.

Consider Oracle Instant Client, a package containing Oracle client libraries required to run OCI, OCCI, and JDBC-OCI applications. Note that Oracle Instant Client comes with a free license for both development and production environments.

You can download a copy of Oracle Instant Client specific to your platform from the Instant Client web page on OTN at:

```
http://www.oracle.com/technology/tech/oci/instantclient/
instantclient.html
```

From the above page, you should download the Basic Instant Client Package that includes all the files required to run OCI, OCCI, and JDBC-OCI applications.

On Windows, perform the following steps to install the Instant Client Package:

- Download a copy of Oracle Instant Client from OTN.
- Unzip the package into a single directory in your file system.
- Add the path to the directory in which you unzipped the libraries to the PATH environment variable.

On UNIX-like platforms, perform the following steps:

- Download a copy of Oracle Instant Client from OTN.
- Unzip the package into a single directory in your file system.
- Set LD_LIBRARY_PATH to the directory in which you unzipped the libraries.

Once you perform the above steps, you can move on and enable the OCI8 extension in your PHP installation.

Enabling the OCI8 Extension in an Existing PHP Installation

On Windows, perform the following steps to enable the OCI8 extension in your existing PHP installation:

- In `php.ini`, uncomment the OCI8 extension line:

  ```
  extension=php_oci8.dll
  ```

- In `php.ini`, set the `extension_dir` directive to the directory in which `php_oci8.dll` resides:

  ```
  extension_dir= c:\php\ext
  ```

- Restart Apache.

On UNIX-like platforms, perform the following installation steps:

- Run configure with Apache2 and OCI8 support:

  ```
  # cd php-5xx
  # ./configure --with-apxs2=/usr/local/apache2/bin/apxs \
  --with-config-file-path=$HOME/apache/conf \
  --with-oci8-instant-client=/home/instantclient10_2 \
  --enable-sigchild
  ```

- Rebuild PHP:

  ```
  # make
  # make install
  ```

- Restart Apache:

  ```
  /usr/local/apache2/bin/apachectl start
  ```

To make sure that the OCI8 extension was successfully enabled, you might run the `testphp.php` script discussed in the *Testing PHP* section earlier in this appendix. This time the output should include the OCI8 section verifying that OCI8 support is enabled.

Installing SQL*Plus Instant Client

Most of the examples in this book assume that you will use SQL*Plus when it comes to performing database administration or creating database objects. Note that SQL*Plus is installed by default when you install the Oracle Database software. So, if you are going to use a local database, you don't need to install SQL*Plus since you already have it. Otherwise, you might take advantage of SQL*Plus Instant Client—the SQL*Plus command-line tool that allows you to communicate with a remote database.

To install SQL*Plus Instant Client on your computer, perform the following steps:

- Download the SQL*Plus Instant Client Package specific to your platform from the Instant Client web page on OTN at:

  `http://www.oracle.com/technology/tech/oci/instantclient/`
  `instantclient.html`

- Unzip the package to the same directory where you unzipped the Basic Instant Client Package files.

- Optionally, set a user environment variable `NLS_LANG` to an appropriate value.

 The `NLS_LANG` parameter is composed of three optional components: language, territory, and character set. To specify it, you use the following syntax: `NLS_LANG = language_territory.charset`. `NLS_LANG` defaults to `AMERICAN_AMERICA.US7ASCII`. For information about supported `NLS_LANG` settings, see Oracle documentation: *Oracle Database Globalization Support Guide*.

That is it. Now you can use SQL*Plus Instant Client to connect to a remote database.

Installing Zend Core for Oracle

As mentioned in Chapter 1, section *Zend Core for Oracle*, you might significantly speed up and simplify the process of making PHP and Oracle software work together by taking advantage of Zend Core for Oracle, a pre-built stack that delivers a rapid development and deployment foundation for Oracle-driven PHP applications, saving you the trouble of separately downloading and installing the required pieces of software.

Once you have completed the following installation steps, you will have a Web/PHP server ready to work with your Oracle database.

Installing Zend Core for Oracle on Windows

Here are the installation steps for Zend Core for Oracle on Windows:

- Log in to your computer as a user of the Administrators group.

- Download Zend Core for Oracle from Zend Network. You can start by visiting the following page:

  `https://www.zend.com/core/oem_registration.php?access_`
  `code=OracleDB`

- After you have downloaded the Zend Core for Oracle package, double-click it to start the installation wizard.

- In the Welcome window, click **Next**.

- In the **License Agreement** window, select **I accept ...** and click **Next**.

- In the **Setup Type** window, you can choose either **Complete** or **Custom** setup options. If you select **Complete**, all of the Zend Core for Oracle components will be installed. Otherwise, you will be able to choose a folder for Zend Core for Oracle installation and components to install. Click **Next** to continue.

- In the **Web Server Selection** window, select the web server to be used. It is recommended that you select the default Apache installed on your computer. Then, click **Next**.

- In the **Web Server API** window, accept the recommended Server API and click **Next**.

- In the **Extension Association** window, choose the extensions that will be associated with the Core PHP installation and click **Next**.

- In the **Password** window, enter a password for accessing the Zend Core for Oracle GUI and click **Next**.

- In the **Ready to Install the Program** window, click **Install** to start installation.

- In the **Installation Complete** window, choose **Yes** for the restart option and click **Finish** to complete the installation and restart the computer.

That is it. Now you should have a Web/PHP that is server ready to work with your Oracle database.

Installing Zend Core for Oracle on Linux

Here are the installation steps for Zend Core for Oracle on Linux:

- Log in to your computer as root.

- Download Zend Core for Oracle from Zend Network. You can start by visiting the following page:

  ```
  https://www.zend.com/core/oem_registration.php?access_
  code=OracleDB
  ```

- After you have downloaded the package, extract Zend Core for Oracle:

  ```
  $ tar -zxf ZendCoreForOracle-v1.3.1-Linux-x86.tar.gz
  ```

- Change directory to ZendCoreForOracle-v1.3.1-Linux-x86:

  ```
  $ cd ZendCoreForOracle-v1.3.1-Linux-x86
  ```

- Start installation:

  ```
  ./install
  ```

- In the **Welcome** screen, click **OK** to continue.

- In the **License Agreement** screen, click **exit**. Then, click **Yes** to accept the license agreement and continue with the installation.

- When prompted, choose the directory for installing Zend Core for Oracle and click **OK**.

- In the next screen, enter a password for accessing the Zend Core for Oracle GUI and click **OK**.

- When prompted, select the web server for Zend Core installation and click **OK**. It is recommended that you select the default Apache installed on your computer.

- In the next screen, accept the selected installation method for the PHP on the web server and click **OK**.

- In the next screen, select a virtual server for the Zend Core GUI and click **OK**.

- When prompted, select to restart the web server to apply the changes.

- In the final screen, click **Exit** to complete the installation and restart the web server.

That is it. Now you should have a Web/PHP that is server ready to work with your Oracle database.

Index

about 73, 74
advantages 75
calling 82
calling, from trigger 85, 86
creating 80, 81
ideal situation 76-79

T

transactional code, developing
code, moving to database 105-109
PHP transactions, controlling 99-105
statement level rollbacks 106-109
triggers, using 105, 106
transaction isolation considerations
about 109
autonomous transactions 118
concurrent update issues 113-118
OCI8 functions, choosing 110-113
transactions 91
about 90
ACID rules 91
handling 289
isolation considerations 109
Oracle, working in 92
overview 89
PHP/Oracle, working in 93-96
transactional code 99
triggers
creating 84, 85
firing 85
stored procedures, calling 85, 86
using 83

V

view
about 69
advantages 69, 70
data complexity, hiding 70, 71
WHERE clause 71, 72
views
column-level security, implementing
192-195
column values, masking 195
column values, masking with DECODE
function 195-198
database access, setting up 191, 192

row-level security, implementing 198-201
Virtual Private Database. *See* **VPD**
VPD
row-level security, implementing 201-204

W

web services
about 295
business logic, building 300
security 319
SOAP web service 299
WHERE clause 71

X

XML data manipulating, Oracle used
about 262
database storage options 263, 264
XML data, retrieving 272-275
XML schemas 267-271
XMLType, using 265, 266
XML processing, with Oracle
about 254
database, moving into 257, 258
Oracle SQL/XML generation functions,
using 254-256
XML data, sorting 258, 259
XSLT transformations, performing 260, 261
XML processing, with PHP
DOM document querying, XPath used 247
PHP extension 244
XML creating, DOM PHP extension used
245, 246
XSLT used 248-254
XQuery
data, querying 290
XML, breaking into relational data 293
XML, constructing 291, 292

Z

Zend Core for Oracle
about 16
features 16
installing 369
installing, on Linux 370, 371
installing, on Windows 369, 370

Packt Open Source Project Royalties

When we sell a book written on an Open Source project, we pay a royalty directly to that project. Therefore by purchasing PHP Oracle Web Development.

In the long term, we see ourselves and you — customers and readers of our books — as part of the Open Source ecosystem, providing sustainable revenue for the projects we publish on. Our aim at Packt is to establish publishing royalties as an essential part of the service and support a business model that sustains Open Source.

If you're working with an Open Source project that you would like us to publish on, and subsequently pay royalties to, please get in touch with us.

Writing for Packt

We welcome all inquiries from people who are interested in authoring. Book proposals should be sent to authors@packtpub.com. If your book idea is still at an early stage and you would like to discuss it first before writing a formal book proposal, contact us; one of our commissioning editors will get in touch with you.

We're not just looking for published authors; if you have strong technical skills but no writing experience, our experienced editors can help you develop a writing career, or simply get some additional reward for your expertise.

About Packt Publishing

Packt, pronounced 'packed', published its first book "Mastering phpMyAdmin for Effective MySQL Management" in April 2004 and subsequently continued to specialize in publishing highly focused books on specific technologies and solutions.

Our books and publications share the experiences of your fellow IT professionals in adapting and customizing today's systems, applications, and frameworks. Our solution-based books give you the knowledge and power to customize the software and technologies you're using to get the job done. Packt books are more specific and less general than the IT books you have seen in the past. Our unique business model allows us to bring you more focused information, giving you more of what you need to know, and less of what you don't.

Packt is a modern, yet unique publishing company, which focuses on producing quality, cutting-edge books for communities of developers, administrators, and newbies alike. For more information, please visit our website: www.PacktPub.com.

Learning Joomla! 1.5 Extension Development

ISBN: 978-1-847191-30-4   Paperback: 200 pages

A practical tutorial for creating your first Joomla! 1.5 extensions with PHP

1. Program your own extensions to Joomla!

2. Create new, self-contained components with both back-end and front-end functionality

3. Create configurable site modules to show information on every page

3. Create configurable site modules to show information on every page

Mastering phpMyAdmin 2.8 for Effective MySQL Management

ISBN: 1-847191-60-6   Paperback: 248 pages

Increase your MySQL productivity and control by discovering the real power of phpMyAdmin 2.8

1. Effectively administrate your MySQL databases

2. Manage users and privileges with MySQL Server Administration tools

3. Get to grips with the hidden features and capabilities of phpMyAdmin

Please check **www.PacktPub.com** for information on our titles

www.ingramcontent.com/pod-product-compliance
Lightning Source LLC
Chambersburg PA
CBHW062036050326
40690CB00016B/2958